"In this rollicking and insightful book, Robert Tracy McKenzie explores the Founders' deep skepticism about human nature and 'democracy,' and shows why the uncritical American turn toward a gospel of populism has had such serious consequences. This is scholarly but accessible history at its best."

Thomas S. Kidd, Vardaman Distinguished Professor of History at Baylor University

"In the spirit of Reinhold Niebuhr, Tracy McKenzie places original sin at the center of American political history. *We the Fallen People* weaves American history, historical thinking, and public theology into a compelling narrative that forces readers to rethink the meaning of our democratic experiment."

John Fea, professor of history at Messiah College and author of *Was America Founded as a Christian Nation?*

"Tracy McKenzie's book *We the Fallen People* is an exercise of deep objective thought that will help Christians process the tumult of American government and politics. McKenzie helps us to think Christianly as American citizens about the future of our democracy. This book couldn't have come at a better time."

Ed Stetzer, executive director of the Wheaton College Billy Graham Center and dean of the School of Mission, Ministry, and Leadership

"Tracy McKenzie has managed to do what few historians can—make the seemingly familiar story of American democracy unfamiliar. *We the Fallen People* leads the reader on a journey to some of the most important events and places that shaped American democracy—the creation of the Constitution, the rise of Jacksonian democracy, and the cultural and political landscape of Tocqueville's *Democracy in America*. In this passage through the American past, McKenzie demonstrates how many Americans have idolized democracy as an intrinsically positive good, often to their own detriment and the destruction of others. Calling on Americans to replace *faith in* democracy with a Tocquevillian *hope for* democracy, McKenzie challenges his readers to hold the same sort of skepticism of human goodness that guided the Founding Fathers. In doing so, he reminds us that the greatest threat to democracy is not a foreign power or domestic political enemy but ourselves."

Trisha Posey, professor of history and honors director at John Brown University

"Robert Tracy McKenzie has incisively identified one of the most subtle and insidious dynamics contributing to the present state of partisanship in America. That is, our stark societal divisions are often fueled by flawed approaches to making sense of the past. The genius of McKenzie's book is in his challenge to us to think both Christianly *and* historically, demonstrating that the two are not mutually exclusive. He shrinks not from the exceedingly difficult task of drawing moral wisdom from history, and he does so with characteristic care and aplomb. *We the Fallen People* helps us to see the past more clearly, giving us the ability to think more rightly about ourselves. These are the indispensable first steps for us as we pursue the common good."

John D. Wilsey, author of *American Exceptionalism and Civil Religion: Reassessing the History of an Idea*

"Robert Tracy McKenzie convincingly argues that the health of a nation depends on its citizens' ability to grasp an old, old idea, that of original sin. America's founders believed it, but it's the rare politician, pundit, or citizen who does today. This is a bracing call for Christians especially to reintroduce this idea into the national conversation and restore some sanity to our public life together."

Mark Galli, former editor in chief of *Christianity Today*

WE THE
FALLEN
PEOPLE

ROBERT TRACY
McKENZIE

We the
FALLEN
People

THE FOUNDERS AND
THE FUTURE OF
AMERICAN DEMOCRACY

ivp
Academic
An imprint of InterVarsity Press
Downers Grove, Illinois

InterVarsity Press
P.O. Box 1400, Downers Grove, IL 60515-1426
ivpress.com
email@ivpress.com

InterVarsity Press® is the book-publishing division of InterVarsity Christian Fellowship/USA®, a movement of students and faculty active on campus at hundreds of universities, colleges, and schools of nursing in the United States of America, and a member movement of the International Fellowship of Evangelical Students. For information about local and regional activities, visit intervarsity.org.

Scripture taken from the New King James Version®. Copyright © 1982 by Thomas Nelson. Used by permission. All rights reserved.

The publisher cannot verify the accuracy or functionality of website URLs used in this book beyond the date of publication.

Cover design and image composite: David Fassett
Interior design: Daniel van Loon
Images: snake cartoon: © John Parrot/Stocktrek Images / Getty Images
       beige craft paper: © Katsumi Murouchi / Moment / Getty Images
       paper: © abzee / E+ / Getty Images
       constitution: © smartstock / iStock / Getty Images Plus

ISBN 978-0-8308-5296-3 (print)
ISBN 978-0-8308-5297-0 (digital)

Printed in the United States of America ♾

InterVarsity Press is committed to ecological stewardship and to the conservation of natural resources in all our operations. This book was printed using sustainably sourced paper.

Library of Congress Cataloging-in-Publication Data
A catalog record for this book is available from the Library of Congress.

P	28	27	26	25	24	23	22	21	20	19	18	17	16	15	14	13	12	11	10	9	8	7	6	5	4	3	2	1
Y	45	44	43	42	41	40	39	38	37	36	35	34	33	32	31	30	29	28	27	26	25	24	23	22	21

For Robyn

Song 5:16

CONTENTS

PROLOGUE

"America Is Great Because . . ."

*B*oiled down, it was an argument about greatness. Donald J. Trump, the surprising Republican nominee for president, promised to "make America great *again*." Hillary Clinton, his Democratic opponent, countered that America is great *already*. "In the end, it comes down to what Donald Trump doesn't get," she told the Democratic National Convention: "America is great—because America is good."[1]

Do you recognize that final phrase? I was watching television that summer night in 2016 as Clinton made her claim to the cheering delegates packed into Philadelphia's Wells Fargo Center. As a historian of the early United States, I knew immediately that the words weren't hers. So did Sean Spicer, a high-ranking adviser in the Trump campaign who would become White House press secretary in another six months. Only the week before, Democrats had pilloried Melania Trump for plagiarizing a sizable chunk of her speech to the Republican National Convention, borrowing from First Lady Michelle Obama, of all people. Now Spicer gleefully accused Clinton of the same offense. Within minutes he had tweeted a "plagiarism alert" to the party faithful: "@hillaryclinton at @DemConvention 'America is great bc America is good,' de Tocqueville 'America is great bc she is good.'"[2]

By "de Tocqueville," Spicer meant Alexis de Tocqueville, the French aristocrat who visited the United States in 1831 and then went home to write his

---

[1]"Transcript, Hillary Clinton's DNC Speech, Annotated," *Los Angeles Times*, July 28, 2016, www.latimes.com/politics/la-na-pol-hillary-clinton-convention-speech-transcript-20160728-snap-htmlstory.html.

[2]Katherine Krueger, "Team Trump Cries 'Plagiarism' into the Void After Clinton's DNC Speech," July 29, 2016, http://talkingpointsmemo.com/livewire/sean-spicer-jeffrey-lord-clinton-plagiarism-de-tocqueville.

two-volume masterpiece of political and social analysis, *Democracy in America*. Clinton's defenders scoffed at the plagiarism charge on the grounds that the phrase is so well known that no reasonable listener would think that Clinton was trying to pass it off as her own. They lambasted "Trump's attack dogs" and retorted that the Democratic nominee was merely "riffing on a famous quote" from a "canonical work" that all educated people should recognize.[3]

In truth, "America is great because she is good" has been a favorite of politicians (and their speechwriters) since the middle of the last century, and we can pinpoint the exact moment when it came to be so. It was the evening of November 3, 1952, and Republican presidential nominee Dwight Eisenhower was in Boston to deliver his final campaign speech before voters went to the polls the following day. Speaking in the midst of the early Cold War with the Soviet Union, the retired five-star general warned the audience of an "organized evil challenging free men in their quest of peace." Then he concluded on a note of hope: the "greatness and genius of America" was equal to the challenge at hand.

What was the source of this "greatness and genius"? Eisenhower explained that "a wise philosopher" had visited the United States "many years ago" with the same question in mind and had arrived at the following answer:

> I sought for the greatness and genius of America in her commodious harbors and her ample rivers—and it was not there. I sought for the greatness and genius of America in her fertile fields and boundless forests—and it was not there. I sought for the greatness and genius of America in her rich mines and her vast world commerce—and it was not there. I sought for the greatness and genius of America in her democratic Congress and her matchless Constitution—and it was not there. Not until I went into the churches of America and heard her pulpits flame with righteousness did I understand the secret of her genius and power. America is great because she is good, and if America ever ceases to be good, she will cease to be great.[4]

Eisenhower's staff made sure to get the text of his remarks to the press, and by the next morning Americans from coast to coast could read the entire speech over breakfast. By dinnertime its author had been elected the nation's next president, millions of Americans had been inspired by the words of the "wise philosopher," and a popular political proverb had been born. Politicians and pundits have been in love with the quote's concluding sentence ever since.

---

[3]Ibid.
[4]*New York Times*, November 4, 1952, 23.

Eisenhower used it repeatedly during his presidency, as did successors Richard Nixon, Gerald Ford, Ronald Reagan, and Bill Clinton, along with vice presidents Spiro Agnew and Mike Pence. At the other end of Pennsylvania Avenue, scores of congressmen and senators have also been fond of it. Over the years, Democratic leaders like Dick Gephardt, Hubert Humphrey, Jim Wright, John Kerry, and Nancy Pelosi have repeated the adage, as have Republicans such as Arlen Specter, Newt Gingrich, Rick Santorum, and Michele Bachmann. Outside of Congress, it's been a favorite of public officials and would-be office-holders, including J. Edgar Hoover, Charles Colson, Ross Perot, Pat Buchanan, Colin Powell, and Ben Carson, as well as of political commentators like Glenn Beck, Rush Limbaugh, and Armstrong Williams.

It's been equally popular outside the DC Beltway—in "fly-over country" or "the real America," depending on your point of view. Even before Eisenhower's inauguration, the editors of *This Week* magazine, a Sunday insert in newspapers across the country, emblazoned the concluding sentence on the front cover and labeled it "words to live by."[5] Within days, an insurance executive in Grand Prairie, Texas, was working it into a talk to the local Rotary Club. The Ladies' Aid Society of Bristol, Vermont, was sponsoring a panel discussion of the phrase. Down in Tuskegee, Alabama, an agent of the US Department of Agriculture was sharing it at a farmers' convention.[6]

In subsequent decades, Americans heard all or part of Tocqueville's reflection in American Legion halls and schools and churches, at PTA meetings and school graduations, and as part of Easter services, Memorial Day ceremonies, and Fourth of July celebrations. We pondered his words in op-ed columns, letters to the editor, church bulletins, newspaper ads, and airport billboards. We absorbed his message at the businessmen's prayer breakfast of Mansfield, Ohio; the annual United Fund awards dinner of Kokomo, Indiana; the Business and Professional Women's Club of San Bernardino, California; and in Mrs. Margaret Smith's first grade class in Traverse City, Michigan.[7]

It's no wonder, then, that when Ronald Reagan hosted a youth delegation at the White House during his presidency, he instinctively turned to Tocqueville's

---

[5]See, for example, *The Des Moines Register*, January 18, 1953, 87.
[6]*Grand Prairie Daily News*, January 25, 1953, 7; *Burlington Free Press*, January 26, 1953, 1; *Montgomery Advertiser*, January 29, 1953, 3.
[7]*Mansfield News-Journal*, May 17, 1963; *Kokomo Morning Times*, February 16, 1965; *San Bernardino County Sun*, February 6, 1970; *Traverse City Record-Eagle*, March 18, 1970; *Anniston* [AL] *Star*, December 21, 1980; *Palm Beach Post*, February 12, 1972; *Genoa* [IL] *Kingston Kirkland News*, August 14, 1980; *Florida Today* [Cocoa, FL], March 26, 1997; *The Clinton* [MS] *News*, April 26, 2007.

observation about the source of America's greatness. It also makes sense that he prefaced the quote with his judgment that the line "has been quoted more than any author has ever had a line quoted."[8] It was an overstatement, but you get the point. With all due respect to Sean Spicer, "America is great because America is good" is arguably the most frequently repeated observation from the most widely cited commentary on American democracy ever written, and Hillary Clinton shouldn't have had to cite Alexis de Tocqueville in repeating it.

Especially since Tocqueville never wrote anything of the kind.

In today's jargon, the whole passage is "fake news"—from the exhaustive search for America's greatness, to the eye-opening encounter with churches aflame with righteousness, to that stirring final declaration that we love so well. Americans have developed a bad habit of crying "Fake news!" in response to anything we'd rather not hear, but I mean it literally. The entire quote is a fabrication.

Is this a big deal? Perhaps not. History is full of famous quotes by famous people who never said or wrote what we attribute to them, and most of the time they're harmless enough. ("I cannot tell a lie." "War is hell." "You can fool some of the people all of the time . . .") But sometimes these inventions are less benign, and "America is great because America is good" is a case in point. It's not just that Alexis de Tocqueville didn't pen these precise words. He didn't come close to believing them.

Neither should we.

---

[8]"Remarks and a Question-and-Answer Session with Members of the American Legion Boys Nation," July 25, 1986, Public Papers of Ronald Reagan, www.reaganlibrary.gov/archives/speech/remarks-and-question-and-answer-session-members-american-legion-boys-nation.

INTRODUCTION

The Consent of the Governed

S ometime in mid-June 1776, Thomas Jefferson mounted the stairs to his rented quarters not far from the Pennsylvania State House in Philadelphia, sat down at his favorite Windsor chair, and penned the opening lines of American Scripture.[1] A century and a half later, the English writer G. K. Chesterton would point to the Virginian's words in the Declaration of Independence as the foundation of American identity. The United States was "a nation with the soul of a church," the Englishman reported after his first visit to America. This wasn't because of Americans' widespread religious faith—Chesterton had almost nothing to say on that score—but because of how they defined themselves. As a nation of immigrants, they believed that the essence of what it meant to be an American had less to do with *birth* than with *belief*. The result, Chesterton marveled, is that "America is the only nation in the world that is founded on a creed."[2]

A century after the Englishman's visit, Americans still know where to find that creed. It begins with the words "We hold these truths to be self-evident," and proceeds to a series of assertions intended to apply to all people at all times in all places. In his original draft, the Sage of Monticello actually packed them into a single, complicated, 114-word-long sentence. (Can you imagine the Founding Fathers on Twitter?) Amid semicolons and subordinate clauses, Jefferson posited five distinct propositions, each introduced by *that*: that we are all created equal; that we are the beneficiaries of God-given rights; that these include the

---

[1]Pauline Maier refers to the entire Declaration of Independence as "American Scripture" in her study of the document. See *American Scripture: Making the Declaration of Independence* (New York: Alfred A. Knopf, 1997).

[2]G. K. Chesterton, *What I Saw in America* (1922; repr., London: Catholic Way Publishing, 2012), 6, 4.

rights to "life, liberty, and the pursuit of happiness"; that governments exist to protect these rights; and that any time a government ceases to uphold its end of the bargain, the people have a right to alter or abolish it.

We keep returning to this "seminal statement of the American Creed," in part, because it speaks of equality and rights and we're a people preoccupied with equality and rights.[3] But we also continue to echo Jefferson's assertions because, however important they are to us, they are *contested* truths. Over the years we have disagreed about what they should mean. Who is to be included in the proposition that "all men are created equal"? What specific rights should be encompassed in the vague categories of "life, liberty, and the pursuit of happiness"? In fact, one way to tell the story of the United States is as an ongoing struggle to define the meaning of Jefferson's ambiguous assertions.

But buried amid Jefferson's five explicit propositions is a sixth, implicit assertion that we can easily overlook. Over the years it's proved to be even more fundamental than the others, but also a lot less controversial, with the result that we tend not to give it much thought. Almost as an aside, in stating the principle that government exists to secure our natural rights, Jefferson suggested that governments "deriv[e] their just powers from the consent of the governed."

By affirming these ten simple words, the signers of the Declaration effectively repudiated not only the reign of George III but of hereditary monarchy in general. And in embracing those same words, colonial patriots rejected Old World absolutism and asserted the sovereignty of the people, insisting that the only legitimate form of government is self-government. They, and we, have never looked back.

It's time that we did, not to undermine our commitment to the consent of the governed but to help it survive. Two and a half centuries after Jefferson took up his pen, Americans are deeply dissatisfied with our ongoing experiment in self-government. Shortly after Donald Trump was sworn in as our forty-fifth president in 2017, pledging to bring power back to the people, a Pew Research poll found that more than three quarters of Americans were either angry or frustrated with the government in Washington.[4]

---

[3]Joseph J. Ellis, *American Sphinx: The Character of Thomas Jefferson* (New York: Alfred A. Knopf, 1997), 54.

[4]Pew Research Center, "Public Trust in Government Remains Near Historic Lows as Partisan Attitudes Shift," May 3, 2017, www.pewresearch.org/politics/2017/05/03/public-trust-in-government-remains-near-historic-lows-as-partisan-attitudes-shift.

At the time, it was tempting to chalk this up to lingering exasperation with a campaign that featured two historically unpopular alternatives for the White House. But the truth was that Americans' dissatisfaction was both deep and long-standing. Popular trust in the federal government had been declining for decades. In the early 1960s, nearly 80 percent of Americans trusted government to do the right thing "just about always" or "most of the time." Who could even imagine that today? By 2000 that proportion had been cut in half. By 2015 it had been cut in half yet again, and by 2019 a scant 17 percent of Americans professed to trust their government.[5] Historians debate the causes of this staggering decline, but none dispute the trend. When it comes to our attitudes toward government, we are deeply dissatisfied.

We are also deeply divided. Political scientists tell us that Congress is more rigidly split along partisan lines than at any time since the Civil War. Political polarization among the rank and file has soared as well. In 1994, 21 percent of Republicans held a "very unfavorable" view of Democrats, while 17 percent of Democrats viewed Republicans in a similar light. By 2017 those proportions had nearly tripled. Fueling this surging contempt is the increasing conviction, held almost equally by Democrats and Republicans, that the opposing party actually poses a threat to the nation. In 2016, a survey sponsored by the Pew Research Center found that 45 percent of Republicans viewed Democrats as "a threat to the nation's well-being." Forty-one percent of Democrats returned the favor.[6]

The upshot is that most of us now find it stressful even to have a conversation with a supporter of the opposing party. (A 2017 poll found that one in six respondents had even cut off communication with a *family member* because of disagreement over the 2016 election.) Thankfully, we seldom have to interact with those who disagree with us, as social media enables us to withdraw into echo chambers of the like-minded. A survey shortly before the 2020 election found that fully two-fifths of respondents didn't personally know a single individual who planned to vote for the candidate they themselves opposed. It's almost impossible to exaggerate our partisan isolation. Interracial marriages are now far

[5]Pew Research Center, "Public Trust in Government Remains Near Historic Lows"; Pew Research Center, "Public Trust in Government, 1958–2019," April 11, 2019, www.pewresearch.org/politics/2019/04/11/public-trust-in-government-1958-2019.
[6]Pew Research Center, "The Partisan Divide on Political Values Grows Even Wider," October 5, 2017, www.pewresearch.org/politics/2017/10/05/the-partisan-divide-on-political-values-grows-even-wider; Ezra Klein, *Why We're Polarized* (New York: Avid Reader Press, 2020), 17.

more common in the United States than weddings of Republicans and Democrats.[7] When it comes to politics, we've become an us-versus-them society.

These twin traits (Americans' distrust of government and of other Americans)
help to explain an even more disturbing trend—namely, an apparent dis-
illusionment with democracy itself. In a national poll conducted shortly before
the 2016 election, 46 percent of respondents agreed that they lacked "faith in
democracy."[8] Admittedly, it's unclear how to interpret such a broad declaration.
Were respondents really just registering frustration with partisan gridlock? Despondent because their preferred candidate seemed likely to lose? Or were they
actually indicating a willingness to accept some more authoritarian alternative?

The latter is at least conceivable. Over the last decade, meticulous assessments
by the World Values Survey, the Pew Research Center, and the Democracy Fund
have found that from a fourth to upward of a third of Americans rate as "good" or
"fairly good" a system that features "a strong leader who does not have to bother
with Congress or elections." The technical term for such a system is *dictatorship*.

I'm skeptical that anywhere near a third of Americans would intentionally
embrace a dictator, but it seems undeniable that our commitment to democracy
is waning, and there is evidence that it is declining most among the young adults
whose job it will be to preserve our democracy in the future. According to the
World Values Survey, roughly three of four Americans born prior to World War
Two find it "essential" to live under a democratic form of government, but that
proportion falls for every subsequent generational cohort. Among "millennials"
—those born after 1980—just under three in ten feel that strongly.[9]

---

[7]Robert J. Samuelson, "Everyone Is Mad at Everyone," *Washington Post*, July 3, 2017; Arthur C.
Brooks, *Love Your Enemies: How Decent People Can Save America from the Culture of Contempt*
(New York: Broadside Books, 2019), 4; Pew Research Center, "Partisanship and Political Animosity in 2016," June 22, 2016, www.pewresearch.org/politics/2016/06/22/partisanship-and-politi-
cal-animosity-in-2016; Philip Bump, "Three-Quarters of Americans Know Only a Few People Who
Support the Candidate They Themselves Oppose," *Washington Post*, September 18, 2020, www.
washingtonpost.com/politics/2020/09/18/three-quarters-americans-know-only-few-people-
who-support-candidate-they-themselves-oppose/.
[8]Nathaniel Persily and Jon Cohen, "Americans Are Losing Faith in Democracy—and in Each Other,"
Washington Post, October 14, 2016, www.washingtonpost.com/opinions/americans-are-losing-
faith-in-democracy—and-in-each-other/2016/10/14/b35234ea-90c6-11e6-9c52-0b10449e33c4_
story.html.
[9]Lee Drutman, Larry Diamond, Joe Goldman, "Follow the Leader: Exploring American Support for
Democracy and Authoritarianism," www.voterstudygroup.org/publication/follow-the-
leader#appendix-a-comparison-of-our-findings-to-2017-survey-by-the-pew-research-center; Yascha
Mounk, *The People vs. Democracy: Why Our Freedom Is in Danger & How to Save It* (Cambridge, MA:

These findings should trouble us, but they ought not to surprise us. Most of us already sense that our public life has gone off the rails, don't we? A 2018 survey sponsored by the Democracy Project found that more than half (55 percent) of Americans believe that American democracy is already "weak," and upward of two-thirds (68 percent) are convinced that it is "getting weaker." A Pew survey from the same year provided more discouraging context, revealing that three-quarters of Americans were "dissatisfied with the way things are going in this country."[10]

And that was before 2020.

Over the course of that trying year, Americans ran a gauntlet of historic calamities: the year began with the impeachment of the president of the United States, followed by the nation's worst health crisis since the Spanish Flu pandemic of 1918–1920, worst economic downturn since the depths of the Great Depression, and worst civil unrest since the turbulent 1960s. As the year wound down, we endured the most divisive presidential campaign since the eve of the Civil War, followed by the most controversial election outcome since the close of Reconstruction. The year culminated with the defeated incumbent pronouncing the voting returns "a fraud on the American public," with nearly two-fifths of registered voters convinced that the presidency had been stolen, and with a large majority of both parties condemning the other for "weakening American democracy."[11]

Prior to this perfect storm, the optimistic among us might have hoped that adversity would unite the nation. It didn't. The trials that we faced didn't overshadow our political differences. They underscored and enlarged them. Scenarios for America's future that would have been unthinkable even a year earlier

Harvard University Press, 2018), 105-11; Richard Wike et al., "Globally, Broad Support for Representative and Direct Democracy: But Many Also Endorse Nondemocratic Alternatives," Pew Research Center, October 16, 2017, http://assets.pewresearch.org/wp-content/uploads/sites/2/2017/10/17102729/Pew-Research-Center_Democracy-Report_2017.10.16.pdf; Michael Albertus and Guy Grossman, "Americans Are Officially Giving Up on Democracy," *Foreign Policy*, October 16, 2020, https://foreign-policy.com/2020/10/16/americans-are-officially-giving-up-on-democracy.

[10]Democracy Project, "The Democracy Project: Reversing a Crisis of Confidence," www.democracy-projectreport.org/report; Pew Research Center, "2020 Pew Research Center's American Trends Panel, Wave 69, June 2020," www.pewresearch.org/politics/wp-content/uploads/sites/4/2020/06/topline-FOR-RELEASE.pdf.

[11]Anthony Salvanto et al., "CBS News Poll: Most Feel Election Is 'Settled' but Trump Voters Disagree," CBS News, December 13, 2020, www.cbsnews.com/news/cbs-news-poll-most-feel-election-is-settled-but-trump-voters-disagree; Fox News poll, December 11, 2020, https://static.foxnews.com/foxnews.com/content/uploads/2020/12/Fox_December-6-9-2020_National_Topline_December-11-Release.pdf.

now suddenly seemed possible. Journalists worried that the final remnant of faith in our political institutions would be shattered forever. Pundits likened our situation to the eve of the Civil War. A prominent cabinet official described American cities wracked by protests as "battle space" that the military must "dominate." A four-star general appalled by the prospect wondered whether we were witnessing "the beginning of the end of the American experiment." Another retired general (recently pardoned by the president) endorsed the imposition of martial law as necessary to forestall a "shooting civil war."[12]

And while most of us were grateful to turn the calendar and leave 2020 behind, the early returns on 2021 were no more encouraging. Only six days into the new year, an angry crowd that had gathered in Washington, DC, for a "Stop the Steal" rally morphed into a violent mob that stormed the US capitol and attempted to prevent the official certification of a new president. Although much of the nation recoiled in horror at the scene, a survey by the American Enterprise Institute conducted afterward found that one in three Americans (and more than half of Republicans) agreed with the statement that "the traditional American way of life is disappearing so fast that we may have to use force to save it."[13]

In short order, the attack on the capitol triggered yet another presidential impeachment (the second in twelve months and the first ever of a president who had already left office), on the grounds that the outgoing executive had actively incited his followers' insurrection. And although a majority of Americans favored the ex-president's conviction in the trial that ensued in February, much of the remainder doubled down on their ardent support of their leader and in their conviction that the new president was illegitimate. By Valentine's Day, almost the only sentiment that unified Americans was the bipartisan belief (shared by 70 percent of Democrats and 66 percent of Republicans) that American democracy "is failing to address the concerns and needs of the public."[14]

---

[12]Elizabeth McLaughlin and Luis Martinez, "Pentagon Defends Defense Secretary's Call to 'Dominate the Battle Space,'" ABC News, June 2, 2020, https://abcnews.go.com/Politics/pentagon-defends-defense-secretarys-call-dominate-battle-space/story?id=71020529; Julian Borger, "'Slide to Illiberalism': Ex-General Joins Chorus of Condemnation of Trump," *The Guardian*, June 4, 2020, www.theguardian.com/us-news/2020/jun/04/trump-military-retired-general-john-allen-protest; Justin Vallejo, "Michael Flynn Calls for Trump to Suspend the Constitution and Declare Martial Law to Re-run Election," *The Independent*, December 3, 2020, www.independent.co.uk/news/world/americas/us-election-2020/michael-flynn-suspend-constitution-martial-law-trump-reelection-b1765467.html.

[13]Daniel A. Cox, "After the Ballots Are Counted: Conspiracies, Political Violence, and American Exceptionalism," American Enterprise Institute, February 2021, www.aei.org/wp-content/uploads/2021/02/After-the-Ballots-Are-Counted.pdf?x91208.

[14]Ibid.

A decade after his visit to the United States, Chesterton concluded that "nothing so much threatens the safety of democracy as assuming that democracy is safe."[15] It's time to stop assuming.

But what do we do? How do we get out of this fix? If I were a politician, here is where I would introduce my list of "real plans for real people" that guarantee "change we can believe in" as we become "stronger together" in order to "make America great again" so that "our best days lie ahead." (And if you were a political junkie, you'd recognize this string of empty phrases as the campaign slogans of George W. Bush in 2000, Barack Obama in 2008, Hillary Clinton and Donald Trump in 2016, and Joe Biden in 2020.) I'm not a politician, however, and I have no simple solution to offer—nor a complicated solution, for that matter.

But these things I believe: First, we must *think deeply* before we can act effectively. Platitudes won't help us. There is no solution to our democratic malaise that can be slapped on a bumper sticker, stitched to a ball cap, condensed into a tweet, or chanted at a rally of "the base." We have more than enough slogans. To thrive, democracy requires grownup conversation.

Second, as scary as it is to realize that the survival of American democracy isn't inevitable, the pressing need of the moment isn't a cultural recommitment to democracy per se. Nor is it to renew our support of a favored political party, policy agenda, or governmental reform. Our first order of business is to reconsider *why* we favor majority rule at all.

Boiled down, there are really only two reasons to believe in majority rule: because we have confidence in human nature or because we don't. The twentieth-century Christian thinker C. S. Lewis put it this way: on the one hand, "you may think all men so good that they deserve a share in the government of the commonwealth, and so wise that the commonwealth needs their advice." Conversely, "you may believe fallen men to be so wicked that not one of them can be trusted with any responsible power over his fellows."

The first view, Lewis insisted, was "the false, romantic doctrine of democracy." The "true ground of democracy" was the latter. Writing in 1943 as the world was convulsed in a death struggle between those who would defend democracy and

---

[15]Chesterton quoted in Kent R. Hill, "Chesterton, Democracy, and the Permanent Things," in *Permanent Things: Toward the Recovery of a More Human Scale at the End of the Twentieth Century*, ed. Andrew A. Tadie and Michael H. McDonald (Grand Rapids, MI: Eerdmans, 1995), 94.

those who sought to destroy it, Lewis confessed that he could only believe in majority rule "because I believe in the Fall of man."[16]

How many Americans today could say the same? How many American *Christians* would agree? For nearly two and a half centuries, Americans have pointed to the consent of the governed as the immutable cornerstone of free government. Yet what we have meant by the "consent of the governed"—how we have defined and defended it—has changed dramatically since the late-eighteenth century.

As a Christian, I agree with Lewis that a deep appreciation of human sinfulness must be the starting point of our thinking about democracy. As a historian, I see little evidence that this has been true for most of our past. The framers of our Constitution, although they rarely spoke in the jargon of orthodox Christianity, nevertheless framed our blueprint of government with human sinfulness in mind. Americans had begun to abandon that sensibility within a generation of the founding, however, precisely as the culture was becoming ever more vibrantly democratic.

Could it be that Americans have embraced democracy for the wrong reason? Might it be that our misguided thinking both worsens our malfunctioning political system and intensifies our mounting frustration? Put differently, is part of the problem of American democracy that we Americans think too highly of ourselves? Could a constructive first step be consciously to redefine ourselves as "We the *Fallen* People"?

My answer to each of these questions is "yes." I'll go further. Although it won't magically unify our polarized society, I'm convinced that a necessary first step to a healthier democracy will be to jettison two of our most deeply held democratic assumptions. We must renounce *democratic faith*, our unthinking belief that democracy is intrinsically just. We must disavow the *democratic gospel*, the "good news" that we are individually good and collectively wise. In the pages that follow, I'll show you why.

Even to consider such a path requires that we cut against the grain of contemporary American values. For starters, we'll have to think deeply about democracy, which is something Americans almost never do. Even as I write this, I can imagine your incredulous response: "Aren't we awash in assessments of

---

[16]C. S. Lewis, "Membership," in *C. S. Lewis: Essay Collection and Other Short Pieces*, ed. Leslie Walmsley (London: HarperCollins, 2000), 336-37; C. S. Lewis, "Equality," in *Present Concerns: Essays by C. S. Lewis*, ed. Walter Hooper (New York: Harcourt Brace Jovanovich, 1986), 17.

American democracy these days? Aren't we bombarded by complaints—on talk radio, cable television, and every form of social media—about partisan gridlock, political corruption, and governmental indifference? And didn't you just cite statistics underscoring how few of us trust government to do the right thing, some even suggesting that we'd be willing to trade democracy for a more authoritarian alternative? Doesn't all this demonstrate that we're *constantly* thinking critically about democracy?"

The short answer is "no." We're inundated with critiques of the American democratic *system*, not of democracy itself. We worry that the will and welfare of the people is being thwarted—by one of the major parties or by both of them; by a dysfunctional Congress, imperial presidency, or unrestrained judiciary; by powerful lobbies, the "1 percent," or the "Deep State." Look closely and you'll find that much of what passes for the careful evaluation of American democracy boils down to a single charge: it needs to be more democratic.

This circular reasoning begs the question of what democracy is and why we should believe in it. When we insist that there's nothing wrong with American democracy that more democracy won't fix, the last thing we're doing is thinking deeply about democracy per se. On the contrary, we're thoughtlessly elevating an ill-defined concept into an unquestioned ideal.

Conservative thinker Irving Kristol observed as much a half century ago in his reflections in *The Democratic Idea in America.* Few Americans have a "democratic political philosophy," Kristol contended, by which he meant a set of more fundamental beliefs and commitments that would guide them in assessing both the pros and cons of democracy. Rather, most of us implicitly subscribe to what Kristol labeled "democratic faith"—an unshakable conviction that democracy is *intrinsically* just and good. This allows us to think critically about particular *democracies* but not about *democracy* per se. As Kristol put it, we find it difficult to wrestle with—even to see at all—"those kinds of problems that flow from, that are inherent in, that are generated by democracy itself."[17]

I'm convinced that the main reason we find it difficult to think critically about democracy is that it requires us to think critically about ourselves. As a culture, we've embraced what Lewis rightly described as the "false, romantic doctrine of democracy." The foundation of that doctrine, the flattering but false assumption on which it is built, is what I call the "democratic gospel," the comforting fiction that we are naturally good.

---

[17]Irving Kristol, *On the Democratic Idea in America* (New York: Harper & Row, 1972), 51.

It's no coincidence that the best known observation from Tocqueville's *Democracy in America* is a specious tribute to our essential goodness. In addition to sounding profound, it affirms what we already believe—or desperately want to believe—about who we are as individuals and as a people. In the words of the New Testament, it proclaims what our "itching ears" want to hear.[18]

It's not like we haven't known for a long time that the famous compliment is a fabrication. In the very same 1953 issue that featured the fraudulent phrase on its cover, the editors of *This Week* asked readers for help in identifying the source of the quote. They explained that they had first assumed that the words were Tocqueville's, but each of the "leading historians and De Tocqueville specialists" that they contacted for verification said, "Not so."[19]

Eighteen years later, after President Richard Nixon cited Tocqueville in reminding the Supreme Court that "if America ever ceases to be good, she will cease to be great," distinguished Harvard historian Arthur Schlesinger Jr. wrote an exasperated and widely reprinted letter to the *Washington Post*. The quote was "obviously forged," Schlesinger noted bluntly, "as phony in 1970 as it was in 1952."[20]

When President Bill Clinton began wielding the quote regularly in the 1990s, political scientist John Pitney exposed "The Tocqueville Fraud" in a national magazine. In a follow-up editorial in the *Los Angeles Times*, Pitney marveled that a president with degrees from Georgetown and Yale relied on "false quotations to convince people that he's intelligent and well-read."[21] Neither the president, nor his wife, apparently, nor very many of the rest of us, was paying attention.

Or maybe we just don't care. That's what Alexis de Tocqueville would conclude, at any rate. He'd be frustrated that we've attributed these famous words to him, but he wouldn't be surprised that we believe them. In the United States "the majority lives in perpetual self-adoration," he observes in volume one of *Democracy in America*.[22] That may be an effective basis for national pride, but it's a poor starting point for thinking deeply about democracy.

---

[18]2 Timothy 4:3.

[19]See, for example, *Des Moines Register*, January 18, 1953, 88.

[20]Reprinted in [Minneapolis] *Star-Tribune*, January 14, 1971, 13.

[21]John J. Pitney Jr., "The Tocqueville Fraud," *The Weekly Standard*, November 13, 1995; John J. Pitney Jr., "As the Great Tocqueville Never Said," *Los Angeles Times*, September 15, 1996.

[22]Alexis de Tocqueville, *Democracy in America*, ed. Olivier Zunz (New York: Literary Classics of the United States, 2004), 295. Unless otherwise indicated, all subsequent citations of *Democracy in America* refer to this edition.

To think *critically* about democracy we must also think *historically* about democracy, and that comes just as unnaturally. Besides being discontented and divided, Americans are also a pervasively present-minded people. For all the popularity of the so-called *History* channel and of historical movies like *Lincoln*, *Hacksaw Ridge*, *Dunkirk*, *The Post*, *The Darkest Hour*, *Harriet Tubman*, and *1917* (the list is long), as a rule we live our lives "stranded in the present."[23] Dismissing the 93 percent of the human race that has gone before us, we press into the future with only the dimmest awareness of the past.

We've been this way a long time. Tocqueville noticed our present-mindedness nearly two centuries ago and saw it as a predictable trait of democratic societies. Such societies are in a "constant state of flux," Tocqueville surmised, which means that the traditional ties that link one generation to the next are weakened or broken entirely. First, men and women lose track of their ancestors, then they gradually cease to care, with the eventual result that "each new generation is a new people." Over time, democracy stimulates a "distinctive distaste for all that is old," Tocqueville concluded, so that "democratic peoples scarcely trouble themselves about what was."[24]

Almost as if on cue, the prominent New York journalist John O'Sullivan trumpeted in 1839 that the United States is "the great nation of futurity." Best remembered today for popularizing the term *Manifest Destiny*, O'Sullivan advised readers of the New York *Democratic Review* to turn their back on the past as they pressed toward the glorious future that God had ordained for his chosen nation. "Our national birth was the beginning of a new history . . . which separates us from the past," O'Sullivan proclaimed. "We have no interest in the scenes of antiquity. . . . The expansive future is our arena."[25]

It may have sold newspapers, but such "chronological snobbery" is as foolish as it is arrogant.[26] Stranded alone in the present, cut off from our past, we cannot understand ourselves by ourselves.

It's one of life's ironies that we are often blissfully unaware of the values that shape us most profoundly. The reason for this begins with the inescapable truth that our lives are short—like a "passing shadow" or a "vapor" that soon vanishes,

---

[23]Margaret Bendroth, *The Spiritual Practice of Remembering* (Grand Rapids, MI: Eerdmans, 2013), chapter one.

[24]Tocqueville, *Democracy in America*, 483, 542, 555, 557.

[25]John L. O'Sullivan, "The Great Nation of Futurity," *The United States Democratic Review* 6, no. 23 (1839): 426-27.

[26]C. S. Lewis, *Surprised by Joy* (New York: Harcourt, Brace, Jovanovich, 1966), 207-8.

to cite two biblical metaphors.[27] Add to this the fact that we rarely think deeply about cultural patterns that haven't changed during our lifetimes. Instead, we see them as "natural," and what we see as natural we quickly take for granted.

My students, to cite one example, find it difficult to think critically about the way that digital devices are affecting us because they've never known a world without them. But we're all the same way. Like the T-Rex in the old *Jurassic Park* movies that couldn't see his prey if it remained perfectly still, we're better at detecting moving objects than stationary ones. Change commands our attention; continuity becomes invisible.

This makes it hard for Americans to see crucial components of our democratic worldview. The moving parts are no problem. We know that the contours of American democracy have changed significantly across the generations, particularly with the expansion of the electorate to include women and people of color. We're similarly alert to the debates that still rage over whether the voices of the rank and file of Americans are effectively heard. Do voter registration laws effectively disfranchise the homeless and non-English speakers? Does the Supreme Court's *Citizens United* ruling give large corporations more influence than the middle class? Would majority rule be served by eliminating the Electoral College?

If we have a blind spot, it's more likely to involve those values where Americans have long been agreed, not where we are politically polarized. When they go unchallenged across generations, areas of agreement gradually morph into "timeless" truths, timeless truths become truisms, truisms become bipartisan platitudes. By that point, all serious thought has died. The values in question may shape us profoundly, but they've become like the air that we breathe, as invisible to us as they are ever present. And we can never think carefully about values we cannot see.

This is where history comes in. We can travel figuratively to a time when many of the values we accept unthinkingly were roundly refuted or new and contested, to a moment when the debates surrounding them were not stagnant and settled but dynamic and alive. This helps us to see afresh "what we habitually take for granted" in our day.[28] The invisible not only becomes visible again; it also becomes *strange* to us, something we can no longer accept mindlessly as obvious

---

[27]Psalm 144:4; James 4:14.
[28]Rowan Williams, *Why Study the Past? The Quest for the Historical Church* (Grand Rapids, MI: Eerdmans, 2005), 25.

and natural. The process can be disorienting, even distressing, but it comes with the possibility of transformation and, in the best case, of wisdom.

In the darkest days of the American Civil War, Abraham Lincoln challenged Americans to "think anew, and act anew" in confronting the crisis before them.[29] Our times demand no less, but I would add a third component to the challenge before us: before we can think anew and act anew, we must *see* anew. That is why I have written this book.

We'll begin in 1787. Part one returns us to a moment in the country's past when the democratic values we take for granted were rejected by the "Founding Fathers" we claim to revere. When the delegates to the Constitutional Convention gathered in Philadelphia that year, they were determined to fashion a "republic"—a "public thing" or a "thing of the people" according to the term's Latin root, *res publica*. (*Respublica est res populi*, John Adams was fond of observing. "The republic is the people.") Yet the framers of the Constitution were also realists to the core. Convinced that a republic was the *best* form of government, they were equally certain that it was not a *perfect* form of government. "Perfection is not the lot of human institutions," delegate Oliver Ellsworth observed. "That which has the . . . fewest faults is the best we can expect."[30]

Foremost among the unavoidable faults of republican government was its extensive reliance on humans. The humans who administered the government would be tempted to "forget their obligations to their constituents and prove unfaithful to their important trust." The humans who composed the electorate would sometimes be "more disposed to vex and oppress each other than to cooperate for their common good." As the Framers saw it, the "diseases most incident to republican government" stemmed chiefly from our flawed human nature.[31] The problem as they understood it is not that we're wholly evil; it's that we're not reliably good.

[29]Abraham Lincoln, *The Collected Works of Abraham Lincoln*, ed. Roy P. Basler, 8 vols. (New Brunswick, NJ: Rutgers University Press, 1953–1955), 5:537.

[30]Nancy Isenberg and Andrew Burstein, *The Problem of Democracy: The Presidents Adams Confront the Cult of Personality* (New York: Viking, 2019), 107; "A Landholder" [Oliver Ellsworth], "To the Landholders and Farmers," *Connecticut Courant*, December 17, 1787, in *The Debate on the Constitution: Federalist and Antifederalist Speeches, Articles, and Letters During the Struggle over Ratification*, ed. Bernard Bailyn (New York: Literary Classics of the United States, 1993), part 1, 521.

[31]Alexander Hamilton, James Madison, and John Jay, *The Federalist Papers*, ed. Clinton Rossiter (New York: Penguin, 1961), 378, 379, 384.

Therein lay the Framers' greatest challenge. They were committed to establishing a republic, and they knew that in any form of government worthy of the name, "the majority must ultimately decide."[32] But a republic is also, and always, a thing of *fallen* people, and that makes majority rule problematic. The majority could be misled by ambitious leaders, follow passion rather than reason, and pursue self-interest at the price of justice. This meant that majority rule was essential in principle and fallible in practice. With a sophistication ill-suited to our contemporary all-or-nothing politics, the Framers held these conflicting views simultaneously, in uneasy tension.

Within little more than a generation this mindset was in full retreat. In part two we'll leapfrog from the 1780s to the 1820s and the election of Andrew Jackson, the first US president without direct ties to the Founders of the Revolutionary generation. In focusing on Jackson's presidency, we'll revisit a time when the democratic values we take for granted were new and raw and conspicuous.

The Americans of Jackson's day still shared the founding generation's commitment to a republican form of government, but they now largely rejected the Founders' qualms about its inescapable imperfections. The man they elected president in 1828 embodied their new optimism. As Andrew Jackson saw things, the solution to effective government couldn't be simpler. "I have great confidence in the virtue of a great majority of the people," he explained to a correspondent on the eve of his election. "As long as the government heeds the popular will, the republic is safe."[33]

But if our ultimate goal is to think more deeply about American democracy, it's not enough merely to observe Americans' newly optimistic understanding of human nature and their insistence on the supremacy of the people's will. In part three, we'll observe Jacksonian democracy in action by exploring two of the most dramatic, and revealing, episodes of Andrew Jackson's presidency: the removal of the Cherokee Nation from their ancestral homeland and Jackson's battle against the largest corporation of his day, the Second Bank of the United States.

Both episodes were fraught with moral significance, and each in its own way raises important questions of palpable relevance to our own democratic, deeply divided age. The removal of the Cherokees is a classic example of what Alexis de Tocqueville called the "tyranny of the majority." It reminds us that, even today,

---

[32]Bailyn, *Debate on the Constitution*, part 1, 201.

[33]John Spencer Bassett, ed., *Correspondence of Andrew Jackson* (Washington, DC: Carnegie Institution of Washington, 1928), 3:412; James D. Richardson, comp., *A Compilation of the Messages and Papers of the Presidents* (New York: Bureau of National Literature, 1897), 4:1515.

democracy can be authoritarian and unjust as well as egalitarian and liberating. And at a time when populism is surging in both Europe and the United States, the "Bank War" both highlights how Andrew Jackson created the original template for a powerful populist and points to our willingness to devalue the rule of law when a strong leader seems to be fighting for our interests.

But the most revealing message of the Jacksonian era was always its relentless defense of democracy on what C. S. Lewis identified as "false, romantic" grounds. This is the democratic gospel, the good news that, in the political sphere, at least, "we the people" aren't fallen at all. We're individually good and collectively wise, and whenever a majority of us agree, our preferences acquire an unassailable moral authority. In the words of George Bancroft, the country's foremost historian at the time, "the Spirit of God breathes through the combined intelligence of the people."[34]

When he wasn't trumpeting the nation's glorious "manifest destiny," journalist John O'Sullivan was preaching a similar democratic dogma. In the very first issue of his influential *Democratic Review*, the editor hailed the "high and holy democratic principle" of confidence in the "sound minds and honest hearts" of the people. Any creed that distrusted human nature was "degrading" and "absurd." "Long enough have we been skeptics with regard to ourselves," echoed the central character in Herman Melville's novel *White-Jacket*. The glorious revelation was that "the political Messiah had come," and "he has come in *us*."[35]

Alexis de Tocqueville—the "wise philosopher" who did *not* comment that "America is great because she is good"—quickly noticed such assumptions when he visited the United States during Andrew Jackson's first term as president. "The vast majority understands republican principles in the most democratic sense," Tocqueville wrote to a cousin two months into his tour of the country. Their faith in democracy rested squarely on their "faith in man's good sense and wisdom" and "in the doctrine of human perfectibility."[36]

In part four, we'll invite one of the most penetrating commentators of this newly democratic age to share with us his fears and hopes for the future of the United States. Tocqueville rejected the positive view of human nature that

---

[34]George Bancroft, "The People in Art, Government, and Religion" (1835), in *Modern Eloquence: Occasional Addresses*, ed. Thomas B. Reed (Philadelphia: John B. Morris and Co., 1900), 7:79.

[35]Joseph L. Blau, ed., *Social Theories of Jacksonian Democracy: Representative Writings of the Period 1825–1850* (Indianapolis: Bobbs-Merrill Co., 1947), 21, 22, 33; Herman Melville, *White-Jacket; or, The World in a Man-of-War* (London: Richard Bentley, 1850), 239.

[36]Tocqueville to Louis de Kergorlay, June 29, 1831, in Alexis de Tocqueville, *Letters from America*, ed. Frederick Brown (New Haven, CT: Yale University Press, 2010), 87.

Americans were coming to see as self-evident, and because of this, he could never wholly embrace Americans' faith in democracy. The rise of democracy was inevitable—of that he had no doubt—but he was equally certain that democracy itself is *morally indeterminate*.

Like human nature generally, as Tocqueville reckoned it, democracy will invariably reflect both "good instincts" and "wicked inclinations." This meant that, although the gradual transition from aristocracy to democracy in the Western world was certain, its consequences were not. The transformation could be a blessing or a curse. It could lead to "servitude or liberty."[37]

And so Tocqueville wrote with fervor, and his words are sometimes hard. "People do not receive the truth from their enemies, and their friends seldom offer it," Tocqueville reminds the readers of *Democracy in America*. "That is why I have told it as I see it."[38] We need to listen carefully to this Frenchman, and we'll invite him to speak to us at length. He has much to say to us, provided we have ears to hear.

But what particularly do we *need* to hear, *now*, and *why*? Before closing, we'll take the time to wrestle with these questions, and in the book's concluding section I'll be bold to offer some pointed answers. Because that's where we're headed, I think it makes sense, even now, to be candid with you about my own commitments and convictions.

First, you should know that I am an American who loves his country. I'm proud to say that my grandfather served in the US Army in World War I, my father was a "tin can sailor" in the US Navy during World War II, and my son is a veteran of the US Marine Corps. I am thankful for the many ways that God has blessed the land of my birth, and I pray that the Lord will continue to bless and guide this nation.

But I am also, and above all, a Christian. I will hasten to add that, if you are a person of a different faith, or of no faith at all, I'm delighted that you've picked up this book, and I hope you'll continue reading. Although they meant well, the culture warriors of the last generation distorted the concept of "Christian history." Pastors and popularizers who looked to the past more for ammunition than enlightenment, they offered tendentious accounts of America's Christian

---

[37]Tocqueville, *Democracy in America*, 282, 834.
[38]Ibid., 480.

heritage that were amateurish, triumphalist, and unabashedly partisan. This is not that kind of book.

But I will not deny that I have a deep burden for the American church. Because I'm convinced that faithful remembering is critical to faithful living, I'm distressed by the "historylessness" that generally characterizes American Christians. Among its other costs, our historical amnesia contributes directly to our dysfunctional engagement with contemporary politics, a pattern distinguished chiefly by its worldly pragmatism and shallowness. I fear we are giving the culture reason to view followers of Christ as simply one more interest group, one more strategically savvy voting bloc willing to trade political support for political influence.

We Americans who seek to follow Jesus need desperately to think more Christianly about our political values, but it's hard to think Christianly about values that we have taken for granted for so long that we're no longer even aware of them. This is where historical knowledge becomes invaluable. At its best, our engagement with the past can help us to see the present—and ourselves—with new eyes.

Alexis de Tocqueville never wrote that "America is great because she is good." He did, however, conclude that "the organization and establishment of democracy among Christians is the great political problem of our time."[39] Two centuries later, the problem has evolved from establishing to perpetuating democracy, but the underlying challenges for American Christians remain unchanged: to think Christianly about democracy, respond rightly to it, and live faithfully within it.

---

[39]Ibid., 360.

Washington Presiding at the Constitutional Convention in 1787

PART ONE

GOVERNING A
FALLEN PEOPLE

*The Founders, the Constitution,
and Human Nature*

IF JAMES MADISON WERE IN COLLEGE TODAY, a conscientious career counselor would break it to our fourth president that he had no future in politics. How would he ever sway voters? Not in person, certainly. Plagued by real and imaginary physical maladies, Madison was uncomfortable in crowds, disliked speaking in public, and detested the thought of appealing for votes. We can't imagine him kissing babies, eating a hot dog at the state fair, or working the crowd into a frenzy at a partisan rally. Even friends described him as "timid" and "stiff," "cold" and "gloomy."[1]

He would fare no better on television. The camera wouldn't be kind to him, not because he was ugly, exactly, but because he was so utterly, relentlessly unimpressive. "Madison at first glance appeared not to merit a second glance" is how a modern historian puts it. "Little and ordinary" was a common verdict among contemporaries. "Little Jemmy" was short and scrawny, and a sympathetic

---

[1]Michael Meyerson, *Liberty's Blueprint: How Madison and Hamilton Wrote the Federalist Papers, Defined the Constitution, and Made Democracy Safe for the World* (New York: Basic Books, 2008), 12; John P. Kaminski, ed., *The Founders on the Founders: Word Portraits from the American Revolutionary Era* (Charlottesville: University of Virginia Press, 2008), 374, 377.

acquaintance tactfully acknowledged that his "form, features, and manner were not commanding."[2] Can you imagine how Donald Trump would skewer him?

Nor would social media be an effective platform. Madison struck many who met him as a "book politician." He was given to "rather too much theory," a sympathetic critic observed, a scholar as much as a statesman. He read widely in multiple languages. He knew the history of the Achaean League, the Helvetic System, and the Amphyctionic Confederacy. He could spell *Amphyctionic.* The world as Madison understood it was complicated, and its serious political problems demanded extended reflection and systematic study, not knee-jerk pronouncements in 280-character increments. Twitter would have appalled him.[3]

James Madison

Today, I'd advise such a student to forget about politics and apply to graduate school. But two and a half centuries ago, intellectualism and politics weren't the matter and antimatter that they are today, and a bookish introvert like James Madison could go on to play an indispensable role in the formation and ratification of the US Constitution. The secret of his unmatched influence—why later generations would remember him as the "Father of the Constitution"— was his ability to meld theory and practice, to enlist the best scholarship of his day in the service of practical problems.

Like most of the fifty-four other delegates to the Constitutional Convention, Madison went to Philadelphia in 1787 with a sense of urgency. The consensus

---

[2]John Ferling, *A Leap in the Dark: The Struggle to Create the American Republic* (New York: Oxford University Press, 2003), 267; Kaminski, *Founders on the Founders,* 377; Joseph J. Ellis, *The Quartet: Orchestrating the Second American Revolution, 1783–1789* (New York: Alfred A. Knopf, 2015), 115; Meyerson, *Liberty's Blueprint,* 11.

[3]Kaminski, *Founders on the Founders,* 377; James Madison to Thomas Jefferson, 24 October 1787, Founders Online, National Archives, https://founders.archives.gov.

was that something had to be done, and done quickly, to save the infant United States from collapse. The intentionally weak Articles of Confederation, erected in wartime, were proving inadequate to the problems of peace. A combination of commercial chaos, financial disarray, local irresponsibility, and internal upheaval threatened to bring down the "frail and tottering edifice," as Alexander Hamilton put it. "It certainly is tottering!" George Washington agreed from Mount Vernon. And should the "fabrick" finally fall, "what a triumph for the advocates of despotism to find that we are incapable of governing ourselves."[4]

But creating "a more perfect union," Madison realized, would require more than simply endowing the central government with sufficient power to address pressing problems. It wasn't enough to clothe the federal government with new authority: the power to tax, to regulate commerce, to raise an army and navy. That was the easy part. The real challenge would be figuring out how to delegate such authority without jeopardizing liberty. This was true because any governmental power necessary to advance the public good could also be perverted "to the public detriment." Granted, the impotence of the central government under the Articles of Confederation invited anarchy, but strengthening its powers would increase "the danger of oppression."[5]

This meant that the *structure* of the new government would be as critical as the powers that it wielded. And so Madison ransacked history, systematically reviewing "ancient and modern confederacies" for lessons that might apply to America. He grappled with the leading theorists of the Enlightenment, poring over crates of dense treatises imported from England, Scotland, and France. The key, he concluded after much study, would be to devise a governmental framework that could compensate for the shortage of virtue among both the people and their leaders. "It may be a reflection on human nature, that such devices should be necessary," Madison later conceded during the debate over the proposed Constitution. "But what is government itself, but the greatest of all reflections on human nature? If men were angels, no government should be necessary."[6]

---

[4]Alexander Hamilton, *Federalist* #15, in Alexander Hamilton, James Madison, and John Jay, *The Federalist*, ed. J. R. Pole (Indianapolis: Hackett, 2005), 81; George Washington to John Jay, 18 May 1786, Founders Online.

[5]Ibid., 219; James Madison to Thomas Jefferson, 17 October 1788, Founders Online.

[6]James Madison, *Federalist* #51, 281.

—1—

ASKING DIFFERENT
QUESTIONS

*I*t's a story that American Christians have long enjoyed repeating—most of it, anyway—and it's not hard to see why. It's packed with drama, it boldly declares Christian truth, and it's not even fabricated—a trait we've learned not to take for granted. See if you recognize it:

It's a sweltering Thursday afternoon in the summer of 1787, and the statesmen gathered behind closed doors in the Pennsylvania State House are discouraged. They have come to Philadelphia on a mission to save the country, but conflicting interests—between North and South, large states and small states, agriculture and commerce—have repeatedly thwarted compromise. Time is running out, tempers are short, and the unthinkable is now increasingly likely: barring a breakthrough, the delegates will have to admit defeat and head home. It is, as James Madison will later recall, a "period of gloom." In the opinion of New York delegate Gouverneur Morris, "the fate of America [is] suspended by a hair."[1]

And then, at this "awful and critical moment," the Constitutional Convention's oldest member asks for permission to address the fractured assembly.[2] *At first glance, Benjamin Franklin is apt to disappoint. A delegate who has met him for the first time this summer describes him as "a short, fat, trenched old man," but Franklin has devoted more than half of his long life to public service, and he commands respect.*[3] *In*

---

[1]James Madison to Jared Sparks, April 8, 1831, in *The Records of the Federal Convention of 1787*, ed. Max Farrand, 3 vols. (New Haven, CT: Yale University Press, 1911), 3:499; Daniel L. Dreisbach, *Reading the Bible with the Founding Fathers* (New York: Oxford University Press, 2017), 137.

[2]William Few, *Autobiography of William Few* (n.d.), in Farrand, *Records of the Federal Convention*, 3:423.

[3]David O. Stewart, *The Summer of 1787: The Men Who Invented the Constitution* (New York: Simon & Schuster, 2007), 33.

Europe, he is hands down the best known and most highly regarded of all Americans. At home, he is second only to George Washington in the prestige and acclaim he enjoys.

But in his eighty-second year, Franklin is long past taking an active role in the convention. Although his mind is still sharp, he is a "physical wreck," plagued by gallstones and gout, and he will address the convention but a handful of times throughout the summer.[4] When he does so, he frequently writes out his remarks in advance and enlists another member of the Pennsylvania delegation to read them on

Benjamin Franklin

his behalf. He has done so today. There is nothing spontaneous about his comments. They are premeditated and serious, devoid of the witticisms for which he is famous.

Acknowledging the "small progress" of the past month, Franklin observes that the convention is "groping, as it were, in the dark, to find political truth." "How has it happened," he asks, "that we have not hitherto once thought of humbly applying to the Father of lights to illuminate our understandings? . . . The longer I live, the more convincing proofs I see of this truth—that GOD governs in the affairs of men. And if a sparrow cannot fall to the ground without his notice, is it probable that an empire can rise without his aid?"

During the Revolutionary War the Second Continental Congress prayed regularly for "divine protection," Franklin goes on to remind his audience, and a "kind Providence" heard and answered their prayers. "Have we now forgotten that powerful Friend?" he asks. "Do we imagine we no longer need its assistance?" If so, their undertaking is doomed. "Except the Lord build the House, they labor in vain that build it," he observes, quoting Psalm 127. Pressing home his point, the venerable patriot concludes with a recommendation: henceforth, the convention should begin each day with prayer "imploring the assistance of heaven, and its blessing on our deliberations."[5]

---

[4]Richard Beeman, *Plain, Honest Men: The Making of the American Constitution* (New York: Random House, 2009), 36.

[5]James Madison, *Notes on Debates in the Federal Convention of 1787* (Athens: Ohio University Press, 1966), 209-11.

It was at this point in the drama that the rest of the cast forgot their lines. Franklin's motion was supposed to be the cue for his fellow delegates to experience deep conviction. Cut to the heart, they were supposed to express remorse and embrace the call to prayer. Instead, they froze or went off script. A handful voiced tepid support. A few raised unconvincing objections. Most sat in silence.

In the end, according to James Madison's meticulous notes of the proceedings, the convention adjourned without even voting on Franklin's motion for prayer. This was a polite way for the delegates to defeat the measure without explicitly rejecting it. Franklin's own summation of the awkward affair was terse and unsparing: "The Convention, except three or four persons, thought Prayers unnecessary."[6] No one mentioned it again.

If we want to understand the rise of American democracy—to see it more clearly and think about it more deeply—then we're going to have to ask different questions about the Constitution. For too long, Christians interested in America's past have been preoccupied with one overarching question: Was the United States founded as a Christian country?[7] Concerning the Constitution specifically, we've wanted to know whether the Framers were Christian men, guided by Christian principles, and determined to establish a Christian government. Not much else has seemed to matter.

There's a logic to our fixation. The questions go to the very heart of how we understand our country and our place within it as people of faith; that makes them integral to our identity. They also promise insight into the Framers' original intent concerning the relationship of church and state. Given the centrality of Supreme Court rulings to religious liberty disputes today, that makes them hugely relevant to public policy. But we need to recognize how difficult these questions are to answer as well as the *damage*—I use the term advisedly—they can inflict on us when we become obsessed with them.

We always confront two obstacles when we try to make sense of the past. The first is a problem of *evidence*: there's almost never enough of it.[8] When it comes to the Constitution, for example, we need to recognize just how hard it is to

[6]Farrand, *Records of the Federal Convention*, 1:452.

[7]For an outstanding introduction to the history of this question, see John Fea, *Was America Founded as a Christian Nation?* (Lexington, KY: Westminster John Knox Press, 2011).

[8]David Bebbington, *Patterns in History: A Christian View* (Downers Grove, IL: InterVarsity Press, 1979), 3.

prove that the document was shaped by Christian thinking or even that the men who crafted it were orthodox believers. Either is a tall order.

Establishing intellectual causation may be the most difficult task a historian ever undertakes. We know from their correspondence, diaries, and libraries that many of the Framers were extraordinarily well read. They were students of theology as well as history, philosophy, science, and ancient literature. They were also practical men of the world with practical concerns about profit and power. Unraveling the interwoven threads of intellectual influence to identify a single strand as paramount is almost impossible.

We should also be leery of the implication that it is a simple thing to substantiate the authentic religious beliefs of figures from more than two centuries ago. "For what man knows the things of a man except the spirit of the man which is in him?" the apostle Paul asks.[9] Compounding the problem is that the Framers typically held their religious views close to the vest. When it came time to fashion a new framework of government in 1787, they produced a document that never refers to God and is silent concerning the religious questions that so divide Americans today. Throughout the convention they abstained from making explicitly religious arguments, and they showed the same reticence during the ratification debates that followed.[10]

Surely this is one reason why Christians have found the story of Franklin's call for prayer so seductive. Right up until its disappointing ending, it seems to constitute the one moment during the Constitutional Convention when the Framers abandoned their reticence and unequivocally declared their faith in God. If the other delegates had only embraced Franklin's recommendation, we could confidently point to the episode as irrefutable evidence of the Framers' faith—perhaps even as a tantalizing hint at God's plan for the United States.

That we have so often remembered the story incorrectly calls our attention to the other major obstacle that interferes with our efforts to understand the past. If the first is a problem of evidence, the second is the "problem of the *historian*"

---

[9] 1 Corinthians 2:11.

[10] A meticulous review of the hundreds of pages of Madison's notes on the Constitutional Convention uncovered only one explicit appeal to the Bible in support of a specific constitutional provision, an allusion by Benjamin Franklin to Exodus 18:21. See Daniel Dreisbach, "The Bible and the Political Culture of the American Founding," in *Faith and the Founders of the American Republic*, ed. Daniel Dreisbach and Mark David Hall (New York: Oxford University Press, 2014), 60. A comprehensive study of 190 major pro-Constitution writings published in 1787–1788 fails to uncover a single explicit allusion to Scripture. See Donald S. Lutz, "The Relative Influence of European Writers on Late Eighteenth-Century American Political Thought," *American Political Science Review* 78 (1984): 194.

—the biases or prejudices that we inescapably bring along on our excursions into the past.[11] Our faulty memory of Franklin's call for prayer reminds us of the temptations that lurk whenever we convince ourselves that the future of American Christianity depends on the history of Christianity in America. The results can sometimes be embarrassing, as the recurring efforts to salvage the "miracle at Philadelphia" amply illustrate.

When Franklin made his plea, almost no Americans were aware of it, and the episode would remain largely unknown for many years after 1787. The delegates had sworn themselves to secrecy during the convention itself, and James Madison, the only delegate to keep a systematic record of the proceedings, chose not to make his notes public until after his death, which didn't occur until nearly a half-century later, in 1836. The first reasonably comprehensive American edition of Franklin's private papers was published as early as 1818, however.[12] Although few Americans would have had access to the expensive, six-volume set, rumors that the Constitutional Convention had "thought prayers unnecessary" eventually began to circulate.

For a country swept up at the time in the spiritual fervor of the Second Great Awakening, the news could be disconcerting. In 1821, for example, a New Hampshire correspondent wrote to John Adams to inquire whether the former president knew anything about the alleged incident. (Adams was not a delegate to the convention and had been in England at the time.) An account of Franklin's call for prayer had recently appeared in the *London Quarterly Review*, of all places, and the writer was distressed to find that the supposed rebuff of Franklin's proposal had become the grounds for English claims that Americans "profess a liberal indifference whether there be any religion in the country, or none."[13]

"Not so!" American Christians insisted, and the easiest way to set the record straight was to substitute a different ending to this story about the country's past. By the middle of the 1820s, newspapers and religious periodicals had begun to circulate a new account of Franklin's proposal based on secondhand testimony first recorded thirty-eight years after the Constitutional Convention.

---

[11]Bebbington, *Patterns in History*, 3.

[12]Benjamin Franklin, *The Works of Dr. Benjamin Franklin, in Philosophy, Politics, and Morals*, 6 vols. (Philadelphia: William Duane, 1808–1818). For Franklin's prepared remarks, as well as his subsequent notation that the convention "thought prayers unnecessary," see 1:474-75.

[13]Nathaniel A. Haven to John Adams, 27 August 1821, Founders Online, National Archives, https://founders.archives.gov. Haven was quoting from "New Churches," *London Quarterly Review* 46 (October 1820): 551.

The source was a relative unknown named William Steele, who claimed to have heard what really happened in a conversation some ten years earlier with a convention delegate who had since conveniently died. In Steele's version, Franklin's proposal "was instantly seconded and carried," and the only delegate "impious" enough to question its wisdom was received with "a mixture of surprise and indignation."[14]

We can excuse early nineteenth-century believers for seizing hold of this comforting ending. Franklin's postscript to the affair was buried in a multivolume collection of his papers that almost no one could afford. Madison's record of the convention had yet to see the light of day. Almost none of the behind-the-scenes correspondence of key delegates was publicly available. In the absence of evidence to the contrary, Steele's secondhand testimony recorded nearly four decades after the fact could be taken seriously, although it never should have been accepted uncritically.

In sum, we can't fault the Christians who swallowed Steele's testimony for not knowing that Franklin himself directly contradicted it. They also had no way of knowing what Madison's record would make clear when it was published: that the mood among delegates grew worse, not better, for days after Franklin's June 28 speech. Nor could they have been aware that George Washington wrote to Alexander Hamilton nearly two weeks after Franklin's plea to complain that affairs were, "if possible, in a worse train than ever."[15]

It's hard to be as charitable toward the numerous modern-day apologists who continue to recycle the myth and insist that Franklin's call for prayer saved the convention and, by extension, the United States. Authors Peter Marshall and David Manuel set the pattern a half-century ago in their fabulously successful interpretation of "God's plan for America," *The Light and the Glory*. After reprinting Franklin's speech in its entirety, Marshall and Manuel skipped the convention's response but insisted (without offering any supporting evidence) that Franklin's plea "marked the turning point" in the convention.[16]

In the intervening decades a host of preachers and media celebrities have echoed this conclusion, including prominent pastor and writer Tim LaHaye,

---

[14]The account first appeared in the letter of William Steele to Jonathan D. Steele, September 1825, and is reprinted in whole in Farrand, *Records of the Federal Convention*, 3:467-73. For examples of contemporary circulation of the letter in whole or in part, see *National Intelligencer*, August 26, 1826, and *Christian Advocate and Journal and Zion's Herald* 33 (April 1832), 129-30.

[15]Beeman, *Plain, Honest Men*, 203.

[16]Peter Marshall and David Manuel, *The Light and the Glory* (Tarrytown, NY: Fleming H. Revell, 1977), 343.

Wallbuilders founder David Barton, popular Christian author Eric Metaxas, and radio host and film critic Michael Medved. Passing over the extensive evidence to the contrary, they insist that Franklin's speech "made a profound impact on the delegates," who viewed his heartfelt plea as "the intrusion of the Almighty" on the country's behalf.[17]

My point is not that the Framers rejected the value of prayer or were hostile to Christianity. Nor am I remotely suggesting that an accurate remembering of Franklin's motion somehow proves that they meant to create a "godless Constitution."[18] But I do want us to see that secular liberals aren't the only ones prone to revise America's past. Desperate to score points against academics who understate Christianity's role in the Founding, all too often Christians have cried "revisionist!" and then jumped into the other ditch, uncritically accepting unverified claims or stretching the evidence to find irrefutable proof of the Founders' born-again convictions. *God doesn't need our exaggerations to accomplish his work.*

There are good ways and bad ways to pay attention to the past, and the debate over America's Christian roots brings out the very worst. The wonder is that we learn anything at all from it. Because so much seems to be at stake in the debate, because we're convinced that we have to *win* it, we end up turning history into an arsenal, a storehouse not of wisdom but of weapons—quotes and anecdotes that we draw like revolvers in a shootout with secular opponents.

Whenever someone at church asks me about the relationship between Christianity and the Constitution, I'm always tempted to reply, "Why do you want to know?" It's a lot like those campaign ads that grow so tiresome before Election Day. Too often what we really want is for the Framers to make a cameo at the end and announce, "We're the Founding Fathers and we approve this message."

I call this the history-as-ammunition approach to the past, and its effects are insidious. Once we set out to prove that the United States was founded as a

---

[17]See Tim LaHaye, *Faith of Our Founding Fathers* (Green Forest, AR: Master Books, 1990), 57, 123-24; David Barton, *Original Intent: The Courts, the Constitution, and Religion* (Aledo, TX: Wallbuilders Press, 1996), 116-18; Eric Metaxas, *If You Can Keep It: The Forgotten Promise of American Liberty* (New York: Viking, 2016), 206; Michael Medved, *The American Miracle: Divine Providence in the Rise of the Republic* (New York: Crown Forum, 2016), 104-7.

[18]Isaac Kramnick and R. Laurence Moore, *The Godless Constitution: The Case Against Religious Correctness* (New York: W. W. Norton, 1996); Brooke Allen, "Our Godless Constitution," *The Nation*, February 21, 2005, 14-20.

Christian country, the temptation to refashion the Founders in our own image becomes irresistible. This doesn't have to be conscious or premeditated. The historical figures that we encounter always resemble us in some ways and differ from us in others, and we quite naturally pick up on the former better than the latter. The history-as-ammunition approach just magnifies this natural tendency.

The result is that, instead of encountering figures from the past who might challenge and change us, we meet our clones in powdered wigs. Sure, they dressed oddly, but deep down the Founders as we imagine them thought as we think, valued what we value, and—not to put too fine a point on it—would vote as we vote. This makes the past politically useful to us, but at a great cost: we learn nothing from it. How could we? The historical figures we've imagined already agree with us in all the ways that matter.

We would be much better served to set aside the question of whether the Framers were *Christian* and focus instead on thinking *Christianly* about the framework of government they constructed.[19] In the rest of this chapter and the next, we'll turn our attention from the Framers' theology to their *anthropology*—from what they thought about God to what they thought about *us*. In essence, we'll take our cue from James Madison, recognizing that our Constitution is, among other things, an extended commentary on human nature.

This means that we'll step away from the politically charged, dichotomous questions at the heart of the Christian America debate: Were the Framers of the Constitution Christians? Were they guided by Christian principles? Was their goal to create a Christian nation? In their stead, we'll ask the following: What were the Framers' views on human nature? How did their views inform the document they bequeathed to us? To what degree were their beliefs about human nature consistent with Christian teaching?

Notice several key features of the questions we'll be pursuing: First, although they shift the focus away from theology to anthropology—from the Framers' beliefs about God to their understanding of humanity—these questions are still *fundamentally religious*. Our faith is never confined solely to what we believe about God; it is also defined by our understanding of human nature and the human condition.

The questions are undoubtedly *historically crucial* as well. If our goal is to understand the rise of American democracy in historical context, as well as to

---

[19]On thinking Christianly, see Harry Blamires, *The Christian Mind* (London: Society for the Propagation of Christian Knowledge, 1963), especially chapter two.

think more Christianly about it in our contemporary context, it's hard to imagine a more fruitful line of questioning. Beyond this, observe that the questions are *open-ended* rather than dichotomous (yes/no questions always promote over-simplification). They also ask us to think in terms of *correlation* or *compatibility* (which can logically be demonstrated) rather than *causation* (which is almost impossible to prove).

Finally, these questions invite us to focus on a subject on which the *historical record is rich*. While it can be exceedingly difficult to pinpoint the Framers' beliefs about God, they spoke and wrote at length concerning their views of human nature. The reason for this is clear. As the infant United States teetered on the brink of collapse by the mid-1780s, the statesmen who would eventually gather in Philadelphia to "form a more perfect union" had no doubt that their country was in the grips of a *moral* crisis. Taught to believe that a republic required "virtue" to survive, they were convinced that the American people weren't virtuous.

In making a case for moral reform in our own day, well-meaning Christian writers often tell the story of the United States as a story of decline from a time when Americans were characterized by a civic-minded commitment to the common good. Eric Metaxas, for example, writes that it was because of this once widespread quality that the Framers of the Constitution could place "tremendous trust in the people." Bemoaning the individualism and self-ishness rampant today, Metaxas exhorts us to become again "the America we were at first."[20]

This would have bewildered the Founders. By the mid-1780s they feared that the country was on the verge of "national humiliation," as one hero of the Revolution put it, and they were convinced that the root cause of that catastrophe was moral. "We are going and doing wrong," lamented future Supreme Court Justice John Jay a year before the Constitutional Convention. "Evils and calamities" would be the result. "We are far gone in every thing ignoble & bad," George Washington echoed in a letter written the day after Christmas 1786. Without decisive action, the country would "sink into the lowest state of humiliation & contempt, & become a byword in all the earth."[21]

---

[20]Metaxas, *If You Can Keep It*, 10, 25.

[21]Henry Knox to George Washington, 23 October 1786, Founders Online; John Jay to George Washington, 27 June 1786, Founders Online; George Washington to Henry Knox, 26 December 1786, Founders Online.

That same month, Mercy Otis Warren, arguably the leading female intellectual in revolutionary America, fumed in a letter to John Adams that their fellow countrymen were undeserving of liberty. Pulling no punches, she reckoned that "the imbecility of human nature" then on display in the United States was as strong "as perhaps may be found in any page of history." Adams could only agree. "Our country men," he concluded to Mercy's husband, James, "have never merited the character of very exalted virtue."[22]

The key word in Adams's assessment was the last one. *Virtue* meant different things in different contexts in Revolutionary America. Most broadly, it could mean any positive trait, as when Washington wondered whether marl "possesses any virtue as a manure" or when a correspondent informed Thomas Jefferson about the "virtues" of Chinese tea.[23] When applied to women, the term often carried the connotation of sexual chastity or modesty. When men aspired to "domestic" virtue, they sought to behave with industry, frugality, and integrity in their homes, businesses, or professions.

But when observers in the 1780s linked the distressing state of the country with a shortage of virtue, they had yet another definition in mind. The virtue they alluded to was a public ideal, not unlike patriotism, embodied in "the willingness of the individual to sacrifice his private interests for the good of the community." As defined by the French philosopher Montesquieu—one of their favorite Enlightenment thinkers—virtue is a "continuous preference of the public interest over one's own." In the words of John Adams, a virtuous patriot lived by the principle that "all things must give way to the public."[24] Conventional wisdom taught that this sort of virtue was essential for a republic to thrive.

And so the Revolutionary generation emphasized it, constantly, making virtue "one of the most revered political concepts of the 18th century."[25] Both before and after the creation of the Constitution, the leading Founders exalted virtue, looked for ways to encourage virtue, and underscored the importance of virtue to the infant republic.

---

[22]Mercy Otis Warren to John Adams, December 1786, Founders Online; John Adams to James Warren, 9 January 1787, Founders Online.

[23]Diary of George Washington, 30 January 1786, Founders Online; Neil Jamieson to Thomas Jefferson, 12 July 1784, Founders Online.

[24]Gordon S. Wood, *Creation of the American Republic, 1776–1787* (Chapel Hill: University of North Carolina Press, 1969), 68; Charles de Secondat Baron de Montesquieu, *Spirit of the Laws*, trans. Anne Cohler et al. (New York: Cambridge University Press, 1989), 36; John Adams to Mercy Otis Warren, 16 April 1776, Founders Online.

[25]Barry Alan Shain, *The Myth of American Individualism: The Protestant Origins of American Political Thought* (Princeton, NJ: Princeton University Press, 1994), 34.

Virtue "is a necessary spring of popular government," Washington would remind the country in his last public address. "Only a virtuous people are capable of freedom," Benjamin Franklin agreed. "Virtue is the only foundation of republics," John Adams postulated. Without it, Framer David Ramsay told his state's ratifying convention, "our growing numbers will soon degenerate into barbarism."[26]

The American who failed to exhibit virtue, Framer William Livingston maintained, "is not only a bad Citizen, but a real Enemy to his country." "When *individuals* consider *their* interests" as opposed to the common good, Framer John Dickinson echoed, "a people is traveling fast to destruction." It followed that public schools must promote virtue, as the prominent physician Benjamin Rush insisted. "Let our pupil be taught that he does not belong to himself," this signer of the Declaration of Independence wrote in 1786. He must forsake all "when the welfare of his country requires it." To the schoolhouse, the Founders added town meetings, militia drills, and religious services as other venues where "the virtues and talents of the people" could be formed.[27]

From across the generations, the Founders' emphasis on self-denial and the common good is rare and refreshing, a stark contrast to today's "naked public square" in which individuals and interest groups look out for number one.[28] But before we conclude that we've discovered a lost golden age, we must realize that the Founders underscored the importance of virtue in part because they found it to be lacking. As they surveyed the state of the country by the mid-1780s, they were convinced that Americans didn't have it, or at least not enough of it.

Observations like these were legion: "There doth not appear to be virtue enough among the people to preserve a perfect republican government." "The people have not wisdom or virtue enough to govern themselves." "It is to be greatly lamented, that there is no more genuine virtue & patriotism among the inhabitants." Virtue "certainly is a principle of too whimsical a nature to be relied

---

[26]Daniel J. Boorstin, ed., *An American Primer* (New York: Penguin, 1966), 221-22; Benjamin Franklin to the Abbés Chalut and Arnoux, 17 April 1787, *Memoirs of the Life and Writings of Benjamin Franklin*, ed. William Temple Franklin, 3rd edition (London: Henry Colburn, 1818), vol. III, pt. 1, 220; John Adams to Mercy Otis Warren, 16 April 1776, Founders Online; Bernard Bailyn, ed., *The Debate on the Constitution: Federalist and Antifederalist Speeches, Articles, and Letters During the Struggle over Ratification* (New York: Literary Classics of the United States, 1993), part 2, 513.

[27]Shain, *Myth of American Individualism*, 43; John Dickinson, "Letters of a Farmer in Pennsylvania" (1768), in *The Writings of John Dickinson: Political Writings, 1764–1774*, ed. Paul L. Ford (Philadelphia: Historical Society of Pennsylvania, 1895), 397; Michael J. Sandel, *Democracy's Discontent: America in Search of a Public Philosophy* (Cambridge, MA: Harvard University Press, 1996), 129, 132; Diary of John Adams, 21 July 1786, Founders Online.

[28]Richard John Neuhaus, *The Naked Public Square: Religion and Democracy in America* (Grand Rapids, MI: Eerdmans, 1984).

on." "Too much has been expected from the virtue and good sense of the people." "There has been an astonishing decay of public virtue among us." "Virtue . . . has an influence only on a chosen few." "We are in the high road to have no virtues left." "The virtue of the people are [sic] vanished." "Virtue . . . has, in a great degree, taken its departure from our land." Americans "do not exhibit the virtue that is necessary to support a republican government."[29]

In sum, the Founders widely believed that self-denial in the service of the common good was in short supply. For evidence, they pointed to the sad state of public affairs.

When advocates of governmental reform insisted that something drastic must be done to save the republic, they regularly pointed to three distressing features of public life. First, because the central government under the Articles of Confederation lacked the power to regulate commerce with foreign nations or to command compliance with international treaties, a coherent foreign policy coordinating the actions of thirteen independent sovereignties was utterly impossible.

Second, because the central government was denied the power to tax, it was staggering financially, unable to honor its debts either to private citizens or foreign governments. Third, there was growing popular resistance to state taxation, and by the winter of 1786–1787 angry citizens across New England were intimidating tax collectors and shutting down county courts in order to forestall tax sales and foreclosures. Anarchy loomed.

Almost everyone who supported the call for the Philadelphia Convention condemned the weakness of the central government under the Articles of Confederation, but it's important not to miss their more fundamental diagnosis. Although each of the concerns listed above could be blamed on defects in the Articles of Confederation, at a more fundamental level each could be understood as resulting from defects in human nature. The core problem, critics

---

[29]Benjamin Lincoln to George Washington, 4 December 1786, Founders Online; David Humphreys to George Washington, 20 January 1787, Founders Online; William Vans Murray, "Political Sketches" (1787), quoted in Shain, *Myth of American Individualism*, 46; William Gordon to George Washington, 20 January 1787, Founders Online; John Jay to Thomas Jefferson, 9 February 1787, Founders Online; Diary of John Quincy Adams, entry for November 26, 1786, Founders Online; Mercy Otis Warren to John Adams, December 1786, Founders Online; John Adams to Elbridge Gerry, 25 April 1785, Founders Online; James Sullivan to John Adams, 16 December 1786, Founders Online; George Washington to John Jay, 18 May 1786, Founders Online; Gordon S. Wood, *The American Revolution: A History* (New York: Modern Library, 2002), 141.

contended, was that neither state governments nor private citizens could be trusted to promote the common good without compulsion. If the apparent failure of the Articles proved anything, it was "the melancholy proof that mankind are not competent to their own government without the means of coercion in the sovereign."[30]

In the realm of foreign relations, the weakness of the central government under the Articles required both states and private citizens to sacrifice their immediate interests voluntarily in the service of the public good. As often as not, they refused. Instead, as John Jay explained to George Washington in the summer of 1786, "personal rather than national interests have become the great objects of attention."[31]

As Secretary of Foreign Affairs under the Articles, Jay was in the process of compiling a report for Congress on the states' compliance with the stipulations of the Treaty of Paris, the agreement with Great Britain that had ended the American Revolutionary War. The gist of Jay's findings was simple: the states weren't complying. Washington was grieved and ashamed. His explanation of their behavior was telling: "We have probably had too good an opinion of human nature in forming our confederation."[32]

Among the least popular provisions of the Treaty of Paris were requirements that the former colonists honor prewar debts owed to English citizens and restore property confiscated during the war from American loyalists. Showing no regard for public honor, state legislatures regularly ignored both obligations, as lawmakers were unwilling to press measures that might upset their constituents. As Jay would later report concerning the treaty, "There has not been a single day since it took effect, on which it has not been violated in America, by one or the other of the states." Because the Articles stipulated that "each state retains its sovereignty, freedom, and independence," the central government could do nothing but stand by and watch.[33]

Critics discerned a similar shortage of virtue underlying the government's dismal financial condition. Given that the Articles of Confederation were created during a war sparked by resentment of British tax policy, it's not surprising that the men who erected that framework were hesitant to clothe their

---

[30]George Washington to John Jay, 10 March 1787, Founders Online.
[31]John Jay to George Washington, 27 June 1786, Founders Online.
[32]George Washington to John Jay, 15 August 1786, Founders Online.
[33]John Jay to George Washington, 27 June 1786, Founders Online.

own revolutionary government with broad taxing authority. Yet, from our twenty-first-century perspective, the mechanism that the Articles envisioned for generating revenue is comical.

Rather than authorizing taxation, the Articles of Confederation invited the central government to make "requisitions" of the states. After determining its annual needs, the Congress would inform the states of the amount of money each needed to donate in order for the government to stay afloat. In theory, each state would then voluntarily comply. It was like a PBS telethon without the commemorative tote bags.

The arrangement worked about as well as you'd expect. By 1786 the central government was reduced to begging. The so-called *United* States—exposed as a loose association of petty independent republics—teetered on the brink of bankruptcy. Thirteen "independent, disunited states" made requisitions "a perfect nihility," Washington lamented, "little better than a jest and a bye word through out the land." The reason this "system of imbecility" failed so miserably, Alexander Hamilton explained, was that the states regularly ignored the common good and yielded to "the persuasive voice of immediate interest or convenience." In sum, they lacked virtue.[34]

The same could be said about the alarming "commotions" plaguing New England by 1786. Contemporaries differed about the "respectability or contemptibility" of the insurgents who were shutting down local courts. Sympathetic observers said that "taxes have been assessed too high and collected too rigidly," and they noted that a shortage of hard money in the countryside made the burden especially heavy on rural taxpayers.

For the most part, this was not the view of future "federalists"—that is, individuals who would soon rally to support a new Constitution. (Opponents of ratification would come to be known as "anti-federalists.") Henry Knox was extreme in characterizing the insurgents as "desperate & unprincipled men" determined to "annihilate all debts" and wage war against "the principles of all government." But probably most future federalists would have echoed the Virginian who discerned in "the disturbances to the North-ward . . . the sure proof of a want of virtue."[35]

---

[34]George Washington to John Jay, 15 August 1786; Alexander Hamilton, *Federalist* #22, in Alexander Hamilton, James Madison, and John Jay, *The Federalist*, ed. J. R. Pole (Indianapolis: Hackett, 2005), 117; Alexander Hamilton, *Federalist* #15, 81.
[35]Henry Knox to George Washington, 23 October 1786; David Stuart to George Washington, 19

From his vantage point in the Confederation Congress in New York, James Madison found the state legislatures as deficient in virtue as the people they represented. In several states, legislators were cravenly capitulating to angry constituents, passing laws postponing the payment of debts or accepting depreciated paper currency as legal tender. For Madison, the "injustice" of such laws called into question "the fundamental principle of republican government, that the majority . . . are the safest guardians both of public good and of private rights."[36]

All of this suggests that, if America had ever basked in a golden age of civic virtue, that time was long past when leading statesmen began calling for a convention to revise or replace the Articles of Confederation. It is more accurate to say, as one historian has concluded, that "the U. S. Constitution emerged from a *crisis* of virtue."[37]

But if the diagnosis was clear, the prescription was not. Logically, one solution would be to increase virtue across the land, infusing public life with a widespread commitment to self-sacrifice for the common good. Another answer, less idealistic, would be to make virtue less necessary by reconfiguring the structure of government itself. Os Guinness helpfully distinguishes between these responses. He labels the first an emphasis on the "informal spirit of liberty," the second an attention to the "formal structures of liberty."[38]

Guinness insists that the Founders embraced both strategies, and in a sense he is right. Beyond their sincere efforts to promote a virtuous citizenry, many also clearly hoped that the new Constitution would make it easier to place virtuous statesmen into office. "The aim of every political Constitution," James Madison observed, "is or ought to be first to obtain for rulers, men who possess most wisdom to discern, and most virtue to pursue the common good of the society." It was Washington's "wish that none but the most disinterested, able and virtuous men may be appointed to either house of Congress." Madison rallied support for the Constitution by suggesting that the Congress under the new government would function as "a chosen body of citizens,

---

December 1786, Founders Online.

[36]James Madison, "Vices of the Political System of the United States," Founders Online.

[37]Thomas S. Kidd, *God of Liberty: A Religious History of the American Revolution* (New York: Basic Books, 2010), 209, italics added.

[38]Os Guinness, *A Free People's Suicide: Sustainable Freedom and the American Future* (Downers Grove, IL: InterVarsity Press, 2012), 19-20.

whose wisdom may best discern the true interest of their country, and whose patriotism and love of justice will be least likely to sacrifice it to temporary or partial considerations."[39]

Yet, for all their praise of virtue, the Founders were realists. They *exhorted* Americans to revere and practice virtue. They didn't *expect* it. When it comes to gauging their reading of human nature, we must see that they thought of virtue as, quite literally, artificial. It doesn't occur naturally in our species. Montesquieu had equated it with a "renunciation of oneself, which is always a very painful thing."[40] It goes against the grain of human nature, and the only way to develop it, the Founders assumed, is through a heroic regimen of prolonged and arduous discipline that few mortals are up to.

Thomas Jefferson, for example—whose view of human nature was rosier than most of his peers—instructed his nephew that virtue was like a muscle that will only "gain strength by exercise." Less optimistic in her outlook, and more representative of her generation, Abigail Adams instructed her son Thomas to think of virtue as "like the stone of Sysiphus." According to Greek myth, Sisyphus was a crafty king who was punished for his deceitfulness by being made to roll a boulder repeatedly up a steep hill for all eternity. Given that human nature is "infirm & liable to err as daily experience proves," Abigail explained to her son, "virtue . . . has a continual tendency to roll down hill & requires to be forced up again by the never ceasing efforts of succeeding moralists."[41] It wasn't an encouraging metaphor.

In actuality, it was defenders of the Articles of Confederation, not proponents of a new constitution, who hoped that the country's problems could be lessened by an increase of virtue. A Massachusetts statesman, for example, wrote to John Adams to condemn those who "vainly" supposed that a stronger central government was essential to the country's happiness. The proper course, he proposed instead, was renewed cultivation of "the love of our country, and attention to the social virtues."[42]

Similarly, a Virginian wrote to James Madison to voice his disagreement with nationalists (like Madison) who were calling for a decided shift of power toward

---

[39]James Madison, *Federalist #57*, 309; George Washington to Benjamin Fishbourne, 23 December 1788, Founders Online; James Madison, *Federalist #10*, 52.

[40]Montesquieu, *Spirit of the Laws*, 35.

[41]Thomas Jefferson to Peter Carr, 19 August 1785, Founders Online; Abigail Adams to Thomas Boylston Adams, 15 March 1787, Founders Online.

[42]James Sullivan to John Adams, 23 October 1785, Founders Online.

the central government and away from the states. "Is there not much less difficulty, and far less danger," he asked Madison, to implement more modest structural changes "and then make an effort, in good earnest, to give purity of manners,
and morals, [and] of course public virtue, a prevalence?"[43]

The answer, federalists agreed, was "no." It was all well and good to imagine a
day when Americans would be exempt from the "weaknesses and evils" intrinsic
to human society, Alexander Hamilton would later note in defending the Constitution, but such fantasies were no basis for effective government. "Is it not
time to awake from the deceitful dream of a golden age?" he asked. Americans

should "adopt as a practical maxim
for the direction of our political
conduct, that we, as well as the
other inhabitants of the globe, are
yet remote from the happy empire
of perfect wisdom and perfect
virtue."[44] To federalists, the primary
lesson of the Articles of Confederation was that the country had expected too much of human nature,
not that an elevation of morals
could cure the country's woes.

Although we may not like to
hear it, proponents of the Constitution repeatedly insisted that,
when it comes to our character,
Americans aren't exceptional. Ham-

Alexander Hamilton

ilton was characteristically blunt: "We have no reason to think ourselves wiser
or better than other men," he averred. "We imagined that the mildness of our
government and *the virtue* of the people were so correspondent, that we were
not as other nations," echoed Henry Knox in a letter to George Washington. "But
we find that we are men, actual men, possessing all the turbulent passions be-
longing to that animal."[45]

---

[43] Arthur Campbell to James Madison, 28 October 1785, Founders Online.
[44] Alexander Hamilton, *Federalist #6*, 27.
[45] Carl J. Richard, *The Founders and the Bible* (Lanham, MD: Rowman & Littlefield, 2016), 269;
   Henry Knox to George Washington, 23 October 1786, Founders Online, italics original.

A Connecticut correspondent aptly distilled this view in a letter to General Washington. "We are already nearly ruined by believing too much—We have believed that the citizens of the United States were better than the rest of the world."[46] Americans weren't unique, these writers insisted. They were human, with all that entails.

And so although they exalted virtue, the Framers of the Constitution didn't convene in Philadelphia to exhort Americans to become again "the America they were at first." Rather, they arrived convinced that government under the Articles of Confederation was failing in large part because it rested on an utterly unrealistic, even utopian understanding of human nature. Whatever steps they might propose, they agreed that their necessary starting point must be a more realistic assessment of the raw material of the republic. The key was to understand human nature rightly.

---

[46]David Humphreys to George Washington, 20 January 1787, Founders Online.

2

"WE MUST TAKE HUMAN NATURE AS WE FIND IT"

*O*ur affairs seem to lead to some crisis—some Revolution—something that I cannot foresee or conjecture," John Jay wrote to George Washington from Philadelphia in the summer of 1786. "We are going and doing wrong," he lamented. "I look forward to Evils and Calamities." The horizon was similarly dark at Mount Vernon, where Washington harbored the same sense of foreboding. Like Jay, he saw that "our affairs are drawing rapidly to a crisis." Like Jay, he confessed that the outcome was "beyond the reach of my foresight." But this much was undeniable: "We have errors to correct."

The chief of these, the general concluded, was that the Founders had "had too good an opinion of human nature" in forming the Articles of Confederation. "Would to God that wise measures may be taken in time to avert the consequences we have too much reason to apprehend." And what would be the key to designing these necessary measures? To Washington the answer was obvious: "We must take human nature as we find it."[1]

But what did that mean? How did the Founders understand human nature? Before we hear them out, I need to offer some final context and an admonition.

First the context: When the Founders referred to traits of "*human* nature," even though they thought of those qualities as universal, in practice they were typically focused on the character of *white males*. They weren't theologians

---

[1]John Jay to George Washington, 27 June 1786, Founders Online, National Archives, https://founders.archives.gov; George Washington to John Jay, 15 August 1786, Founders Online.

deliberating about the condition of human beings before a righteous God, as important as that question is. They were statesmen debating how best to structure government in order to preserve liberty and perpetuate a republic. When they mused about human nature, in other words, it was commonly with an eye to political questions, not theological ones, and politics in the late-eighteenth century was predominantly a white male domain.

Today we would rightly reject such a truncated conception of civil society. In the late-eighteenth century it was conventional wisdom, grounded on two long-standing axioms of republican political philosophy. The first was the contention that voting is not a right—for anyone—but rather a privilege conferred on those who will exercise it responsibly. Although this view began to be challenged during the American Revolution, the Founders supported it almost unanimously. In the words of James Wilson, a signer of both the Declaration of Independence and the Constitution, they viewed the vote as "a darling privilege of free men" that should only be extended "as far as considerations of safety and order will permit."[2]

The second principle was that "safety and order" permitted only the economically independent to vote. A century and a half earlier, Englishman Henry Ireton had articulated the new orthodoxy: "If there be anything at all that is the foundation of liberty," the son-in-law of Oliver Cromwell declared, "it is this, that those who shall choose the law-makers shall be men freed from dependence upon others."[3]

Property owners not only had a "permanent fixed interest" in the community that seemed to entitle them to a voice in its public affairs. Their economic independence also supposedly freed them from manipulation by landlords or employers or creditors who might otherwise use their economic leverage to control their votes. Property requirements for voting were ubiquitous in colonial America, and after the onset of the American Revolution all but two of the thirteen new state governments extended them in some form. In so doing, they excluded between 30 and 40 percent of adult white males from the franchise.

The logic behind such laws becomes clearer when we recall that elections in the seventeenth and eighteenth centuries were public rituals. Voters cast their ballots openly or, as often as not, announced their preferences orally before their

---

[2]Alexander Keyssar, *The Right to Vote: The Contested History of Democracy in the United States*, rev. ed. (New York: Basic Books, 2009), 8.

[3]Jack P. Greene, *Imperatives, Behaviors, and Identities: Essays in Early American Cultural History* (Charlottesville: University of Virginia Press, 1992), 251.

assembled friends and neighbors. The plausible assumption was that, in such a context, community members dependent on others for their daily bread could be manipulated or intimidated by those who controlled their livelihoods. "Such is the frailty of the human heart," John Adams observed, that "Men who have no Property . . . talk and vote as they are directed by Some Man of Property."[4]

So it was that individuals under the dominion of another were "deemed to have no will of their own," as Montesquieu explained. Allowing such a person to vote, the great English jurist William Blackstone elaborated, would effectively "give a great, an artful, or a wealthy man, a larger share in elections than is consistent with general liberty." From our vantage point, an obvious solution would have been to implement a secret ballot, but at the end of the American Revolution that reform was still more than a century in the future. For the Founders, the safest path was to follow the advice of philosopher John Locke and deny full participation in civil society to anyone "subjected to the Will or Authority of any other Man."[5]

Locke's maxim was technically colorblind, but it had the practical effect of reinforcing existing hierarchies of race and gender. Whereas the insistence on economic independence disfranchised a sizable *minority* of white males, it disqualified both enslaved people and married white women *entirely*. The essence of slavery is to be "subjected to the Will or Authority" of another, and in the eighteenth century the law defined marriage in much the same way. Under a legal principle known as coverture, women forfeited all control of their property to their husbands upon marrying, and this meant that they simultaneously forfeited any claim to full participation in the political community.

The year before he served as a delegate to the Constitutional Convention, Judge Oliver Ellsworth of Connecticut explained the connection in a case before his court. Married women were "placed in the power of a husband," he noted, "whose solicitations they cannot resist, and whose commands . . . it is their duty to obey." In such a vulnerable condition, Ellsworth concluded, their professed votes could "afford but very uncertain evidence of the real wishes of their hearts."[6]

---

[4]John Adams to James Sullivan, 26 May 1776, Founders Online.
[5]Charles de Secondat Baron de Montesquieu, *Spirit of the Laws*, trans. Anne Cohler et al. (New York: Cambridge University Press, 1989), 160; Keyssar, *Right to Vote*, 8; Greene, *Imperatives, Behaviors, and Identities*, 251.
[6]Linda K. Kerber, *Women of the Republic: Intellect and Ideology in Revolutionary America* (Chapel Hill: University of North Carolina Press, 1980), 143.

Note the circular arguments that banished both black slaves and white wives from political society. First, the law denied them the right to control property. Next, it denied them the privilege of voting because they weren't property owners. There's no evidence that the Founders agonized over this reasoning.

Although Abraham Lincoln would be correct when he later insisted that the majority of the Founders hoped to see slavery eventually die out, it's equally true that they took black inferiority for granted. The more extreme among them echoed the author of the Declaration of Independence. A decade after writing that "all men are created equal," Thomas Jefferson concluded that blacks are "inferior to whites in the endowments both of body and mind." The differences were not the product of environment, he hypothesized, but "real distinctions which nature has made."[7]

Those with more moderate views would have agreed with North Carolinian David Ramsay, soon to be a delegate to the Constitutional Convention. Ramsay thought Jefferson had "depressed the negroes too low," and he countered that "all mankind" are "originally the same and diversified by accidental circumstances." But whether they viewed African Americans as intrinsically inferior or inferior as a consequence of their enslavement, the Founders shared a common inability to envision a biracial society in which emancipated slaves had an equal voice in the republican task of self-government.[8]

Nor could they imagine such a role for their own wives. When Abigail Adams wrote to her husband in 1776 to "Remember the Ladies" in the new framework of government he would help to create, she pointedly questioned why her sex should "hold ourselves bound by laws in which we have no voice or representation." John Adams had no answer and deflected with a joke about the "Despotism of the Peticoat." His friend Richard Henry Lee, a fellow signer of the Declaration of Independence, was almost alone among prominent Founders in his willingness to support limited voting rights for white married women. Politics had been seen as the province of males since the days of Aristotle. The Founders saw no reason for change.[9]

---

[7]Thomas Jefferson, *Notes on the State of Virginia*, in *The Portable Thomas Jefferson*, ed. Merrill Peterson (New York: Penguin, 1975), 192-93, 186.

[8]Joseph Ellis, *American Dialogue: The Founders and Us* (New York: Alfred A. Knopf, 2018), 26, 227.

[9]Abigail Adams to John Adams, 31 March 1776, Founders Online; John Adams to Abigail Adams, 14 April 1776, Founders Online; Gary Nash, *The Unknown American Revolution: The Unruly Birth of Democracy and the Struggle to Create America* (New York: Viking, 2005), 289.

Frederick Buechner reminds us that when we are born into the world, there is simultaneously a world born in us.[10] We are immersed into cultural contexts that affect our innermost beings, shaping what we know, how we think, what we take for granted, and what we struggle to accept. We naturally tend to assume "that 'what is' is what was meant to be."[11] Even the most far-sighted among us transcend the world we inherit but partially; none of us escapes its influence entirely. From hindsight, we see how this was true of the Founders. Some later generation will see how this has been true of us.

Which brings us to the admonition: Americans have long found it difficult to think about the nation's Founders with discernment. We eschew nuance and complexity for an all-or-nothing dogmatism that either venerates the Founders or views them with disdain. Let's strive to do better.

And so if you've been conditioned to revere the Founders, be careful. If you've been accustomed to think of them as infallible, don't. In theological terms, that's idolatry. I want you to listen to the Founders, not canonize them.[12] They weren't saints. They were flawed. They had blind spots, many of which are now glaringly obvious. That's why at the end of this chapter we'll take time to assess their views in the light of Scripture and historic Christian teaching rather than accept them uncritically.

Similarly, if you're tempted to dismiss the Founders out of hand, think again. I get why you might feel this way. Given that our views with regard to race and gender differ so dramatically from the Founders, it can seem sensible to question whether they have anything to say to our twenty-first-century world. But bear this in mind: When we discern truths that our ancestors could not see, it doesn't necessarily mean that we are wiser than they were. It may only mean that their blind spots were different from ours, in which case they may see much that we cannot.

So what *was* the Founders' understanding of human nature? In an age in which we're accustomed to being flattered by politicians seeking our support, it can be jarring to hear the candid comments of the individuals we revere as "Founding Fathers." At their most extreme, they could be dark indeed. The arch patriot Samuel Adams spoke for most of his peers in asserting that "ambitions and lust

---

[10]Frederick Buechner, *The Sacred Journey: A Memoir of Early Days* (New York: HarperCollins, 1982), 9.

[11]Margaret Bendroth, *The Spiritual Practice of Remembering* (Grand Rapids, MI: Eerdmans, 2013), 49.

[12]Ellis, *American Dialogue*, 224.

for power . . . are predominant passions in the breasts of most men." Today we tend to think of ambition as a positive trait, but in the eighteenth century the term denoted an inordinate desire to rise in influence and social status, whatever the cost. It was the very opposite of virtue, as reflected in a common saying, "When virtue is lost, ambition succeeds."[13]

Echoing Adams, Alexander Hamilton railed against "the folly and wickedness of mankind." Patrick Henry confessed to "dread the depravity of human nature." Roger Sherman characterized humans as "prone to evil and adverse to the good." Sam Adams's cousin John decried the extent of "rascality," "venality," "corruption," "avarice," and "ambition" (there's that word again) to be found "among all ranks and degrees of men." George Mason lamented "the natural lust for power so inherent in man."[14]

Benjamin Franklin added the "love of money" to the love of power, identifying "avarice and ambition" as the "two passions which have a powerful influence in the affairs of men." George Washington maintained that "the motives which predominate most in human affairs [are] self-love and self-interest." John Jay offered the most succinct assessment: "The mass of men are neither wise nor good."[15]

We can read assertions like these and assume that the Framers of the Constitution must have viewed human beings as unrelievedly "evil." That would be a mistake. Like so much of their understanding of the world, the Framers' assessment of human nature was complicated. In Hamilton's words, they were convinced that "the supposition of universal venality in human nature is little less an error in political reasoning than the supposition of universal rectitude."[16]

In other words, the Framers scoffed at the contention that men and women are basically good, but they also rejected the view that we are relentlessly depraved.[17] No simplistic generalization can capture their position, and that's a

---

[13]Bernard Bailyn, *The Ideological Origins of the American Revolution* (Cambridge, MA: Harvard University Press, 1967), 60; John Adams to Elbridge Gerry, 25 April 1785, Founders Online.

[14]Alexander Hamilton, *Federalist #78*, in Alexander Hamilton, James Madison, and John Jay, *The Federalist*, ed. J. R. Pole (Indianapolis: Hackett, 2005), 418; Carl J. Richard, *The Founders and the Bible* (Lanham, MD: Rowman & Littlefield, 2016), 271; Mark David Hall, "Roger Sherman: An Old Puritan in a New Nation," in *The Forgotten Founders on Religion and Public Life*, ed. Daniel L. Dreisbach et al. (Notre Dame, IN: University of Notre Dame Press, 2009), 247; Merrill Peterson, *Adams and Jefferson: A Revolutionary Dialogue* (New York: Oxford University Press, 1976), 6.

[15]Thomas S. Kidd, *Benjamin Franklin: The Religious Life of a Founding Father* (New Haven, CT: Yale University Press, 2017), 227; George Washington to Joseph Jones and James Madison, 3 December 1784, Founders Online; John Jay to George Washington, 27 June 1786, Founders Online.

[16]Alexander Hamilton, *Federalist #76*, 405.

[17]For a survey of psychological studies that arrive at essentially the same conclusion, see Christian B. Miller, *The Character Gap: How Good Are We?* (New York: Oxford University Press, 2018).

disadvantage to them and a challenge to us, for the temptation to caricature their views is almost irresistible. Alexis de Tocqueville would have understood why. "An idea that is clear and precise even though false," he observes in *Democracy in America*, "will always have greater power in the world than an idea that is true but complex."[18]

That may be, but for the Framers there was no alternative. A republican form of government as they understood it *logically required* a complex understanding of human nature, and there was no point in hiding the fact. On the one hand, they were forming a *government*, and they were the inheritors of a long philosophical tradition that traced the origins of all government to inescapable flaws in human character. On the other hand, they were fashioning a *republican* government—a thing of the people grounded in popular consent—and that presupposed a certain qualified confidence in the capacity of humans to govern themselves.

When James Madison observed that, "if men were angels, no government should be necessary," he was merely repackaging an axiom that most American political thinkers had long taken for granted. In the opening paragraphs of the revolutionary pamphlet *Common Sense*, for example, the patriot radical Thomas Paine had reminded the American colonists that, while the development of society is prompted by "our wants," the emergence of government is made necessary by "our wickedness." If our consciences spoke to us clearly and we obeyed them consistently, "man would need no other lawgiver."[19]

In the seventeenth century, English political philosophers like Thomas Hobbes and John Locke had made Paine's point by speculating about a prehistoric "state of nature," a time before the development of civil laws and governments with the coercive power to enforce them. Hobbes had equated the state of nature to a state of war, a never-ending struggle of "everyone against everyone," each distrusting the other, striving for power, living in fear. Locke's state of nature was comparatively less horrific, but he still inferred that, because "the greater part" of humanity are "no strict observers of equity and justice," life in the state of nature would be "full of fears and continual dangers."[20]

The result, according to this conventional wisdom, was that humans flee the state of nature at the earliest opportunity. They willingly sacrifice a measure of

---

[18]Tocqueville, *Democracy in America*, 186.

[19]Thomas Paine, *Common Sense*, ed. Isaac Kramnick (New York: Penguin, 1976), 65.

[20]Thomas Hobbes, *Leviathan*, ed. Edwin Curley (Indianapolis: Hackett, 1994), 80; John Locke, *Two Treatises of Government* and *A Letter Concerning Toleration*, ed. Ian Shapiro (New Haven, CT: Yale University Press, 2003), 102, 154.

the liberty that they naturally enjoy in exchange for the greater peace and security that government promises. Seen in this light, the very existence of government was a continual reminder that men and women can't live together in harmony on their own. Or as Madison condensed the point, we need government because we're not angels.

But we're not devils either, at least according to the Framers' calculus. If humans are wholly evil, they reasoned, then government grounded in the consent of the governed makes no sense. Rather than a free republic, such a dark view of human nature would justify monarchy or dictatorship. If we're really wholly evil, "nothing less than the chains of despotism" could prevent us "from destroying and devouring one another."[21]

Madison captured the Framers' complicated perspective this way: "As there is a degree of depravity in mankind which requires a certain degree of circumspection and distrust: So there are other qualities in human nature, which justify a certain portion of esteem and confidence." Notably, Madison went on to observe that "Republican government presupposes" the latter "in a higher degree than any other form."[22]

This is why the Framers *didn't* assume that humans are wholly evil. What they did say—over and over again—is that few of us are virtuous. As New Jersey delegate William Livingston put it, "It is extremely difficult, for the best of men, to divest themselves of self-interest." The reason for this is simple, New York delegate James Wilson explained: "It is the nature of man to pursue his own interest, in preference to the public good."[23]

This is the relentless theme of *The Federalist*, the collection of eighty-five essays that Hamilton, Madison, and Jay authored in defense of the proposed Constitution during the fall and winter of 1787–1788. Writing under the pseudonym "Publius," the trio collaborated to fashion the strongest possible case for the new framework of government. Although the authors were hardly impartial, within a generation Thomas Jefferson could characterize *The Federalist* as "an authority to which appeal is habitually made by all . . . as evidence of the general opinion of those who framed, and of those who accepted the

---

[21]James Madison, *Federalist #55*, 304.

[22]Ibid.

[23]Barry Alan Shain, *The Myth of American Individualism: The Protestant Origins of American Political Thought* (Princeton, NJ: Princeton University Press, 1994), 123; Bernard Bailyn, ed., *The Debate on the Constitution: Federalist and Antifederalist Speeches, Articles, and Letters During the Struggle over Ratification* (New York: Literary Classics of the United States, 1993), part 1, 68.

Constitution of the United States, on questions as to its genuine meaning."
Today *The Federalist* remains "the single most important resource for interpreting the Constitution," and scholars praise it as "the one American work that unequivocally belongs in the great canon of Western political theory."[24]

In the pages of *The Federalist*, Publius explains human nature in terms of a "hierarchy of motives."[25] The most common and most powerful is *passion*, the influence of prejudice and irrational emotion. Passion typically channels our basest desires, and when left unchecked, it frequently harms others as well as ourselves. Next comes *interest*, the rational but selfish pursuit of personal welfare. Interest doesn't have to be purely material, although Madison noted that "in the popular sense of the term" it most commonly equated with "the immediate augmentation of property and wealth."[26] Least common is *reason*, by which the authors meant not just rational thought per se but rational thought in the service of the common good. Reason, as the authors use the term, is indispensable to the exercise of virtue.

THE

FEDERALIST:

A COLLECTION

OF

E S S A Y S,

WRITTEN IN FAVOUR OF THE

NEW CONSTITUTION,

AS AGREED UPON BY THE FEDERAL CONVENTION,
SEPTEMBER 17, 1787.

IN TWO VOLUMES.

VOL. I.

NEW-YORK:

PRINTED AND SOLD BY J. AND A. M‘LEAN,
No. 41, HANOVER-SQUARE.
M, DCC, LXXXVIII.

Title page of *The Federalist*, 1788

Time and again, *The Federalist* reminds us of the predominance of passion and interest over reason. "Momentary passions, and immediate interests" control human conduct more than "considerations of . . . justice," Hamilton observed.

---

[24]Michael Meyerson, *Liberty's Blueprint: How Madison and Hamilton Wrote the Federalist Papers, Defined the Constitution, and Made Democracy Safe for the World* (New York: Basic Books, 2008), x, ix; Jack N. Rakove, "Introduction," in Alexander Hamilton, James Madison, and John Jay, *The Federalist: The Essential Essays*, ed. Jack N. Rakove (Boston: Bedford/St. Martin's, 2003), 3. Hamilton authored fifty-one of the essays, Madison authored twenty-nine, and Jay, who fell ill shortly after the project began, contributed five.

[25]Daniel Walker Howe, "The Political Psychology of *The Federalist*," *William and Mary Quarterly*, 3rd ser., vol. 44 (1987): 491.

[26]Gordon S. Wood, *The Idea of America: Reflections on the Birth of the United States* (New York: Penguin, 2011), 140.

This is why we have government in the first place: "because the passions of men will not conform to the dictates of reason and justice without constraint." Reason is "timid and cautious," Madison explains. Its "mild voice" is "too often drowned" out in public debate by those clamoring for "immediate and immoderate gain."[27]

In sum, *The Federalist* insists that we are preeminently self-interested beings. We may pursue our personal advantage irrationally, shooting ourselves in the foot with foolish, reckless schemes. We may pursue it prudently, taking rational steps to enhance our well-being. Either way, the underlying priority remains the same. The "stern virtue" that places the common good above self-interest "is the growth of few soils," according to Publius.[28] For the rest of us mortals, *self-interest* is in the driver's seat.

By the mid-1780s, then, America's Founding Fathers were under no illusion that the country was great. Its potential was unlimited, but they knew that America *wasn't* great, in no small part because American citizens, like humans generally, *weren't* good. They lacked virtue. Making the proper allowances for this defect became, quite literally, the Framers' springboard to a "more perfect union."

As much as they continued to praise and promote virtue, the Framers who gathered at Philadelphia in 1787 didn't craft the Constitution for a virtuous people. Their recognition that we are self-interested by nature informs every article, every section, every line of the document that they created. It explains their ambiguity toward governmental power, their preoccupation with checks and balances, and above all, their distrust of democracy.

Accepting, though not celebrating, the truth that we are essentially selfish creatures, the Framers thought of the maintenance of free government as a tightrope walk between the evils of anarchy and despotism. When government is too weak, the outcome is reminiscent of when "there was no king in Israel" and "everyone did what was right in his own eyes."[29] That description of anarchy from the Old Testament was a decent summation of government under the Articles of Confederation, as the Framers reckoned it.

But history taught that anarchy couldn't exist indefinitely. John Jay warned that the resulting insecurity of person and property would tempt "orderly and

---

[27]Hamilton, *Federalist* #6, 24; Hamilton, *Federalist* #15, 79; Madison, *Federalist* #49, 274; Madison, *Federalist* #42, 230.
[28]Alexander Hamilton, *Federalist* #73, 391.
[29]Judges 17:6.

industrious" individuals "to consider the charms of liberty as imaginary and delusive." The "disgust and alarm" among responsible citizens would "prepare their minds for almost any change that may promise them quiet & security." By 1786, rumors were reaching Mount Vernon that "even respectable characters" were speaking of a "monarchical form of government without horror." The country "was apt to run from one extreme into another," George Washington worried. Eventually, Americans would exchange liberty for despotism as the price of order and safety.[30]

It was to forestall this predictable transition from anarchy to despotism that the Framers clothed the central government with greater authority to promote the common welfare. This is why they packed the Constitution with new powers for the central government, most notably the authority to levy taxes, regulate commerce, and maintain a standing army. But the Framers always thought of power as a two-edged sword. If anarchy is the seedbed of despotism, the antidote to anarchy comes with its own "danger of oppression." As Publius observed, *any* governmental power "to advance the public happiness" is simultaneously power "which may be misapplied and abused."[31]

Few themes loomed larger during the ratification debates than the tendency of selfish human beings to abuse power. Statesmen suspicious of the Constitution warned that powers ceded to the federal government could never be reclaimed, given the "fascination of power" that bewitches officeholders. "Men are unwilling to relinquish powers which they once possess," they reminded their countrymen. What is worse, "the unerring experience of ages" proves that those invested with power "are ever disposed to increase it."[32]

Exactly a century later, the English statesmen and historian Lord Acton made his now famous observation that "power tends to corrupt, and absolute power corrupts absolutely." The Framers would have agreed—sort of. "Wherever there is an interest and *power* to do wrong," James Madison observed in a letter to Thomas Jefferson, "wrong will generally be done."[33] The Framers grounded the Constitution on the assumption that power predictably corrupts our *behavior*. They would have denied that it necessarily has this effect on our *hearts*.

---

[30]John Jay to George Washington, 27 June 1786, Founders Online; George Washington to John Jay, 15 August 1786, Founders Online.

[31]James Madison to Thomas Jefferson, 17 October 1788, Founders Online; James Madison, *Federalist* #41, 219.

[32]Bailyn, *Debate on the Constitution*, part 1, 90; part 2, 761, 169.

[33]John Emerich Edward Dalberg-Acton, *Historical Essays and Studies*, ed. J. N. Figgis and R. V. Laurence (London: Macmillan, 1907), 504; James Madison to Thomas Jefferson, 17 October 1788, Founders Online, emphasis added.

Consider that when individuals or governments lack the power to trample on the rights of others, it isn't an expression of virtuous restraint when they fail to do so. Similarly, if a change of circumstances empowers them to act on selfish inclinations that were always present, it's misleading to blame power itself as the sole cause. The Framers agreed that when we're given power it typically alters how we act. But when it comes to our hearts, they knew that power doesn't change our nature so much as expose what's already there. And part of what is already there, both supporters and opponents of the Constitution agreed, is a hunger for power that grows logically out of our self-interested nature.

Since we want nothing so much as to rule ourselves and please ourselves, we're drawn to power because it enables us to get what we want. In building his case for ratification, Alexander Hamilton acknowledged the "love of power" built into the "constitution of man." Antifederalist critics agreed that a "thirst for power" was one of the preeminent passions "in the history of mankind." They deplored "the natural lust of power." They lamented that "the love of power and superiority is as prevailing in the United States at present as in any part of the earth."[34] Where defenders and critics parted ways was in the federalist contention that the Constitution contained sufficient safeguards against the abuse of power.

"We are not to expect perfection in this world," Washington wrote to the Marquis de Lafayette in the aftermath of the Philadelphia convention. Tyranny can emerge under any form of government, Washington conceded, including republics. There is no failsafe mechanism that can guarantee otherwise. The good news was that "mankind, in modern times, have apparently made some progress in the science of government." The statesmen at Philadelphia had gleaned principles from that "science" to create a framework "with more checks and barriers against the introduction of tyranny . . . than any government hitherto instituted among mortals."[35]

From his diplomatic post in London, John Adams similarly praised the new plan of government. It respected "all the great principles necessary to order, liberty, and safety," he exulted to John Jay.[36] Adams particularly admired the

---

[34]Alexander Hamilton, *Federalist #15*, 79; Bailyn, *Debate on the Constitution*, part 2, 514, 608, 593.
[35]George Washington to Marquis de Lafayette, 7 February 1788, Founders Online.
[36]John Adams to John Jay, 16 December 1787, Founders Online.

proposal's two-house legislature in conjunction with a strong executive and independent judiciary. He had long been convinced that such a balance and separation of powers was essential to sustain a free government.

Eleven years earlier, Thomas Paine had recommended in *Common Sense* that the united colonies adopt a simple continental government consisting solely of a unicameral legislature. Adams had "regretted . . . to see so foolish a plan recommended to the people of the United States." He was positively despondent when the country embraced such foolishness and incorporated it into the Articles of Confederation. "A people cannot be long free, nor ever happy, whose gov-

ernment is in one assembly," he had written then. The absence of any check on its power would allow such a simple government to expand inexorably until it became an engine of tyranny.[37]

As for Paine, the best that Adams could say was that the heavy-drinking polemicist was better "at pulling down" than at building. Paine's argument for independence had merit, Adams conceded. But his plan for continental government was nothing more than a "poor, ignorant, malicious, short-sighted, crapulous mass."[38] (That last adjective may not mean what

John Adams

you think it means. In the late eighteenth century it alluded to the excessive influence of alcohol. Adams was implying that Paine—who rarely took up his pen without a decanter of brandy close at hand—was drunk when he wrote *Common Sense*. He probably was.)

---

[37]Diary of John Adams, Spring 1776, in Founders Online; John Adams, *Thoughts on Government, Applicable to the Present State of the American Colonies*, April 1776, in John Adams, *Revolutionary Writings, 1775–1783*, ed. Gordon Wood (New York: Literary Classics of the United States, 2011), 51; John Adams to Abigail Adams, 19 March 1776, Founders Online.
[38]John Adams to Thomas Jefferson, 22 June 1819, Founders Online.

Paine's contempt for any check on the power of the legislature made sense only on the assumption that political actors would be guided by virtue. Adams knew better. "All men would be tyrants if they could," he had observed in a 1763 essay on "man's lust for power." A generation later, he remained convinced that "religion, superstition, oaths, education, laws, all give way before passions, interest, and power." The solution, Adams maintained in words reminiscent of *The Federalist*, was for "power [to] be opposed to power, and interest to interest."[39]

In contrast to Paine's "crapulous mass," the "Report of the Convention at Philadelphia" represented "the greatest single effort of national deliberation that the world has ever seen," Adams gushed to his son-in-law. The secret of the delegates' success, he explained, was that they had rejected the injurious notion "that a certain celestial virtue, more than human, has been necessary to preserve liberty." A "well-ordered constitution" could go a long way toward compensating for the defects in human nature, Adams observed. Indeed, it was more than possible that a republic could exist "even among highwaymen [i.e., bandits], by setting one rogue to watch another."[40]

Even among highwaymen. If widespread virtue among the people and their elected leaders is the indispensable pillar of free government, then the statesmen who convened in Philadelphia in 1787 had no reason for optimism and no solution to offer. Their hope was grounded primarily in their ability to fashion a government that could compensate for "the defect of better motives." "The science of politics . . . has received great improvement," Publius trumpeted. Now there are "powerful means by which the excellencies of republican government may be retained."[41]

Chief among these is the system of checks and balances that we learn about in junior high civics class and rarely think about afterward: the division of the legislative branch into two houses, the executive's power to veto acts of the legislature, the legislature's role in approving executive treaties, and so forth. Nearly two and a half centuries later, these "constitutional securities" fairly shout to us the Framers' understanding of human nature.[42] They were created as safeguards against selfish citizens and ambitious rulers, for a world in which "wrong will generally be done" whenever the incentive and power to do wrong coincide.

---

[39]John Adams, "An Essay on Man's Lust for Power," Founders Online; Richard, *Founders and the Bible*, 266.

[40]John Adams to William Stephens Smith, 26 December 1787, Founders Online.

[41]James Madison, *Federalist #51*, 281; Alexander Hamilton, *Federalist #9*, 42.

[42]Nathan Dane to Melancton Smith, 3 July 1788, in Bailyn, *Debate on the Constitution*, part 2, 850.

The Framers' "great difficulty" was to give the central government the necessary power to avoid anarchy and promote the general welfare without creating at the same time a Frankenstein's monster that could devour our liberty. It was an awesome twofold task. As Madison summarized it, they had to "enable the government to control the governed" while simultaneously obliging the government "to control itself."[43]

This is where checks and balances come in. "Ambition must be made to counteract ambition," Madison famously noted in explaining the Constitution's separation of powers in *Federalist* #51. "If men were angels" such precautions would be unnecessary. In the world we actually live in, they come in handy.[44]

The Framers weren't as pessimistic as the New York federalist who thought it safest to "say all men are dishonest." Nor would they go as far as the influential British philosopher, David Hume, who recommended that, "in contriving any system of government, and fixing the several checks and controls of the constitution, every man ought to be supposed to be a knave." Though comparatively less cynical, they did take for granted that "enlightened statesmen will not always be at the helm," and so they planned accordingly.[45]

During the state-level debates on ratification, defenders of the Constitution frequently pointed to its checks and balances as evidence that the Framers had found a way to make virtue less necessary. Writing under the pseudonym "Americanus," a federalist writer contended that the Philadelphia convention had designed a government "founded on the broad basis of human nature." Its plan of separation of powers, checks and balances, and frequent elections required "none of those heroic virtues which we admire in the ancients, and to us are known only by story. The sacrifice of our dearest interests, self-denial, and austerity of manners, are by no means necessary."[46]

Federalist Noah Webster made much the same argument. Praising the safeguards built into the Constitution, Webster proclaimed that "virtue . . . never was and never will be, till men's natures are changed, a fixed, permanent principle and support of government." The proposed Constitution was superior to the Articles of Confederation because the Framers had made allowances for this

---

[43]James Madison, *Federalist* #51, 281.
[44]Ibid.
[45]Bailyn, *Debate on the Constitution*, part 2, 808; Mark Ellingsen, *Blessed Are the Cynical: How Original Sin Can Make America a Better Place* (Grand Rapids, MI: Brazos Press, 2003), 55; James Madison, *Federalist* #10, 51.
[46]"Americanus III," in Bailyn, *Debate on the Constitution*, part 1, 441.

inviolable truth. Following Washington's advice to "take human nature as we find it," they had fashioned a framework for government that would deter a degeneration into tyranny "so long as there shall remain *any* virtue in the people."[47]

Nowhere does the Framers' understanding of human nature come through more clearly than in their fundamental suspicion of democracy. The delegates at Philadelphia were wholeheartedly committed to preserving a republic—a thing of the people grounded in the consent of the people—but rejecting monarchy isn't the same thing as embracing democracy, and with very few exceptions the Framers wanted nothing to do with the latter.

Enlightenment political philosophy taught that a republic could theoretically encompass any form of government in which the sovereign power was exercised by more than one person. It was an elastic concept. As one historian has noted wryly, "Republicanism was simply what monarchism was not." While this ruled out dictatorship and absolute monarchy, it left a host of alternative arrangements still on the table. Alexander Hamilton, for example, recommended that both senators and the president be elected for life. "Is this a republican system?" he asked his fellow delegates. "It is strictly so, as long as they remain elective."[48]

Hamilton's proposal went nowhere, but neither did the suggestions of a handful of delegates that the convention construct a "democracy." In the ancient world, "democracy" referred to what today we might label "direct democracy"— a system of government in which every eligible citizen participates personally in every political decision. The Framers struggled to find anything good to say about such an arrangement. Their study of history taught them, as Madison observed, that "such democracies have ever been spectacles of turbulence and contention; have ever been found incompatible with personal security or the rights of property; and have in general been as short in their lives as they have been violent in their deaths."[49]

Given the size of the United States, of course, direct democracy, at least at the national level, was never a viable option in 1787. As John Adams noted in defense of the Constitution, the people as a whole "can never act, consult, or reason

[47]"A Citizen of America" [Noah Webster], in ibid., part 1, 158; George Washington to Marquis de Lafayette, 7 February 1788, Founders Online, italics added.

[48]Linda K. Kerber, "The Republican Ideology of the Revolutionary Generation," *American Quarterly* 37 (1985): 475; Edward J. Larson and Michael P. Winship, *The Constitutional Convention: A Narrative History from the Notes of James Madison* (New York: Modern Library, 2005), 51.

[49]James Madison, *Federalist* #10, 52.

together, because they cannot march five hundred miles, nor spare the time, nor find a space to meet."[50]

That was true, no doubt, but the Framers also rejected *representative* democracy. As Adams made clear, it was a truism that the new government would necessarily rely on some form of representation. But this foregone conclusion left unanswered two critical questions: How much of a voice would the people have in choosing their representatives? And would these representatives, however chosen, be constrained by the opinions of their constituents?

In a republic, James Madison explained in *Federalist* #38, the officeholders administering the government could be chosen by the people either directly or indirectly. The Framers mostly opted for the latter. As a modern political scientist observes, "This new constitution, born in celebration of 'republican government,' did not grant anyone the right to vote."[51] The closest that the Framers came was in Article I, section 2, in which they stipulated that the qualifications for voting for the House of Representatives should be identical to those that the states individually imposed for elections to the state assemblies.

The Framers agreed to this provision knowing full well that the vast majority of states at the time imposed property or tax-paying requirements to vote. As we've already seen, these restrictions collectively disqualified between 30 and 40 percent of the adult white male population, not to mention women, the enslaved, and most people of color generally. Such restrictions notwithstanding, the proportion of citizens able to participate was probably higher than anywhere else in the world at the time, and the Framers felt no hesitation in designating the House of Representatives as "the grand depository of the democratic principle of the government."[52]

In all other branches of the new government, however, the influence of the people would be decidedly remote. Senators would be chosen not by the people directly but by the state legislatures. The president would be chosen not by the people directly but through the agency of an "electoral college." This meant that, in most instances, members of the House of Representatives would choose the president, selecting from among a pool of finalists determined by "electors" appointed in some unspecified manner by state legislators elected by adult white male property holders. Federal judges would be chosen not by the

---

[50]Yascha Mounk, *The People vs. Democracy: Why Our Freedom Is in Danger & How to Save It* (Cambridge, MA: Harvard University Press, 2018), 56.

[51]Keyssar, *Right to Vote*, 4.

[52]Larson and Winship, *Constitutional Convention*, 18.

people directly but by a president elected by members of the House of Representatives selecting among finalists identified by electors appointed by state legislators placed in office by a significantly restricted electorate.

Confused yet? As convoluted as it was, there was method in the Framers' madness. They proposed such a complicated system in order to erect a republican form of government simultaneously "derived from the great body of the society" and significantly shielded from popular pressure. As Alexis de Tocqueville would recognize a half century later, their goal was to construct a government that "represents the majority without being necessarily the slave of its passions."[53] This was no simple task. The complexity of the solution reflects the magnitude of the challenge.

And why did the Framers go to such lengths to shield officeholders from popular pressure? Because they were convinced that there would be occasions "when it may be necessary and proper to disregard the opinions which the majority of the people have formed." A New York federalist went so far as to estimate that "there are a thousand things which an honest man might be obliged to do, from a conviction that it would be for the general good, which would give great dissatisfaction to constituents."[54]

There are two basic ways to conceive of representatives' duty to their constituents. On the one hand, they can function much like a professional *agent*. A sports agent, for example, seeks the best deal that he can for his client; he gives advice freely, but in the end it's the client who calls the shots. An agent who disregards his client's instructions deserves to be fired. On the other hand, a representative can function like a *trustee*. A court may appoint a trustee to manage a minor's inheritance, for instance, and it is her job to manage the funds in the best interest of the beneficiary, not to take orders from a teenager.

The Framers unapologetically advocated the latter view. A responsible representative would "take care to inform himself" of the electorate's "dispositions and inclinations." He "ought to be acquainted with the interests and circumstances of his constituents" and cultivate "a sympathy with the wants and wishes of the people." But this most decidedly did *not* require that he simply channel the voice of the majority. A dedicated public servant would be characterized by a zeal for the public welfare, not by a slavish obedience to the public's preference.[55]

---

[53]James Madison, *Federalist #38*, 207; Tocqueville, *Democracy in America*, 1:291.

[54]Bailyn, *Debate on the Constitution*, part 2, 766, 793.

[55]Alexander Hamilton, *Federalist #35*, 185; James Madison, *Federalist #56*, 305; Bailyn, *Debate on the Constitution*, part 2, 512.

It is the "*dispassionate* voice of the people" that constrains and informs public policy, Framer David Ramsay reminded the South Carolina ratification convention. The checks and balances of the Constitution were designed to translate "the sober second thoughts" of the people into "the law of the land," not their passions and transient impulses. "It is the *reason* of the public alone that ought to control and regulate the government," Publius bluntly insisted in *The Federalist*. "The passions ought to be controlled and regulated by the government."[56]

When a New York opponent of the Constitution suggested that Congress should express the "feelings" of the people, federalist Robert R. Livingston erupted: "What! Shall the unjust, the selfish, the unsocial feelings be represented? Shall the vices, the infirmities, the passions of the people be represented? Government, Sir, would be a monster." It's worth noting that his opponent quickly backtracked, clarifying that representatives ought to be governed not by the people's feelings but by their "true interest."[57] No Framer of the Constitution disagreed.

The problem was that the people's "true interest" would sometimes be "at variance with their inclinations." At times the people would err on their own, Madison noted, as "the passions of the unthinking" and "the prejudices of the misthinking" pointed them toward policies they would later regret. At other times they might be deceived, Hamilton observed, "beset as they continually are by the wiles of parasites and sycophants, by the snares of the ambitious, the avaricious, [and] the desperate."[58]

When such occasions arise, the Framers maintained, the officeholder's duty is clear: to thwart the will of his constituents. Because they were comparatively vulnerable to popular pressure, members of the House of Representatives could expect to be penalized by their constituents if they did so. To put it differently, it would require great virtue for a member of the House to serve the people wisely. For that reason, the Framers pinned their hopes elsewhere, most especially on the Senate and the executive.

Because the Senate wasn't popularly elected, the Framers expected it to be filled with individuals of greater age, experience, and wisdom than their counterparts in the House. They opposed popular election of the Senate precisely in the hope that it would be able to proceed "with more coolness, with more

---

[56]Bailyn, *Debate on the Constitution*, part 2, 507, italics added; James Madison, *Federalist* #49, 276, italics added.
[57]Bailyn, *Debate on the Constitution*, part 2, 777, 782.
[58]James Madison, *Federalist* #41, 219; Alexander Hamilton, *Federalist* #71, 383.

system, and with more wisdom than the popular branch." During the struggle for ratification, federalists portrayed the new framework as balancing "the wisdom of the Senate" against "the voice of the people . . . heard in the House of Representatives."[59]

Madison endorsed this role explicitly in the pages of *The Federalist*. The Senate would occasionally serve "as a defense to the people against their own temporary errors and delusions," he explained in *Federalist* #63. In a marvelous expression of the Framers' conflicted views about democracy, Madison noted that "the *cool* and *deliberate* sense of the community" should "*ultimately* prevail" in a free society. There's an element of optimism in this guarded pronouncement, an expression of faith that, in the long run, both the majority and their representatives can agree on policies that genuinely promote the common good.

That's in the long run. In the meantime, there will be "particular moments . . . when the people, stimulated by some irregular passion, or some illicit advantage, or misled by the artful misrepresentations of interested men, may call for measures which they themselves will be the most ready to lament and condemn." In those instances, Madison explained, the Senate's role would be to "suspend the blow meditated by the people against themselves, until reason, justice and truth can regain their authority over the public mind."[60] In sum, the division of the legislature into two branches would serve two purposes: to protect the people from the government and to protect the people from themselves.

The new office of president could serve in this latter role also. In his explication of the executive branch in *The Federalist*, Alexander Hamilton reminded readers that "the republican principle demands that the *deliberate* sense of the community should govern the conduct" of officeholders. "But it does not require an unqualified complaisance to every sudden breeze of passion," he went on to clarify, "or to every transient impulse which the people may receive from the arts of men, who flatter their prejudices to betray their interests."[61]

Hamilton noted that opponents of the Constitution worried that the proposed four-year term of the president would render the executive too independent of the people, especially at the beginning of his term when the next election was far in the future. A shorter term, these critics argued, would ensure that the president would be more responsive to popular opinion. But this was

---

[59]Larson and Winship, *Constitutional Convention*, 35; Bailyn, *Debate on the Constitution*, part 2, 521.
[60]James Madison, *Federalist* #63, 339, italics added.
[61]Alexander Hamilton, *Federalist* #71, 382-83, italics added.

precisely why a longer term was necessary, Hamilton countered, and those who thought otherwise simply didn't get "the purposes for which government was instituted." They didn't understand "the true means by which the public happiness may be promoted."[62]

Rather than a weak executive marked by "servile pliancy"—one who would constantly bow to every wind of opinion—wisdom called for a courageous president willing to stand against the clamor of the majority when the general welfare required that. Although hopefully infrequent, occasions would inevitably arise when the president's job would be to "withstand the temporary delusion" of the people "in order to give them time and opportunity for more cool and sedate reflection."[63]

So here's a question: When was the last time you heard a candidate for office promise, if elected, to "withstand your delusions" and protect you from the adverse consequences of your poor judgment? What political future would a candidate brazen enough to do so possibly have? To read the Framers' defense of the representative's role as trustee is to glimpse a world far removed from our own.

To borrow from the categories Abraham Lincoln would make famous in the Gettysburg Address, the Framers of the Constitution were determined to erect a framework of government "for the people," one that would effectively promote the general welfare. They proudly considered their handiwork a government "of the people," since by their reckoning they were honoring the republican principle of the "consent of the governed." But they made no pretense of creating a government strictly "by the people." That was never their intention, and they were not being hypocritical in declining to do so.

Academic historians sometimes explain the Framers' aversion to democratic rule as an expression of elitist arrogance. One influential study, for example, reduces the Constitution in its original form to "a slur on the capacities of ordinary citizens."[64] From this perspective, the Constitutional Convention was essentially a reactionary coup by men in powdered wigs defending upper-class privilege.

---

[62]Ibid., 382.
[63]Ibid., 382, 383.
[64]Woody Holton, *Unruly Americans and the Origins of the Constitution* (New York: Hill & Wang, 2007), 278.

In truth, the Framers *were* elitist, and they would have been the first to admit it. In part, their suspicions of democracy were grounded in their assumption that the rank and file of citizens lacked *discernment*. This was not a commentary on their innate intelligence or their moral character but rather a recognition that few Americans in the late eighteenth century possessed the education, information, and time for study required to make informed decisions about national politics.

The delegates at Philadelphia constantly reminded one another of this. "The people cannot know and judge of the characters of candidates," Maryland's John Mercer observed. "The worst possible choice will be made." They "lack information and are constantly liable to be misled," agreed Roger Sherman of Connecticut. "The people are uninformed," echoed Elbridge Gerry of Massachusetts, and as a result "the popular mode of electing the chief magistrate would certainly be the worst of all." George Mason concurred, declaring that "the extent of the country renders it impossible that the people can have the requisite capacity to judge of the respective pretensions of the candidates."[65]

In the Framers' defense, the extent of the country *was* daunting. In 1787 the United States was as large as Great Britain, Ireland, France, Germany, and Italy combined. Within this vast expanse, the barriers to information were enormous. There were no political parties to serve as conduits of political news and perspectives, and the small number of newspapers in the country still focused primarily on local news.

Most national news circulated—to the degree that it circulated—through irregularly published pamphlets pitched to sophisticated readers or, more commonly, through the personal correspondence of prominent statesmen. It's not so surprising then, that Mason, who actually favored the direct election of members of the House of Representatives, insisted that "it would be as unnatural to refer the choice of . . . chief magistrate to the people as it would to refer a trial of colors to a blind man."[66]

This is not to suggest that if the internet had been invented two centuries earlier the Framers would have been fine with direct democracy. They wouldn't have. The Framers' discomfort with a democratic form of government went far beyond their concerns about barriers to information. At a more fundamental level, it was a logical extension of their conviction that power is always a threat to liberty, *whoever* wields it.

---

[65]Larson and Winship, *Constitutional Convention*, 110, 17-18, 99, 93.
[66]Ibid., 93.

The colonists who had protested British tyranny in 1776 had conceived of the struggle for liberty as a perpetual contest between "the people" and their rulers. Viewed in this light, tyranny can only exist when it is inflicted on the people by the enemies of the people. The Framers' key insight was that such a conception is too narrow. Oppression could come as readily from the people as from the prince. "Wherever the real power in a government lies," James Madison explained to Thomas Jefferson shortly after the Constitution was ratified, "there is the danger of oppression." And where was the power? As Madison surveyed the American political landscape in 1788, the answer was clear: "In our governments the real power lies in the majority of the community."[67]

Any other answer meant that the United States was not a republic. Time after time, the Framers insisted that this was the litmus test of republican government. "In free republics . . . the will of the people makes the essential principle of the government," Hamilton informed his fellow New Yorkers. All of the powers granted to the new government could be traced "to one great and noble source, THE PEOPLE," James Wilson announced at a public rally in Pennsylvania.[68] It is "indispensable in a republic, that all authority should flow from the people," Charles Pinckney reminded the South Carolina ratification convention. As Publius summed up the matter, the "genius of republican liberty" allowed for no other locus of power.[69]

Yet the people, just like their elected leaders, were also subject to all the imperfections of a fallen human nature. As one federalist put it, "Is not history as full of the vices of the people, as it is of the crimes of the kings?"[70] Critics of the Constitution during the ratification debates (much like devotees of the Tea Party movement in recent years) often overlooked this point. They fell into the trap of portraying "the people" as intrinsically virtuous. Only the scoundrels in government, they implied, could be corrupted by power. Just "drain the swamp," in other words, and all will be fine.

Pennsylvania federalist Benjamin Rush mocked this view in a letter to Framer David Ramsay. Is it true that government officeholders are "the receptacles of *all* the depravity of human nature?" he asked rhetorically. "By no means," he replied in answer to his own question. "The people do not part with their full proportions of it." We know this by "revelation," Rush observed (by which he meant the teaching of Scripture), as well as by "reason" (that is, the lessons of

---

[67]James Madison to Thomas Jefferson, 17 October 1788, Founders Online.
[68]Ibid.; Bailyn, *Debate on the Constitution*, part 2, 766; part 1, 803.
[69]Bailyn, *Debate on the Constitution*, part 2, 585; James Madison, *Federalist #37*, 194.
[70]Benjamin Rush to David Ramsay, 19 April 1788, in Bailyn, *Debate on the Constitution*, part 2, 418.

history and experience). "The present *moral* character of the citizens of the United States," he concluded, "proves too plainly that the people are as much disposed to vice as their rulers."[71]

This is not a popular view today, but it's an axiom at the heart of the Constitution as the Framers conceived it. Because *none* of us is naturally virtuous, because we're *all* subject to the lure of self-interest, because *each of us* is vulnerable to the intoxication of power, power is *always* a threat to liberty. This holds true whether that power is wielded by a king, an aristocratic elite, or the rank and file of the community. But because the Framers presupposed that in a republic "the people are the fountain of all power," it was the power of the people that the Framers feared most.[72]

Nothing shows the Framers' ambivalence toward democracy more clearly than their view on how to protect individual rights in a free society. They accepted that government could be oppressive—who could doubt that? But the form of oppression they thought most likely involved a popular majority using governmental power to indulge its passions or promote its interests at the expense of the minority. This was "the disease most incident to republican government," the threat that inevitably looms over any society committed to "the consent of the governed" as its organizing principle.[73]

"This is a truth of great importance, but not yet sufficiently attended to," James Madison explained to Thomas Jefferson in 1788. Jefferson, then in Paris as American ambassador to the court of Louis XVI, was preoccupied with potential "abuses of power issuing from a very different quarter." The delegates at Philadelphia, in contrast, had recognized that in a truly free society "the invasion of private rights is *chiefly* to be apprehended, not from acts of government contrary to the sense of its constituents, but from acts in which the government is the mere instrument of the major number of the constituents."[74]

Madison spelled out his reasoning most fully in *Federalist* numbers 10 and 51, surely two of the most profound expressions of political philosophy ever penned in the United States. Majority oppression isn't a danger in homogeneous societies

---

[71]Ibid.

[72]Samuel Holden Parsons to William Cushing, 11 January 1788, in Bailyn, *Debate on the Constitution*, part 1, 748.

[73]James Madison, *Federalist* #10, 54.

[74]James Madison to Thomas Jefferson, 17 October 1788, Founders Online.

where everyone has the same material interests or passions, Madison notes. The problem is that civilized, free societies never match that description. Men and women divide into different factions with different interests, prejudices, opinions, and political agendas. The infant United States, for example, included a range of religious sects, as well as an assortment of economic groups—landholders, tenants, wage laborers, manufacturers, merchants, financiers—each "actuated by different sentiments and views."[75] What if any one of these groups should constitute a majority?

To Madison, the answer was indisputable. "If a majority be united by a common interest," he observes in *Federalist* #51, "the rights of the minority will be insecure."[76] This single, simple sentence embodies the Framers' philosophy in microcosm.

Note the realism. *Whenever* a majority emerges with interests or passions at odds with those of the rest of the society, the rights of other citizens *will be* insecure. As Madison expressed it privately, "Wherever there is an interest and power to do wrong, wrong will generally be done." Exhortations to virtue wouldn't change this fundamental truth. As Publius put it, "If the impulse and the opportunity be suffered to coincide, we well know that neither moral nor religious motives can be relied on as an adequate control."[77]

But if private virtue was unlikely to protect the minority in such instances, governmental protection of the minority was positively dangerous. It was one thing for an individual officeholder to stand up to an unjust popular majority bent on indulging its passion or interest, but sooner or later that officeholder could be turned out of office by the direct or indirect pressure of a disgruntled electorate. The only *reliable* way for government to protect minorities from majorities, Madison realized, is to give government power "independent of the majority."[78] The only problem with that solution is that power "independent of the majority" contradicts the principle of "consent of the governed." As Madison observed, it is the hallmark of absolute monarchy and dictatorship.

Do you see the conundrum? Because none of us is reliably good, a majority with interests at odds with the rest of society poses a threat to the minority.

---

[75]James Madison, *Federalist* #10, 50.

[76]James Madison, *Federalist* #51, 282.

[77]James Madison to Thomas Jefferson, 17 October 1788, Founders Online; James Madison, *Federalist* #10, 51.

[78]James Madison, *Federalist* #51, 283.

Because none of us is reliably good, a government with power independent of the majority poses a threat to everyone.

If there is a "republican remedy" to this dilemma, Madison argued that it lay in the likelihood that the United States would be so large and so diverse that it would be divided and subdivided into so many competing factions that no one of them could command the support of a majority of voters. "The security for civil rights," such as it was, rested precariously on this "multiplicity of interests." In sum, the Framers believed that they had crafted a government grounded in the consent of the governed but operating in a society in which, they fervently hoped, cohesive majorities would rarely exist.

Before we wrap up this chapter, we should pause briefly and think Christianly about the Framers' view of human nature. It's not enough to *describe* it accurately, although that's a critical first step. If our ultimate objective is not head knowledge but wisdom, then it's essential that we also *evaluate* what we have seen, scrutinizing the Framers' understanding in the light of Scripture and church teaching.

As I explained in the previous chapter, we'll intentionally sidestep the controversial question of whether the Framers were Christian men whose Christian convictions primarily guided them as they crafted the Constitution. We'll pose instead a question that is just as important but far easier to answer: Were the Framers' views on human nature *compatible* with an orthodox Christian understanding? The answer, beyond doubt, is "Yes!" The Framers didn't use explicitly religious language in articulating their understanding of human nature, nor did they appeal explicitly to Scripture to justify their assessments, but their evaluation of humans as preeminently self-interested is easy to harmonize with the orthodox Christian understanding that we are all sinful by nature.

G. K. Chesterton once observed that the latter "is the only part of Christian theology which can really be proved," by which he meant that you don't have to accept the authority of Scripture to be persuaded of it. Far from an abstraction, the ubiquity of sin is "a fact as practical as potatoes," Chesterton wrote, a reality we would "see in the street" even if we never opened a Bible.[79]

If Chesterton was right, then we can't automatically attribute the Framers' skeptical view of human nature to Christian teaching. They may have based their views on insights from philosophy, literature, or history, or simply from what

---

[79]G. K. Chesterton, *Orthodoxy* (1908; repr., New York: Image Books, 2001), 8-9.

they saw "in the street" as they went about their lives. John Witherspoon, Presbyterian minister and signer of the Declaration of Independence, acknowledged as much when he observed that "those who have been the most conversant in public life and have obtained most of what is called a knowledge of the world have always the worst opinion of human nature."[80]

Whatever influences formed the foundation for their view, this much we can say with confidence: the Framers' perception of men and women as naturally driven by self-interest accorded comfortably with what Christians of that day accepted as an unassailable tenet of the faith. It echoed an understanding of human nature rooted in Scripture, rearticulated by Augustine, reaffirmed by the great Protestant confessions, and reinforced from countless American pulpits.

Historically, Christians have grounded their understanding of human nature on two doctrinal pillars: the concepts of *imago Dei* and original sin. The former teaches us that we bear the image of God. We occupy a unique place in God's created order—"a little lower than the angels" according to the psalmist.[81] We bear the divine imprint in the sense that we possess, among other things, an eternal soul, the faculty of reason, and a "capacity for moral goodness."[82] We're not just animals with a more developed cerebral cortex. There's a precious dignity inherent in our status as God's image bearers. This intrinsic human dignity is consistent with the Framers' hopes that a republic could not only survive but flourish.

But the second pillar instructs us that our rejection of God's rule has defaced the divine image we each bear, marring though not obliterating it entirely. Since the disobedience of our first parents—traditionally referred to as "the fall"— each of us enters the world as a natural rebel against our rightful ruler. This is what is meant by "original sin": the "sin that's already inside us, already dwelling in us . . . at our very conception."[83] If the dignity of *imago Dei* gives us hope that a government of the people might flourish, the corroding effects of original sin persuade us never to take self-government for granted. Given humankind's fallen state, a free and just society is as fragile and unnatural as it is precious.

Scripture testifies repeatedly to this human fallenness. In the Old Testament we read the psalmist's declaration, "There is none who does good, no, not one."

---

[80]Richard, *Founders and the Bible*, 267.
[81]Psalm 8:5.
[82]Gregory A. Boyd and Paul R. Eddy, *Across the Spectrum: Understanding Issues in Evangelical Theology*, 2nd ed. (Grand Rapids, MI: Baker Academic, 2009), 100.
[83]Alan Jacobs, *Original Sin: A Cultural History* (New York: HarperCollins, 2008), xiii.

"There is no one who does not sin," King Solomon confesses before the Lord's altar. "There is not a just man on earth who does good and does not sin," echoes the Preacher of Ecclesiastes. "The heart is deceitful above all things, and desperately wicked," laments the prophet Jeremiah. "All we like sheep have gone astray," concurs Isaiah, "we have turned, every one, to his own way."[84]

The refrain continues when we turn to the New Testament. Its "good news" is glorious because "all have sinned and fall short of the glory of God." "We all stumble in many things," James insists. We are naturally "foolish, disobedient, [and] deceived," according to the apostle Paul. "If we say that we have no sin, we deceive ourselves," John the apostle maintains, and we "make [God] a liar." Most powerful of all is the categorical declaration of Christ himself: "No one is good but One, that is, God."[85]

Augustine of Hippo, the fifth-century Christian leader and theologian, did not invent the concept of original sin but sought to summarize and systematize what he discerned in Scripture. As a result of our first parents' "sinful presumption," Augustine observed in the *City of God*, human nature was fundamentally changed. It was "vitiated"—that is, made defective or corrupted. The result, as the psalmist confessed, is that each of us is "brought forth in iniquity."

In Augustine's terminology, this means that each of us comes into the world characterized by "recalcitrance" (a stubborn resistance to authority) and "concupiscence" (a desire for worldly pleasure).[86] Boiled down, our overriding motives from birth are to rule ourselves and please ourselves. In the terminology of the Founders, none of us is naturally inclined to virtue. To deny ourselves in order to promote the good of others is a contradiction of the willful self-interest that naturally propels us through life.

The great orthodox confessions of the Reformation similarly underscored the centrality of original sin to the human condition. Across the sixteenth and seventeenth centuries, gatherings of Protestant theologians repeatedly asserted the ubiquitous effects of the fall on the unregenerate human heart. Apart from the work of the Holy Spirit, we are full of "distrust, contempt, and hatred of God" according to the Second Helvetic Confession (1536), "inclined to all wickedness" in the words of the Heidelberg Catechism (1563), "corrupt in all [our] ways" in the view of the Belgic Confession (1561). With the exception of Christ, according

---

[84]Psalm 14:3; 1 Kings 8:46; Ecclesiastes 7:20; Jeremiah 17:9; Isaiah 53:6.
[85]Romans 3:23; James 3:2; Titus 3:3; 1 John 1:8, 10; Matthew 19:17.
[86]Saint Augustine, *City of God*, trans. Gerald G. Walsh et al., abridged ed. (New York: Image Books, 1958), book 13, chapter 3, 272; Psalm 51:5.

to the Canons of Dort (1619), "all the posterity of Adam . . . have derived corruption from their original parent" and are characterized by "blindness of mind . . . and perverseness of judgment." The result, the Westminster Confession (1647) summarized, is that we are "wholly defiled in all the parts and faculties of soul and body."[87]

The Reformed confessions taught that these tendencies persist even among Christians who are being regenerated by the work of the Holy Spirit. They tended to distinguish between the act of *justification*, in which God imputes the righteousness of Christ to the believer, and the process of *sanctification*, in which the Spirit gradually empowers the believer to live more and more in accordance with God's law. They agreed that the latter process is always incomplete in our lifetime, and as a general rule it is woefully incomplete. The Westminster Larger Catechism expressed this forcefully, pointing to "the remnants of sin" that abide in all believers until death. These lead to "perpetual lustings of the flesh against the spirit; whereby they are often foiled with temptations, and fall into many sins."[88]

Underscoring the importance of this doctrine, the renowned evangelist of the Great Awakening, George Whitefield, told American audiences that a deep sense of personal sinfulness was a prerequisite to salvation. Has the Holy Spirit made you "to see and feel . . . that you are conceived and born in sin?" he would inquire. "If you have never felt the weight of original sin, do not call yourselves Christians." A generation later, Reverend John Witherspoon declared that "nothing can be more absolutely necessary to true religion than a clear and full conviction of the sinfulness of our nature and state. Without this, all that is said in scripture of the wisdom and mercy of God in providing a Saviour is without force and without meaning."[89]

And what did this sin nature mean, practically? Churchgoers were instructed by their pastors that, since the fall, "sin had intoxicated man with the principle of self-love." They were reminded from the pulpit how "deep and universal is the present innate Depravity of human Nature." They heard repeatedly that, without the aid of Christ, they were capable of nothing good, "not even a good thought much less a good desire." Lest they grow complacent, they were pressed to acknowledge that the natural person is "a poor, indigent, frail and helpless being;

---

[87]Joel R. Beeke and Sinclair B. Ferguson, eds., *Reformed Confessions Harmonized* (Grand Rapids, MI: Baker Books, 1999), 46-48.
[88]Ibid., 105.
[89]Jacobs, *Original Sin*, 133; Richard, *Founders and the Bible*, 264-65.

his reason corrupt, his understanding full of ignorance and error, his will and desires bent upon evil."[90]

A century after the delegates at Philadelphia finished their work, the renowned English historian James Bryce completed a multivolume study of US politics and government titled *The American Commonwealth*. In commenting on the underlying philosophy of the Constitution, the future ambassador to the United States summed up his assessment with one pithy observation: "It is the work of men who believed in original sin."[91] Perhaps.

Whether the Framers believed in that doctrine literally and in its fullest theological sense is hard to prove. They rarely spoke of sin at all, much less original sin, and to say that the checks and balances that they incorporated in the Constitution were biblical in origin would be a stretch.

Yet two conclusions are beyond dispute: first, the Framers held an understanding of human nature largely consistent with biblical truth; second, they went to elaborate lengths to design the Constitution with this understanding in mind. The point is not that the Framers' view of human nature was perfectly identical to orthodox Christian teaching about original sin. It wasn't. Some of the Framers, for example, held out the possibility that, in rare instances, humans might overcome "the selfish bias inseparable from human nature" and exercise a pure and undiluted virtue.[92] Christian orthodoxy taught that this was always an illusion—"there is none who does good, no, not one."

For our purposes, however, what is striking is how much the two views overlapped. When the Framers insisted that none of us is naturally inclined to virtue, Christians around the country could cheerfully respond, "Amen!" In the 1780s, the dogma of original sin was still an "unimpeachable truism" among American believers.[93] Given the depravity of human nature, who could marvel that virtue was in short supply?

"What is government itself," James Madison would inquire in *Federalist* #51, "but the greatest of all reflections on human nature?" This was no mere rhetorical flourish. For the statesmen who gathered in Philadelphia to "form a more perfect union," it was a profound and unassailable truth. To succeed, they must fashion

[90]Shain, *Myth of American Individualism*, 130, 200, 221, 224.
[91]James Bryce, *The American Commonwealth* (London: MacMillan & Co., 1888), 1:407-8.
[92]Richard, *Founders and the Bible*, 265.
[93]Shain, *Myth of American Individualism*, 129.

a framework of government grounded in a correct understanding of human nature. If it was to be a republic—and this was their fervent goal—it would be a republic peopled largely by self-interested citizens deficient in virtue. In Christian terms, the Framers' challenge at Philadelphia was to design a framework of government for people who would be *fallen* as well as free. It was no small task.

The County Election

PART TWO

THE GREAT REVERSAL

"The People's Candidate"
Exalts the People's Virtue

ANDREW JACKSON SCRAWLED HIS EARLIEST surviving letter from the village of Jonesborough, North Carolina (now Tennessee), on August 12, 1788, some six months after James Madison penned *Federalist #51*. Here is what he wrote:

> Sir: When amans feelings & charector are injured the ought to Seek aspeedy redress; . . . My charector you have Injured; and further you have Insulted me in the presence of a court and a larg audianc I therefore call upon you as a gentleman to give me Satisfaction for the Same. . . . I hope you can do without dinner untill the business done; for it is consistant with the charector of agentleman when he Injures aman to make aspedy reparation; therefore I hope you will not fail in meeting me this day from yr obt st Andw. Jackson.[1]

The United States had just officially ratified the proposed new Constitution (without North Carolina's concurrence), but Jackson was preoccupied with more personal affairs as the summer wound down. Barely out of his teens, a minimally trained and utterly inexperienced new lawyer, he had just been publicly humiliated

---

[1] Andrew Jackson to Waightstill Avery, August 12, 1788, in *The Papers of Andrew Jackson*, ed. Sam B. Smith, Harriet Chappell Owsley, Harold D. Moser, et al., 10 vols. (Knoxville: University of Tennessee Press, 1980–2016), 1:12.

in one of his first court cases. The opposing counsel, a prominent North Carolina attorney named Waightstill Avery, had had the audacity to ridicule Jackson's legal argument, and now the young hothead was demanding "satisfaction": either an apology or a duel. Avery was not about to apologize.

And so that evening, just before dusk, the two combatants met for an "interview" on the field of honor. They were a mismatched pair. At forty-seven, Avery was well into a distinguished public career. He was well educated, a graduate of the College of New Jersey (now Princeton), at a time when not one in a thousand adult American males could boast a college degree. He was influential: after moving to North Carolina, Avery had become a patriot leader during the Revolution, then went on to serve as attorney general, adviser to the governor, state legislator, and militia colonel. And he was refined, at least as that quality was measured in the Carolina mountains. He knew some Latin, read widely, and came to court in knee breeches and a powdered wig.

Then there was his opponent. As he sighted down his gun barrel, Avery would have seen a youth twenty-six years his junior: tall, rail-thin and gangly, with a pock-marked face and a shock of reddish-brown hair with a mind of its own. The son of poor Irish immigrants to the South Carolina backcountry, Andrew Jackson had been orphaned at fourteen. Alone in the world, reckless and headstrong, he soon earned the reputation of a first-class hellion. A neighbor recollected that he was "the most roaring, rollicking, game-cocking, horse-racing, card-playing, mischievous fellow" the community had ever known.[2] A gentleman in his own mind, Jackson faced Avery with boundless self-regard but otherwise with few connections, little money, and less education.

As the sun dropped toward the horizon, the duelists leveled their pistols at one another, took careful aim . . . and missed. Intentionally. It was the ultimate anticlimax, no doubt, but a common conclusion to such ritual encounters. Both parties demonstrated courage and upheld their honor, and both went home unharmed.

History would show that it was an uncommon outcome where Jackson was concerned, however, for he rarely drew his weapon without blood being shed. Sometimes the blood was his own. Twice he was severely wounded in such engagements; he would carry the offending bullets in his body for decades. Sometimes the blood was his opponent's, as when he killed a Tennessee planter after a dispute that began in an argument over a horse race before progressing to the question of his wife's chastity.

---

[2]Sean Wilentz, *Andrew Jackson* (New York: Times Books, 2005), 18.

But in a deeper sense, Jackson's duel with Avery *was* an apt harbinger of the future. Looking closely, we can glimpse traits permanently etched into his character. Time would prove Andrew Jackson brave, determined, enterprising and self-confident, willing to stand up against anyone and anything who challenged the principles he claimed to honor. It would also reveal that he was hungry for glory, averse to introspection and systematic thought, passionate, impulsive, dogmatic, self-righteous, violent, quick to take offense, resistant to authority, and impatient with the rule of law.

If there is a common thread unifying both the strengths and weaknesses of this future president of the United States, it was Jackson's supreme, unshakable belief in his own righteousness. After reading thousands of documents that Jackson wrote or dictated, I have yet to unearth a single instance in which he acknowledged a character flaw or confessed a moral offense. He was seemingly incapable of admitting wrong. If anything, as a modern biographer puts it, "he was ever convincing himself of his moral infallibility."[3]

When Washington society lauded him and his name began to be suggested as a candidate for high office, Jackson wrote to his wife Rachel, "I assure you Vanity has no seat in my bosom." To a sycophantic supporter, he humbly admitted that he had been unfailingly selfless in his public career: "In nothing in which I have been engaged; did I ever look to myself." He informed one old friend that "no man can command his temper better than I" and another that "I have always made it a rule when I speak, to speak the truth." "I take principle for my guide," he explained to a protégé, "always secure in the rectitude of my conduct." And when it became clear that he would be a serious contender for the presidency, he confessed to a relative, "I have no fear but my charector will stand the test of the most exact scrutiny. . . . I am at perfect peace with myself."[4]

The flip side of this moral self-assurance was Jackson's equal certainty that anyone who crossed him was a scoundrel. In theory, he accepted the possibility of a principled opponent. In practice, he rarely met one. Political disagreements were personal to Jackson, and personal disagreements were moral. They underscored the chasm between his own rectitude and the ambition and animosity of his adversaries.

No one ever differed with Andrew Jackson over banking or tariffs or slavery or territorial expansion or Native American treaties or cabinet appointments

---

[3]Andrew Burstein, *The Passions of Andrew Jackson* (New York: Vintage Books, 2004), 155.
[4]Jackson, *Papers of Andrew Jackson*, 5:352, 370, 378; 6:358, 98; 5:372.

from decent motives or an honest difference of opinion. His opponents were "villains" (or "villians" by his spelling). They were "vile," "wicked," "sordid," and "despicable," not honorable adversaries but *enemies*—his enemies and the enemies of the American people.[5] And so Jackson reviled them, denouncing them as "common sewers," "arch fiends," "base calumniators," "minions of corruption," "cowardly miscreants," and "designing demagogues."[6]

The American people elected Andrew Jackson president four decades after his duel with Waightstill Avery, during a period that historians have labeled variously as the "Age of Jackson," the "Age of Democracy," or the age of "Jacksonian Democracy."[7] If Jackson didn't cause the rise of democracy in the United States, he undeniably benefited from it, reinforced it, and symbolized it. In the sphere of national politics, Jackson's public career intertwined with key trends that marked a decided break with the Founders' world: a significant expansion of the electorate, the emergence of something like modern political parties and campaign techniques, and a dramatic increase in popular political participation.

But there is a second and more important sense in which Jackson embodied the rise of democracy in the United States. In his typically dogmatic and inconsistent way, Jackson championed a new understanding of human nature that would become central to democracy as Americans have understood and experienced it. This makes him a fitting symbol of the age that bears his name, and arguably of ours as well.

In 1787, the Framers of the Constitution had gathered in Philadelphia in response to "a crisis of virtue." As a solution, they fashioned a framework of government for *fallen* people. They assumed that each of us has the potential to behave virtuously, and we may even do so at times, but we're naturally prone to passion and guided by self-interest.

Four decades later, Andrew Jackson turned this assessment upside down. Most men and women are naturally virtuous, Jackson insisted, the only exceptions being the designing demagogues and hypocritical scoundrels who questioned his character or thwarted his agenda. To paraphrase C. S. Lewis, Jackson's message was that the American people were so good that they deserved a voice in government and so wise that the government needed their counsel.

And the people loved him for it.

---

[5]Ibid., 7:151, 6:488, 7:642, 6:479.
[6]Ibid., 6:454, 488, 471, 472, 482, 87.
[7]John Fea, *Believe Me: The Evangelical Road to Trump* (Grand Rapids, MI: Eerdmans, 2018), 168.

3

"THE PEOPLE THOUGHT GEN. JACKSON WORTHY"

*A*mericans have typically ignored the past, but the mid-1820s was an exception. Between 1824 and 1826 they were positively captivated by the past, in awe of the Founding generation and the void their passing would leave behind. More than at any other moment in our history, the country seemed keenly sensitive to the passage of time and acutely aware of a profound sense of loss.

Two key events fueled this nostalgia. The first came in August 1824 with the arrival of the Marquis de Lafayette for a yearlong tour. In 1777, then nineteen-year-old Marie-Joseph Paul Yves Roch Gilbert du Motier, Marquis de Lafayette had abandoned a life of wealth and privilege and crossed the Atlantic to fight alongside American colonists in the contest for liberty. Serving with Washington on battlefields from Brandywine to Yorktown, the dashing Frenchman had won the love and respect of his commanding general and the undying gratitude of the American people. Now he had returned.

As Lafayette crisscrossed the country for a succession of rallies and banquets and parades, adoring audiences heard repeatedly that the aging hero was not only a champion of liberty. He was not only a true friend of America. Lafayette, the man whom the Father of His Country had loved liked a father, was the *last surviving* general of the Continental Army. And at each celebration, the now sixty-six-year-old grandfather was greeted and escorted by local veterans of the Revolution embodying their own bittersweet message. Dignified and proud, they were also feeble and stooped—living monuments to the revolutionary generation and poignant reminders that it was passing away.

A year after Lafayette's departure, a second defining event, "eerie and exhila-rating," drove home this inescapable truth.[1] On July 4, 1826, John Adams and Thomas Jefferson died within hours of each other. The timing struck everyone. That two of the three remaining signers of the Declaration of Independence, as well as the second and third presidents of the country, would pass away precisely on the country's fiftieth anniversary had to be more than a wonderful coinci-dence. Surely there was Design in it. From his home outside Nashville, Andrew Jackson spoke for thousands in wondering whether the remarkable timing might not be an omen of "the approbation of Divinity."[2]

If the long-departed Washington had been the Sword of the American Revo-lution, Adams and Jefferson had been the Tongue and the Pen.[3] Adams had been an early, outspoken, and untiring voice for independence in the Continental Congress, while Jefferson had earned immortal fame as the principal author of the Declaration. Now all three were gone. The result was a palpable sense that a heroic age was coming to a close. The revolutionary generation that had struggled to achieve liberty was giving way to a new generation charged with maintaining it. How that rising generation would stack up against its predecessor was the question of the day.

John Quincy Adams

John Quincy Adams knew one way that it would differ. He shared his insight in a speech, mostly for-gettable and now forgotten, de-livered in the House of Represen-tatives on March 4, 1825. On that gray Friday morning, the fifty-six-year-old secretary of state had left his house on F Street in Wash-ington for the capitol, where in a

[1] Andrew Burstein, *America's Jubilee: How in 1826 a Generation Remembered Fifty Years of Indepen-dence* (New York: Alfred A. Knopf, 2001), 228.

[2] Andrew Jackson, in *The Papers of Andrew Jackson*, ed. Sam B. Smith, Harriet Chappell Owsley, Harold D. Moser, et al., 10 vols. (Knoxville: University of Tennessee Press, 1980–2016), 6:191.

[3] Merrill Peterson, *Adams and Jefferson: A Revolutionary Dialogue* (New York: Oxford University Press, 1976), 3.

brief ceremony in the House of Representatives he had been sworn in as the sixth president of the United States.

In his forty-minute inaugural address, Adams invited his audience to look "back to that generation which has gone by and forward to that which is advancing." He lavished praise on the Constitution, that "revered instrument." He paid tribute to the wisdom of its Framers, "those illustrious benefactors" who had bequeathed such a "precious inheritance" to posterity. And then, almost in passing, Adams declared something that none of his predecessors had ever suggested in a public document or speech: the United States was now a "representative *democracy*."[4]

As he offered this assessment, Adams knew full well that the "illustrious benefactors" who fashioned the Constitution in 1787 had both feared "representative democracy" and actively opposed it. He also knew, perhaps better than anyone, that a democratic mindset was fast becoming deeply entrenched among the rising generation. He was, after all, at the center of the episode that exposed the seismic shift taking place.

The presidential election of 1824 was one of the most important in American history because it was one of the most revealing. More than any other presidential contest, it demonstrated how the architects of the Constitution actually expected the executive to be chosen. But more than any other event of the era, it also revealed how strongly Americans had come to disagree with the Founding Fathers they supposedly revered. Scarcely a generation after the ratification of the Constitution, a critical mass of Americans now rejected the Framers' philosophy of government, their conception of civic virtue, and their understanding of human nature.

The election of 1824 didn't cause these changes, and it's an exaggeration to say that it "unleashed the democratic storm that had been building for years."[5] But it did lay bare the degree to which Americans had been gradually embracing a new mindset, and it undoubtedly reaffirmed and accelerated the trend.

---

[4]James D. Richardson, comp., *A Compilation of the Messages and Papers of the Presidents* (New York: Bureau of National Literature, 1897), 2:860-62, emphasis added; William J. Cooper, *The Lost Founding Father: John Quincy Adams and the Transformation of American Politics* (New York: W. W. Norton, 2017), 223; Burstein, *America's Jubilee*, 150.

[5]Robert V. Remini, *The Legacy of Andrew Jackson: Essays on Democracy, Indian Removal, and Slavery* (Baton Rouge: Louisiana State University Press, 1988), 14.

From our twenty-first-century perspective, the contest looks bizarre. Not two but *four* major candidates squared off in the general election. Party affiliation was meaningless. Not one of the candidates had a national following, and none came close to commanding a majority of the Electoral College vote. This sent the top three finishers to a runoff in the House of Representatives, where congressmen chose the second-place candidate as the best individual for the job. But this strange-looking process was not only perfectly constitutional. It was more or less what the Framers had anticipated.

What seems bizarre to us today appeared predictable to the Framers in 1787 for a simple reason: they didn't anticipate the emergence of modern political parties, much less the development of a mature two-party system. Formal parties hadn't existed in colonial America, and none of the Framers regretted that. As a whole, our Founding Fathers were keenly suspicious of parties. In the best case, they hoped to do without them entirely. Barring that, they would accept them as necessary evils, institutions to be tolerated, not encouraged.

James Madison, for example, grouped parties with "factions," organized coalitions that he condemned as the source of innumerable "mischiefs" and a threat to popular government. John Adams feared "a division of the republic into two great parties . . . as the greatest political evil under our Constitution." Thomas Jefferson denounced unthinking loyalty to party as "the last degradation of a free and moral agent" and famously declared, "If I could not go to heaven but with a party, I would not go there at all." And before stepping down from the presidency after two terms in office, George Washington reaffirmed these views by alerting the country to "the baneful effects of the spirit of party."[6]

Washington had offered his solemn warning knowing that Congress and even his own cabinet were badly divided over a number of important issues, and he feared that these divisions might solidify into permanent factions. They soon did. When the president announced in September 1796 that he would not accept a third term, it was as if he had fired a starter's pistol for the ensuing campaign. Less than three months later, the country witnessed its first contested

---

[6]James Madison, *Federalist* #10, in Alexander Hamilton, James Madison, and John Jay, *The Federalist*, ed. J. R. Pole (Indianapolis: Hackett, 2005), 49; Richard Hofstadter, *The Idea of a Party System: The Rise of Legitimate Opposition in the United States, 1780–1840* (Berkeley: University of California Press, 1969), 2, 122-23; Daniel J. Boorstin, ed., *An American Primer* (New York: Penguin, 1966), 220.

presidential election, pitting the Federalist John Adams against the Democratic-Republican Thomas Jefferson.[7]

For the next twenty years the Federalist and Democratic-Republican parties competed for control of the young government. They were distinguished by profound differences in economic vision, constitutional interpretation, and international strategy. Federalists favored a pattern of economic growth that balanced agriculture, commerce, and manufacturing. They advocated the purposeful use of federal power as a means to that end, and they believed that a liberal interpretation of the federal government's implied powers under the Constitution's "necessary and proper clause" was essential to national flourishing and consistent with the original intentions of the Framers. And when war broke out in the 1790s between the two most powerful nations in the world at that time—Great Britain and France—the Federalists added to these policy positions a decided tilt toward the British.

The Democratic-Republicans reversed each of these positions. "Those who labour in the earth are the chosen people of God, if ever he had a chosen people," Jefferson famously observed, and his party tended to oppose initiatives that might weaken the country's identity as a land of farms and farmers.[8] The Jeffersonians generally feared the growth of federal power, believed that a strict construction of the Constitution was essential to preserve the rights of the states and the liberties of the people, and sided with the French in their war with Great Britain. Never in our history have two major parties differed so starkly over so many issues of so much significance.

But this "First Party System," as historians label it, lasted barely a generation. Never grassroots movements, both the Federalists and the Democratic-Republicans were top-down coalitions strongest at the national level, and even there they lacked much of the institutional apparatus and structure that we would expect today of a political party deserving of the name.

What is more, neither party really conceived of itself as a party. Both sides justified their partisan activity as a necessary but temporary recourse, one that they had reluctantly adopted in order to save the country from an internal enemy. Once they had discredited and vanquished the other party, they would disband

---

[7]The Jeffersonian faction often called themselves simply "Republicans" rather than "Democratic-Republicans," but I use the longer term consistently to avoid confusing this early party with the Republican Party of Abraham Lincoln that came into being during the 1850s.

[8]Thomas Jefferson, *Notes on the State of Virginia*, in *The Portable Thomas Jefferson*, ed. Merrill Peterson (New York: Penguin, 1975), 217.

and the country could return to a state of nonpartisan harmony. And when the Federalists fell into disrepute after their opposition to the War of 1812, it looked for a moment like this might happen.

In 1816 the Democratic-Republican James Monroe won the presidency in a landslide over the Federalist nominee, Rufus King. After sweeping victories in the midterm elections of 1818, Democratic-Republicans outnumbered Federalists in Congress by almost 6:1, and by 1820 the Federalists were so anemic that they allowed Monroe to go unopposed in his bid for a second term as president. While pockets of self-identified Federalists survived in a few locales, the Federalists had ceased to exist as a viable national party.

But then, instead of stacking their arms and retiring in triumph, the Democratic-Republicans opted to stick around and fight among themselves. With no party to oppose them in 1824—and therefore no chance of losing the election for Monroe's successor—there was no incentive for the party to rally around a single candidate, nor for presidential aspirants to bow out gracefully in the interest of party unity.

So it was that not one but four Democratic-Republicans professed to carry the party's banner in the general election that fall. Because the Framers wanted nothing to do with parties, the Constitution says nothing about how party candidates should be nominated. Since 1796, Democratic-Republicans in Congress had held a caucus in election years to discuss potential candidates and agree on an individual to endorse. In 1824 a minority gathered on Valentine's Day to repeat the process, proposing as the party's nominee the congressional favorite, Secretary of the Treasury William H. Crawford of Georgia. Crawford had been the second choice of the caucus in 1816 when James Monroe had narrowly won their endorsement, and his supporters believed that it was now rightfully his turn.

But roughly two-thirds of the Democratic-Republicans in Congress, including many who favored Crawford's election, now condemned the process as illegitimate. Some believed on principle that it needed to be more open. It was one thing when two viable parties were contesting the election, but now that there was only one party in the field, for the Democratic-Republicans in Congress to select the party's nominee would be tantamount to their electing the president. The general election would be meaningless.

But congressmen who favored someone other than Crawford for the presidency now had every incentive to attack the caucus as well. With no chance of losing the White House to a Federalist, they saw no reason to acquiesce in

Crawford's nomination. And so they turned to another extraconstitutional method for identifying nominees, using sympathetic state legislatures to pass resolutions in favor of alternative candidates.

The field got crowded quickly. Joining Crawford as serious candidates were Secretary of War John C. Calhoun, Secretary of State John Quincy Adams, Speaker of the House Henry Clay, and of course Andrew Jackson, recently elected US senator from Tennessee. Calhoun, the youngest of the group at forty-two, could afford to wait and bowed out in exchange for the vice presidency. Each of the other four very much wanted to be president, could count on strong support from at least one region of the country, and was disinclined to step aside. The stage was set.

By modern standards, the "campaign" that followed was hardly a campaign at all. Reckoning ambition as a character flaw, the Founders had believed that those who desired power couldn't be trusted with it. From this it followed that a virtuous statesman never *sought* the responsibility of public office; he *accepted* it out of a sense of duty when his country called. The ideal candidate was a "Mute Tribune," a gifted leader who was indifferent to political success and refused to speak on his own behalf.[9] The tradition of the Mute Tribune was fading by the 1820s, but it still held fast in presidential contests, with the result that none of the candidates in 1824 even once openly appealed for votes. Study on that for a moment.

Yet if the candidates refused to speak, their supporters didn't hesitate. They spoke frequently and passionately, and they experimented with a range of new techniques aimed at mobilizing public opinion. Campaign newspapers, biographies, and broadsides began to emerge, along with campaign buttons (of a sort), rallies and parades, local conferences and conventions. Because the candidates remained silent and all claimed to belong to the same party, their policy positions were seldom well known and often overlapped. More central to the campaign were experience, character, and above all, image.

The images that mattered most were those of Adams and Jackson. They would be the top vote getters in 1824, and the only candidates on the ballot in the rematch of 1828. Neither would have fared well in today's nonstop campaigning. Adams freely confessed that he was "reserved, cold, austere, and forbidding."

---

[9]M. J. Heale, *The Presidential Quest: Candidates and Images in American Political Culture, 1787–1852* (New York: Longman, 1982), 4.

Others who knew him added that he was "stiff," "clownish," "coarse," and "dirty," despite his regular practice of swimming naked in the Potomac River. They sniffed that "he had neither the manners nor the appearance of a gentleman."[10]

By contrast, Andrew Jackson could be positively dashing—from a distance. He cut a majestic figure on horseback or saluting from a balcony, but by the mid-1820s he had lost so many teeth that he couldn't enunciate clearly and found it "very unpleasant" to speak in public.[11] (There was more than one reason to play the Mute Tribune.) The good news for both candidates was that few Americans would ever lay eyes on them or hear them speak.

If the election came down to experience in government, the choice between Adams and Jackson was stark. As one historian observes, "By the standards of his day," Jackson "was the least qualified man ever to run for the presidency." He had served briefly in Congress in the 1790s, resigning before his term expired, and again for a few months in the winter of 1823–1824, but no one could identify a single piece of legislation to his credit, or even a noteworthy speech, for that matter. A New Hampshire congressmen was only stating the obvious when he observed that Jackson "has no reputation as a Statesman."[12]

Quincy Adams, conversely, had by 1824 devoted nearly four decades of his life to government service. In addition to six years in the Senate, he had served lengthy separate stints as US minister to the Netherlands, to Russia, to Prussia, and to Great Britain, and he had spent the last eight years as arguably the most successful secretary of state in US history, in which capacity he had been the primary architect of the Monroe Doctrine.

The task for the Jackson campaign, then, was to minimize the importance of political experience. To do so, the general's boosters fashioned the first instance in presidential politics of "deliberate image building and mythmaking."[13] Part of their strategy was conventional. They would portray Jackson as a worthy heir of the Founding Fathers who had demonstrated his merit through a lifetime of virtuous service. In Jackson's case, this meant service on the field of battle rather than in the halls of government.

---

[10]Donald Ratcliffe, *The One-Party Presidential Contest: Adams, Jackson, and 1824's Five-Horse Race* (Lawrence: University Press of Kansas, 2015), 7-8, 61, 59.

[11]Jackson, *Papers of Andrew Jackson*, 6:220.

[12]Lynn Hudson Parsons, *The Birth of Modern Politics: Andrew Jackson, John Quincy Adams, and the Election of 1828* (New York: Oxford University Press, 2009), 2; Ratcliffe, *One-Party Presidential Contest*, 133.

[13]David S. Heidler and Jeanne T. Heidler, *The Rise of Andrew Jackson: Myth, Manipulation, and the Making of Modern Politics* (New York: Basic Books, 2018), 6.

Not long after his duel with Waightstill Avery, Jackson had left the Carolinas for the Tennessee frontier and a tiny hamlet then known as Nashborough. It proved to be the perfect locale for an inexperienced but ambitious lawyer, and he had prospered. Lawyer's fees, political connections, and extensive land speculation had led to wealth and influence, and then eventually to a political appointment as general over the Tennessee militia. It was as *General* Jackson, then, that he had served his country during the War of 1812 while Adams was drinking tea with European diplomats.

Jackson first commanded Tennessee volunteers against British-aligned Creek "Red Sticks" in present-day Alabama, a campaign that culminated in a decisive victory at the Battle of Horse-shoe Bend in March 1814. He then led a combination of militia and regular army units to a stunning defeat of a far larger British force at the Battle of New Orleans the following January. Overnight, Jackson became a national celebrity.

Andrew Jackson

Jacksonians both underscored the general's military record and embellished it. To begin with, they insisted that Jackson had risked his life for his country in not one but *two* wars, not only the War of 1812 but also the American Revolution before that. Magnifying his supposed involvement in a local skirmish with the British back in 1780 (when Jackson was all of thirteen), they rejoiced to have found "another *Hero of Seventy-Six.*" When the Redcoats had threatened his backcountry community, Jackson had "marched to battle," making him "the last of those valiant establishers of the liberty of our Republic" who could ascend to the presidency.[14]

---

[14]Sharon Ann Murphy, "The Myth and Reality of Andrew Jackson's Rise in the Election of 1824," in *A Companion to the Era of Andrew Jackson*, ed. Sean Patrick Adams (Oxford: Blackwell, 2013), 274, 277; [John Eaton], *Letters of Wyoming, to the People of the United States, on the Presidential Election, and in Favor of Andrew Jackson* (Philadelphia: Simpson and Conrad, 1824), 6.

They similarly magnified the significance of Jackson's undeniable victory at New Orleans a generation later. The Battle of New Orleans actually occurred two weeks after a peace treaty with the British had been negotiated in Belgium (by John Quincy Adams, no less), but nothing could restrain the Jackson campaign from proclaiming that the general had "saved the nation" in its second war for independence. Jackson's campaign biography declared that no man alive was more responsible for the survival of the United States. Patriotism and gratitude dictated that every true American vote for "the Champion, the Defender, the Deliverer of his Country."[15]

This line of argument, however embroidered, was still essentially traditional. The country's first president, after all, had initially won the respect of Americans by defending them on the battlefield. Jacksonians were simply contending that their candidate deserved the same regard as "the immortal Washington." But the Jackson campaign made a second major claim that stretched forward into our world rather than backward toward the Founders'. Andrew Jackson, they announced, stood alone as "the People's Candidate."[16]

Like a lot of political slogans, this one was vague enough to allow for a variety of meanings. In context, it's clear that they weren't portraying Jackson as a common man of humble birth, although that must have been tempting. From our perspective, the arc of Jackson's life, from unlettered orphan to wealthy national celebrity, was a campaign consultant's dream. But although the day was not far distant when politicians would routinely boast of their lowly origins (even when they had to invent them), Jackson's 104-page campaign biography said almost nothing about his early life.

Nor were the Jacksonians claiming that their candidate currently lived in humble simplicity, inviting voters to think of the general, even now, as a reflection of themselves. Only four elections later, in 1840, supporters of William Henry Harrison would invent the myth that their candidate for the presidency lived in a crude log cabin and spent his days reclining on a "buckeye bench" and swigging hard cider with passersby. To their credit, the Jackson campaign didn't take that route.

[15]*Letters of Wyoming*, 14.
[16]Ibid., 1, 15, 94; Ratcliffe, *One-Party Presidential Contest*, 177.

It would have been hard to pull off. By 1824, Jackson was comfortably ensconced in the "one percent" of his day and did nothing to hide the fact. At "the Hermitage," Jackson's plantation east of Nashville, the general welcomed guests to a Greek Revival mansion adorned with spiral staircase, Parisian wallpaper, Chinese carpets, canopied beds, and crystal chandeliers.

In the formal dining room they would eat off of French china and sip coffee from a silver service crafted in Philadelphia. In the adjacent parlor, with its mahogany tables and mantelpiece of Italian marble, the ladies could play a piano that cost more than most yeoman farms. And venturing behind the great house, they could see Jackson's other valuable property: his carriages, thoroughbred race horses, and the more than one hundred human beings who tended his cotton and corn.

In context, the claim that the general was "the People's Candidate" originally meant only that he was *not* the nominee of the Congressional caucus. If elected, he wouldn't owe his office to a group of elite politicians in Washington. Invariably, though, the contention that Jackson was "the People's Candidate" (the candidate the caucus had rejected) shaded into the broader assertion that he was "the *choice* of the people" (the candidate the electorate preferred).[17] This

The Hermitage, home of Andrew Jackson as it would have appeared around the time of his death.

[17]*Letters of Wyoming*, 1, italics added.

was a harder case to make. Jackson was hardly the only alternative to Crawford (the choice of the caucus), and in a day before opinion polls, there was really no way to substantiate the claim that Jackson was the people's choice until after the election.

What is most significant is not that the Jacksonians lacked evidence for their claim but that they wanted to make it at all. The national popular vote hadn't even been recorded in the eight presidential elections prior to 1824, and there was nothing in the Constitution to suggest that it should be otherwise. In Article II, section 1, the Framers had stipulated that the executive should be chosen by "electors" appointed by each state "in such manner as the Legislature thereof may direct." They likely expected these individuals to be handpicked by the legislatures, and they certainly intended that they would "think for themselves" in choosing the best candidate.[18]

Yet much had changed since 1787. Most notably, the states had gradually shifted toward the popular election of presidential electors. As late as 1800, the state assemblies chose the electors in roughly three quarters of the states (11 of 16). By 1824 the proportion had fallen to one in four (6 of 24). What is more, a tradition was growing of having electors commit to a candidate in advance so that a vote for a particular elector was tantamount to a vote for the presidential candidate himself. For the first time in history, the 1824 election would roughly approximate a popular referendum on the presidency. The popular vote mattered now.

Its meaning was also changing, and the Jacksonians were leading the way in redefining it. The Framers of the Constitution had assumed that "the people are as much disposed to vice as their rulers." The Jackson campaign countered that moral corruption was a disease largely limited to "leading men" who "practice intrigue" and "seek after office." This made "public opinion . . . the safest guarantee of freedom." It meant that the surest bulwark of American liberty was "the good sense and sober reflection of the American people."[19]

Implicit in such claims was the assumption that "the people" were naturally both virtuous and discerning—they sincerely desired to promote the common good, and they reliably possessed the information and mental acuity necessary to wise judgment. To hear Jacksonians tell it, almost the only circumstance

---

[18]Ratcliffe, *One-Party Presidential Contest*, 201.
[19]Benjamin Rush to David Ramsay, 19 April 1788, in Bernard Bailyn, ed., *The Debate on the Constitution: Federalist and Antifederalist Speeches, Articles, and Letters During the Struggle over Ratification* (New York: Literary Classics of the United States, 1993), part 2, 418; *Letters of Wyoming*, 2, 14, 52.

that could mar these innate qualities was extended political experience or an extensive education.

In 1824 the Jackson campaign introduced a tactic common in American politics today—namely, "running against Washington, D.C."[20] When he wasn't on the battlefield being "the Deliverer of his Country," Andrew Jackson had had the good sense to stay far away from the capital as much as possible. This was because he "has a soul that towers above intrigue," Jackson's campaign biography explained. His countrymen would find him not in Washington but "where the chief magistrate of the nation should always be sought for, in private life."[21] Taken literally, this maxim suggested that the ideal president should have no prior political experience at all. Jackson came close.

The Jacksonians' denigration of political experience shaded into an anti-intellectual assault on education of any kind, and future candidates would learn "to conceal their intellect rather than proclaim it."[22] John Quincy Adams was one of the best and most broadly educated Americans ever to hold public office, then or since. He had traveled to Europe with his father at the age of eleven, and while John Adams was occupied as an American diplomat, young John Quincy studied in several countries and worked on his languages, eventually learning Latin, Greek, French, German, and Dutch. He accepted his first government post at the age of fourteen—as private secretary to the American minister to Russia—before returning to complete his education at Harvard.

To the Jacksonians, such accomplishments amounted to less than nothing. They scorned Adams as a "closet scholar" who had learned only from books. Notwithstanding his far-flung travels, "his classical acquirements," and his "high literary attainments," he knew little of the world and even less "of man as he is." All of Adams's training paled in comparison to Jackson's "native strength of mind," a quality they praised without ever quite defining. Whatever it was, it was adequate to the demands of the presidency, the duties of which "are not of that cumberous, mental responsibility and character, which many are in the habit of supposing."[23]

---

[20]Daniel Walker Howe, *What Hath God Wrought: The Transformation of America, 1815–1848* (New York: Oxford University Press, 2007), 207.
[21]*Letters of Wyoming*, 5, 51.
[22]Parsons, *Birth of Modern Politics*, xviii.
[23]*Letters of Wyoming*, 58, 59, 88, 90.

From the outset of the 1824 campaign, the smart money was always on the election ending in a runoff. There were simply too many strong candidates in the contest for one of them to win a majority in the Electoral College. In the likely event that no candidate claimed a majority, the Constitution directed that the top three finishers proceed to a runoff in the House of Representatives, where each state delegation would cast a single vote, and a majority would be required to select a winner. With twenty-four states in the Union in 1824, a successful candidate would need the support of thirteen states to claim victory.

As expected, each of the four candidates did well enough in the general election to ensure that no one of them could claim a majority in the Electoral College. Adams swept New England and New York, while Jackson won Pennsylvania and New Jersey and divided the South with Crawford and the West with Clay. The final official tally showed Andrew Jackson with 99 electoral votes, John Quincy Adams 84, William C. Crawford 41, and Henry Clay 37.

Jackson's 99 votes gave him a clear *plurality* in the Electoral College (roughly 38 percent of the total), but they fell far short of the 131 votes needed for the required *majority*. Although constitutionally irrelevant, the popular vote totals followed a similar pattern. Jackson received 40 percent of the approximately 360,000 votes recorded, Adams 33 percent, and Crawford and Clay 13 percent each.[24]

The outcome in the Electoral College meant that the House would choose from among Jackson, Adams, and Crawford in a runoff scheduled for early February. As the odd man out, Clay "quickly shifted from candidate to president-maker," as one historian puts it.[25] In the interim between the general election and the runoff, the Speaker of the House endorsed Adams publicly, encouraged the states that had originally supported him to move into the Adams column (even though Adams had garnered few votes in those states), and did his best to persuade other state delegations to follow suit. In the end, thirteen state delegations opted for Adams on the first ballot in the House, making the candidate who had finished *second* in the general election the next president of the United States.

Before going to bed that night, John Quincy Adams prayed to the "father of mercies" that his election would "redound to his glory and to the welfare of my Country."[26] The next day he took a step that he genuinely believed was consistent with both but which historians ever after have considered a colossal

---

[24]Donald Ratcliffe, "Popular Preferences in the Presidential Election of 1824," *Journal of the Early Republic* 34 (2014): 71. Due to rounding, the percentages of the official popular vote do not total 100.
[25]Cooper, *Lost Founding Father*, 215.
[26]John Quincy Adams, *Diaries*, ed. David Waldstreicher (New York: Library of America, 2017), 2:94.

political mistake. Adams offered the position of secretary of state to Henry Clay, and Clay, after deliberating for a couple of weeks, accepted. The "optics," to use a modern phrase, could not have been worse.

If Adams thought about the possible fallout, he didn't care. He and Clay had served together on the commission that negotiated the Treaty of Ghent ending the War of 1812, he respected his diplomatic skills, and he genuinely viewed Clay as the most qualified, readily available candidate for the post. Much of the country, unfortunately, concluded from the circumstantial evidence that Clay had sold his support to the highest bidder and that Adams had bought the presidency with a cabinet post.

But not just any cabinet post. In the country's young history, the position of secretary of state had regularly functioned as a stepping stone to the presidency. (Jefferson, Madison, Monroe, and now Adams had each served in the position prior to becoming president.) To those inclined to see wrongdoing, John Quincy Adams had not only bought the presidency. He had brazenly named as his successor his partner in crime.

For two centuries, Americans have let the so-called Corrupt Bargain overshadow everything else about the election of 1824, and that's exactly what the Jacksonians would have wanted. But to gauge the true significance of the runoff in the House, we first need to give some more thought to the general election. The charge that Adams and Clay had struck a deal to win Adams the presidency gained its explosive power from the claim that, in so doing, they had thwarted the popular will. But had they? Was Andrew Jackson truly "the choice of the people" in 1824?

The short and surprising answer is "Not really." Remember that the official tally gave Jackson only 40 percent of the popular vote in the general election, which is another way of saying that a sizable majority of those who voted wanted someone *other* than Andrew Jackson to become president. This was a simple truth that Jackson's supporters almost immediately forgot or intentionally obscured.

From across the country came a crescendo of complaints that the House had acted "in known opposition to the People's choice." Outraged Jacksonians wrote to the general to condemn the crime. A Tennessee legislator charged that "the voice of the nation was stifled." A Louisiana correspondent berated the House for overturning "the will of a great majority," which had been "so emphatically pronounced." The outcome contradicted "the known will of the majority of this nation" according to a Kentucky supporter; it "deprived the people of their

President," in the words of a New Yorker. "That the great Body of the people" had preferred Jackson "*none can doubt*," another correspondent insisted. That "the express wishes of this Nation was unheeded, *none will deny*."[27]

These claims were demonstrably false. They were also wonderfully effective.

For his part, Jackson had no trouble embracing the new dogma and appears to have convinced himself that it was true. Shortly after the general election, Jackson confessed to a correspondent that he was indifferent to the outcome. "Having been supported by the *majority* of the people," he could accept whatever came with equanimity. "I have this consolation," he confided in another letter, "that by the voice of a *majority* of the people, my pretensions have been preferred." And once the House had finished its work, Jackson joined the chorus complaining that the popular will had been thwarted. Although he claimed not to desire the office himself, he professed to "weep for the liberty of my country," knowing that John Quincy Adams had become president "contrary to the voice of *the nation*."[28]

But it's worth restating: 40 percent is not a majority, and it was an expedient fiction to equate Jackson's plurality of support with "the voice of the nation."[29] Unwilling to acknowledge that "the people" had not rallied behind the general, the Jacksonians, including Jackson himself, adopted a simple strategy: when the truth is inconvenient, deny it—repeatedly, dogmatically, indignantly.

In reality, the most popular choice in the general election had been "none of the above." Barely a fourth of eligible voters—approximately 27 percent—had bothered to participate. Jackson had actually won only a *plurality* of a *small minority*—40 percent of the ballots cast by the 27 percent of the electorate who went to the polls. A little arithmetic tells us that "the choice of the people" in 1824 received the votes of barely *one-tenth* of the electorate (10.8 percent). A lot of Americans admired Andrew Jackson as a successful "Indian fighter" and war hero, but there is zero evidence that the House's selection of John Quincy Adams overturned a massive groundswell of support for "the People's Candidate."

What the outcome of the runoff did do, and that beyond question, is give Jackson's "base" a profound sense of grievance and a potent issue for the next campaign.

---

[27]Jackson, *Papers of Andrew Jackson*, 6:30, 290, 49, 64, 33, 112.

[28]Ibid., 5:455, italics added; 6:14, 20, 194, italics added.

[29]Donald Ratcliffe has recently argued plausibly that Jackson would not even have had a national *plurality* if popular election had been the norm of all the states in 1824. See Ratcliffe, "Popular Preferences in the Presidential Election of 1824," 71.

Over the years, historians have failed to uncover any evidence of an actual agreement between Adams and Clay. They agree that Clay's decision to accept the cabinet post was a monumental blunder, given the accusations that were sure to follow, but they dismiss the charge of a "corrupt bargain" as "dubious," "unsubstantiated," and "unfair."[30]

At the time, prominent pro-Jackson politicians such as Martin Van Buren (Jackson's handpicked successor as president) and Missouri senator Thomas Hart Benton conceded that the accusation was spurious. It didn't matter. Outrage is a powerful motivator, and the charge wouldn't die. The rank and file of Jackson men were certain that the election had been stolen by corrupt politicians.

So was Andrew Jackson. Throughout his life, Jackson assumed the worst of anyone who challenged him. Clay's decision to oppose his election could be explained only by a defect in Clay's character. The general was in the Senate on the day that Clay publicly announced his support for Adams, and within hours he had written to a close friend that the Speaker of the House had shown a "want of principle" and proved himself a "political weathercock."[31]

Soon Jackson was recycling unsubstantiated rumors of "intrigue, corruption, and sale of public office." When Clay subsequently accepted the post of secretary of state after Adams's election, the news only confirmed what Jackson already knew in his bones. Clay had betrayed the people's trust in exchange for "thirty pieces of silver," he wrote to an old friend. "*Like Judas of old*" he had "*sold himself & his influence* to Mr. Adams."[32]

Clay had anticipated a backlash. Four days after announcing that he would support Adams, the Speaker had penned a letter to a prominent friend in Virginia, a judge named Francis Brooke, and asked him to publish the communication in a local newspaper. (In the context of the 1820s, this was as close as a prominent office holder could come to holding a press conference.) He was in a delicate and highly critical position, Clay told Brooke, and whatever course he followed with regard to the runoff, he was sure to make a lot of people angry. He had proceeded according to the rule that he always followed when facing such difficult decisions: he had examined his *conscience*. That "faithful guide" had persuaded him that "I ought to vote for Mr. Adams."[33]

[30]Sean Wilentz, *Andrew Jackson* (New York: Times Books, 2005), 48; Ratcliffe, *One-Party Presidential Contest*, 254; Donald B. Cole, *Vindicating Andrew Jackson: The 1828 Election and the Rise of the Two-Party System* (Lawrence: University Press of Kansas, 2009), 19.

[31]Jackson, *Papers of Andrew Jackson*, 6:20.

[32]Ibid., 6:23, 30, 32.

[33]Harry L. Watson, ed., *Andrew Jackson vs. Henry Clay: Democracy and Development in Antebellum America* (Boston: Bedford/St. Martin's, 1998), 158.

Clay explained that he had ruled out William Crawford in part because of the state of his health—Crawford had suffered a serious stroke in late 1823 from which he was still recovering—and in part because he had finished so far behind the other finalists. He had decided against Jackson, on the other hand, because he feared that elevating a "military chieftain" to such a position of power might ultimately threaten the republic. Clay closed his letter by predicting that his stance would call forth "all the abuse, which partisan zeal, malignity, & rivalry can invent." But then he concluded with a rhetorical question: "What is a public man worth, if he will not expose himself" to criticism "for the good of his country?"[34]

None of the Framers could have said it better. Writing in the 1820s, Clay was speaking in the republican vernacular of the 1780s. Although he never used the word *virtue*, the concept pervaded his explanation to Judge Brooke. Disregarding the transient popular passions of the moment, he had examined his conscience and followed its dictates in the pursuit of the common good, even when he knew that the people would punish him for it.

Was this a principled stand or an 1820s version of "spin"? There's no doubt that Clay very much wanted to be president (he was a candidate for the office three times), and he surely viewed Jackson, another popular westerner, as a formidable rival. But this much is equally certain: if he had quietly declined Adams's offer of a cabinet post—so that the cloud of the "Corrupt Bargain" didn't overshadow his words as we read them—we'd be taking his explanation, and his warning, a lot more seriously.

Henry Clay

Keep in mind first of all that Clay had done nothing unconstitutional. As a member of the House of Representatives, neither he nor any congressman was bound by the original preferences

---

[34]Ibid.

of his state when choosing a winner in the runoff. (None of the candidates could have ever received a majority if all of the congressmen had followed such a rule.) This didn't prevent Jacksonians from condemning Clay for disregarding "his obligations to the constitution" by his "daring and open infraction of the Representative duty."[35] Such charges betrayed both ignorance of the Constitution and an all-too-familiar assurance that it surely says whatever we need it to say at the moment.

Beyond this, note that Clay's objections to Jackson were entirely plausible. It's both ironic and revealing that the man who would become the symbol of American democracy struggled with authoritarian tendencies for much of his life. As a military commander, Jackson was a stern disciplinarian who brooked not the slightest challenge to his authority. During his 1814 campaign against the Creeks in Alabama, Jackson ordered the execution of a seventeen-year-old volunteer for leaving his guard post and speaking disrespectfully to an officer. During his subsequent defense of New Orleans, he ordered the execution of six militiamen who had earlier contended—probably correctly—that their terms of service had expired and attempted to return home.

Yet this same disciplinarian chafed under the authority of others. In 1813, as a commander of Tennessee militia engaged in operations in present-day Mississippi, Jackson disobeyed a direct order from the secretary of war to disband his force and marched his men back to Tennessee instead. Later the same year, Jackson led an unauthorized invasion of Spanish Florida on the grounds that the British were using Pensacola as a staging area for future operations against Louisiana.

In command at New Orleans at the close of 1814, Jackson declared martial law prior to the British campaign for that city and refused to revoke it until well after formal notification had arrived of the end of the war. When a member of the Louisiana legislature published an editorial condemning him for abuse of power, Jackson had him arrested. When a federal judge issued a writ of habeas corpus for the legislator's release, Jackson ordered that the judge be seized and exiled beyond American lines.

Commissioned as a general in the regular US Army for his exploits during the War of 1812, in 1818 Jackson again invaded Spanish Florida without official authorization, this time on the grounds that the region provided a haven for Seminoles engaged in raids into southern Georgia. Surrounding the territorial capital at Pensacola, he promised the Spanish governor that he would

---

[35]Jackson, *Papers of Andrew Jackson*, 6:33.

"put to death every man found in arms" if Spanish troops tried to defend their seat of government.[36]

While Jackson rejoiced at ending the "depredations of our frontier," his civilian superiors were less than delighted.[37] Not only had the popular general rashly invaded Spanish territory. Along the way he had captured and executed two British citizens he believed to be inciting the Seminoles, trying them by court martial and without benefit of counsel. In sum, Jackson's unauthorized foray threatened not one but two international incidents. Members of President James Monroe's cabinet recommended that Jackson be reprimanded or even court-martialed, while Congress summoned him to Washington to testify at an inquiry into his recent conduct.

It was during these congressional hearings in 1819 that Henry Clay first raised the alarm about Jackson. In an impassioned speech in support of a resolution to censure the general, the Speaker reviewed the history of "military chieftains" who first won the people's applause and then subverted their liberty. "Greece had her Alexander, Rome her Caesar, England her Cromwell, France her Bonaparte," Clay reminded his colleagues. "If we would escape the rock on which they split, we must avoid their errors."[38]

In his defense, Jackson claimed that the War Department had given prior approval for his campaign, but he was never able to document it. A recent examination of the episode concludes that "Jackson did not merely exceed his instructions" in invading Florida. "He violated his orders in every particular with remarkable enthusiasm."[39]

Six years later, Clay was again warning the country about its popular hero, explaining that he was unwilling to elevate a "military chieftain" to the nation's highest office for fear that it would lead the country down a path "which has conducted every other republic to ruin."[40] No one in 1824 or 1825 seriously expected Andrew Jackson to become an American Caesar, marching on Washington at the head of an army and proclaiming himself emperor. But that was never really Clay's point. What Clay was alluding to, both in 1819 and again in 1825, was Jackson's long-standing habit of resisting accountability, disregarding

---

[36]H. W. Brands, *Andrew Jackson: His Life and Times* (New York: Anchor Books, 2005), 337.

[37]Nancy Isenberg and Andrew Burstein, *The Problem of Democracy: The Presidents Adams Confront the Cult of Personality* (New York: Viking, 2019), 332.

[38]Watson, *Andrew Jackson vs. Henry Clay*, 142.

[39]Heidler and Heidler, *Rise of Andrew Jackson*, 99-100.

[40]Watson, *Andrew Jackson vs. Henry Clay*, 158.

authority, and challenging the rule of law. Clay didn't imagine these character traits, and he wasn't alone in fearing them.

Predictably, Jackson defended himself by attacking Clay. When Clay had introduced his resolution to censure him back in 1819, the general had written to his wife that the Speaker had chosen to "abandon principle" in the cause of "self-aggrandizement." Six years later, when Clay announced that he could not support a "military chieftain" for president, Jackson complained to an old friend that Clay had opted to "abandon principle . . . for self agrandisement." Nothing really had changed in his response except the spelling.[41]

The general elaborated on his defense in a much longer letter to New York politician Samuel Swartwout (who promptly shared it with a New York City newspaper). As Clay had done in his letter to Brooke, Jackson underscored his own virtue. He had demonstrated virtue by risking his life for "the honor safety & glory of our country"—something Henry Clay had never done. He had exhibited virtue by refusing to promote his own candidacy—something Clay could never claim. Jackson knew that the sanctimonious Speaker of the House was influenced by "selfish views & considerations" rather than the "workings of an honest conscience."

Above all, Jackson was gratified that, unlike Clay, he had done nothing "to prostrate that fundamental [principle] which maintains the supremacy of the people's will." He would "retire again to my farm" with his principles intact, he told Swartwout. Unscarred by Clay's baseless insinuations, he would submit to "a purer tribunal"—namely, "the Judgment of an enlightened patriotic & uncorrupted people."[42]

Jackson's letter to Samuel Swartwout appeared in the *New York National Advocate* on the same day that John Quincy Adams—now *President* Adams—announced that the United States had become a "representative democracy." Note that Adams didn't say simply that the country was a "democracy." Although American political culture was becoming more "democratic" by the 1820s, decades would pass before *democracy* would predominate in popular usage.

To begin with, the word still carried pejorative connotations. The Founders had associated the term with the direct democracy of classical Greece—a model

[41]Brands, *Andrew Jackson*, 351; Jackson, *Papers of Andrew Jackson*, 6:20.
[42]Jackson, *Papers of Andrew Jackson*, 6:41-42.

in which every eligible citizen participated directly in each major political decision. Such democracies, James Madison cautioned, were "spectacles of turbulence and contention" and "incompatible with personal security or the rights of property." They "never possessed one feature of good government," echoed Hamilton. "Their very character was tyranny."[43]

Democracy could also be ambiguous. The Founders had sometimes used the word not only to describe a simple model of government but also to identify an element within a more complicated form of government that balanced monarchy, aristocracy, and democracy: the influence of the one, the few, and the many. By this line of thinking, the House of Representatives was the domain of "the democracy" within the larger framework of constitutional government. It was through that chamber, presumably, that the voice of the people would be most clearly heard.[44]

This habit of equating "the democracy" with "the great body of the people" contributed to yet another meaning for the ambiguous term. When a political party later began to coalesce around the person of Andrew Jackson, supporters frequently would refer to the new institution not as "the Democratic Party" but as "the Democracy," and eventually their opponents did as well. This meant that references to "democracy" could easily take on a partisan tinge.

The least imprecise label, then, and the one that Adams used in his inaugural address, was "representative democracy," and it's crucial that we understand how he and his contemporaries understood the phrase. As we already know, the Framers were resolved to create a republic, a "public thing" in which all legitimate power flowed from popular consent. They also took as a given that the republic they were creating would necessarily rely on some form of representation. And yet they were categorically opposed to "representative democracy." So what distinguishes a representative democracy, which the Framers abhorred, from a representative republic, which they sought to perpetuate and render "more perfect"?

These are slippery terms, and there's no point in our trying to come up with absolute definitions intended to hold in all times and places. But it's a simple thing to observe some of the glaring ways that the republican mindset of the Framers differed from the democratic assumptions of the generation that followed. Four seem particularly important.

---

[43]James Madison, *Federalist* #10, 52; Bailyn, *Debate on the Constitution*, part 2, 768.
[44]Bailyn, *Debate on the Constitution*, part 1, 260.

First, there was now a widespread sentiment that voting was a right for all adult white males rather than a privilege accorded those who, by virtue of substantial property ownership, had a "stake" in the society and were (hopefully) immune to manipulation and coercion. At the time of the American Revolution, a conservative estimate would be that 60 percent of adult white males were enfranchised. Over the course of the next two generations, state after state relaxed its property requirement for voting. By 1824, the proportion of adult white males who possessed the vote had risen to between 80 and 90 percent.

This meant that a growing proportion of Americans responded to the election of 1824 from the starting point of assumed *right*. If the congressional caucus was equivalent to "the great whore of Babylon" (Andrew Jackson's analogy), it was in large part because (in Jackson's words), it subverted the people's "direct right of electing the president."[45]

Voices from around the country reiterated the point. The caucus represented a "usurpation of the people's rights," declared the *Richmond Enquirer*. It wrested from the people "the most important right pertaining to their freedom," the *Nashville Gazette* agreed—namely, "the right of choosing their chief magistrate."[46] And if the people possessed such a right, it called into question not only the congressional caucus but the Electoral College and the House runoff as well.

Invariably, the correct assertion that the caucus was nowhere explicitly sanctioned in the Constitution shaded into the false insistence that the Constitution expressly authorized the people to elect the president. A pro-Jackson meeting in Knoxville, Tennessee, for example, preemptively blasted the caucus in 1823 on the grounds that "the right to choose and decide is vested in the people by the constitution itself." A pro-Jackson meeting in Baltimore denounced the caucus as a "usurpation of the rights of the people" as defined in "our constitution." Jackson himself echoed the claim. "In the adoption of our Constitution," he wrote in a message to be shared at a public rally, "the people secured to themselves the right of choosing their own agents to administer the government."[47]

Except that they didn't.

Second, by the 1820s there had been a sea change in the common understanding of the responsibility of government officeholders to their constituents. As we noticed earlier, the Framers thought of government officials as *trustees*

---

[45]Jackson, *Papers of Andrew Jackson*, 6:14.

[46]Ibid., 5:328; Murphy, "Myth and Reality," 273; Thomas Coens, "The Early Jackson Party: A Force for Democratization?," in Adams, *Companion to the Era of Andrew Jackson*, 239.

[47]Coens, "Early Jackson Party," 245, 240; Jackson, *Papers of Andrew Jackson*, 6:183.

charged with a solemn obligation to promote the common welfare. By the 1820s, Americans increasingly thought of government officeholders as public *agents*, hired representatives whose primary function was to implement the wishes of the taxpayers who paid their salaries.

Anger at the outcome of the 1824 election evoked a cascade of dogmatic re-definitions of the proper role of the people's representatives. The *Nashville Republican* condemned the outcome of the runoff on the grounds that "the Constitution declares that a majority shall rule, and he who is the favorite of the people . . . must be elected by Congress." A Pennsylvania correspondent wrote to Jackson to rail against those congressmen who had inflicted "open insult" and "deep injury" on their constituents by disregarding their preferences. They should have "the finger of scorn pointed at them wherever they go."[48]

A Kentucky officeholder similarly insisted that "all Public men should smart for not doing that which their people wants." Another upper-South politician found relevant guidance in the Scripture's injunction to servants to obey their masters. The representative "who knows his masters will and fails, or refuses to obey it, deserves to be beaten with many stripes."[49]

This changing understanding of the role of the representative was closely related to a radical transformation of the traditional understanding of virtue, which is the third key difference between democratic and republican assumptions during this era. In 1787, the Framers of the Constitution had conceived of virtue as self-denial in the service of the common good. When popular opinion is misguided, the virtuous statesman must be prepared to stand against it, regardless of the cost. Virtuous senators would sometimes have to "suspend the blow meditated by the people against themselves." A virtuous president would occasionally need to "withstand the temporary delusion" of the electorate.[50]

A generation later, virtue increasingly meant self-denial in the service of the public's preferences. From the Jacksonian perspective, the officeholder who voted against the wishes of his constituents was now the very definition of a scoundrel.

We can catch a glimpse of this new understanding in Jackson's letter to Samuel Swartwout, but the best expression that I've come across lies in the pages of the pro-Jackson *Washington Gazette*. In an article titled "Mr. Clay and His Conscience," the editor ridiculed Clay's explanation that his devotion to the republic

---

[48]Heidler and Heidler, *Rise of Andrew Jackson*, 198; Jackson, *Papers of Andrew Jackson*, 6:30.
[49]Jackson, *Papers of Andrew Jackson*, 6:64, 84.
[50]James Madison, *Federalist* #63, 339; Alexander Hamilton, *Federalist* #71, 383.

had dictated his opposition to Jackson. It wasn't virtue that drove Clay's decision. "The selfish ambition of Henry Clay is visible in every line of his letter," the editor contended. His sanctimonious appeal to his "conscience" was "but a thin disguise to a foul purpose."

But the *Gazette* made clear that, even if Clay was sincere, even if he genuinely feared giving a man like Jackson more power, he had committed an unpardonable sin by opposing the candidate whom the people preferred. "Mr. Clay, in denouncing that Hero, sets himself up in judgment against the sense and the voice of the People," the editor thundered. "If the People thought Gen. Jackson worthy, is it for Henry Clay to pronounce him unworthy?" The answer was clear. "No. Henry Clay himself has inflicted the deepest wound on the fundamental principle of our government. *He* has insulted and struck down the majesty of the People."[51]

Above all, these evolving understandings—of the basis of the franchise, of the role of the representative, of the definition of virtue—were inextricably intertwined with a dramatically new conception of human nature. The Framers had grounded their convictions about government on their fundamental belief that humans are essentially selfish and prone to passion. By the 1820s, Jacksonian rhetoric frequently assumed exactly the opposite. As it emerged in Jacksonian America, the gospel of democracy is that men and women individually are basically good, and collectively they are reliably wise, with the result that the will of the majority is infused with an unassailable moral authority.

This wasn't inevitable. Following C. S. Lewis, we can imagine Americans in the 1820s and 1830s opposing the freedom of elected officials to thwart the will of the majority because of their belief in human fallenness. By such reasoning, humans' innate selfishness and propensity to abuse power would make it dangerous to give elected officials such latitude. Instead, American politics increasingly reflected the dogma that the American people were so "enlightened patriotic & uncorrupted" that their will must be absolute. The will of the people "is our oracle," Jacksonian writer George Bancroft proclaimed the year after John Quincy Adams entered the White House. "This, we acknowledge, is the voice of God."[52]

---

[51]Watson, *Andrew Jackson vs. Henry Clay*, 160, 161.
[52]Robert Wiebe, *Self-Rule: A Cultural History of American Democracy* (Chicago: University of Chicago Press, 1995), 38.

— 4 —

"A TRIUMPH OF THE VIRTUE OF THE PEOPLE"

*I*t's an exaggeration to say that the 1828 presidential campaign began the moment the House selected John Quincy Adams as president—but not much of one. The paramount issue in 1828 would be the validity of the outcome of the election of 1824, and for four solid years the supporters of "the People's Candidate" attacked it, relentlessly accusing Adams and Clay of stealing the election and defrauding the public. The only way to right such a monstrous wrong would be to put the Hero of New Orleans in the White House, and almost no one doubted that, if he lived, Andrew Jackson would be a candidate for president in 1828.

That was fine with the general. Jackson lingered in Washington just long enough to vote against Henry Clay's confirmation as secretary of state, then he shook the dust off his feet and headed for home. (He would officially resign his seat before the next session.) Honored at numerous towns and cities along the way, he finally arrived at Nashville in mid-April 1825, where an artillery salute announced his arrival and a military parade escorted him to a public dinner on his behalf. In brief remarks, Jackson reminded the throng that he hadn't sought the presidency. He didn't desire it. But if his country should call him to the office, his sense of duty forbade him to decline "public favour" when offered.[1]

In the context of the day, this was equivalent to staging a rally at Trump Tower and announcing his candidacy before a gaggle of cameramen and reporters. When the Tennessee legislature formally nominated the Hero of New Orleans

---

[1]Andrew Jackson, in *The Papers of Andrew Jackson,* ed. Sam B. Smith, Harriet Chappell Owsley, Harold D. Moser, et al., 10 vols. (Knoxville: University of Tennessee Press, 1980–2016), 6:63.

later that fall, it simply made official what everyone already assumed. In the meantime, Jackson retired to the Hermitage and made "planning his next run at the White House . . . his full-time job."[2] The election was three years away, and Jackson's hat was already in the ring.

It was different with Adams. For his part, the country's sixth president appears to have thought about reelection hardly at all, except occasionally to remind himself that his prospects were poor. John Quincy Adams may have been the hardest-working individual ever to occupy the White House, but he directed none of that effort toward developing a personal following or a political movement. For four years he simply went about the business of governing, rarely leaving Washington, rarely even straying from his office except on Sundays, when his custom was to attend not one but two religious services.

On a typical weekday, the president would rise at 5:00 a.m., read in his Bible and a biblical commentary, walk around the Capitol or swim in the Potomac for an hour to an hour and a half, study newspapers and reports and write in his diary until a late breakfast, then endure a seven- to eight-hour gauntlet of appointments until a quiet dinner at 5:30 with his wife. Dinner done, he would return to his desk until late in the evening, perhaps relaxing with a few minutes of Cicero or Tacitus (in the original Latin) before turning in around eleven.

It was a grueling, unglamorous regimen, but then Adams had been taught from his earliest memories that there was no higher calling than a life of public service. His father, in the son's estimation, had "served to great and useful purpose his Nation, his Age, and his God." John Adams's firstborn aspired to nothing less.[3]

If Andrew Jackson spent much of his time in Washington fantasizing about retirement, John Quincy Adams spent much of his time fearing it, for it signified to him a life devoid of "useful purpose." Descendant of the Puritans that he was, at the end of his presidency he regretted that his "services to my fellow creatures" were not "such as they ought to have been," but then his standard had been severe and uncompromising: to devote "all the faculties of my Soul . . . to the Improvement, Physical, Moral and Intellectual of my Country."[4]

He would do anything for his country—except play politics or become the leader of a party. Adams had entered office keenly aware that, by his own calculation,

---

[2]Daniel Walker Howe, *What Hath God Wrought: The Transformation of America, 1815–1848* (New York: Oxford University Press, 2007), 251.

[3]John Quincy Adams, *Diaries*, ed. David Waldstreicher (New York: Library of America, 2017), 2:131.

[4]Ibid., 2:211, 193.

"perhaps two thirds of the whole people [were] adverse to the result."[5] What was worse, the proportion of federal employees who opposed his election was likely that great or greater. Recognizing this, Henry Clay approached Adams at the outset of his administration and suggested the propriety of removing from office all current presidential appointees who openly opposed the chief executive. More specifically, he recommended that Adams begin by replacing a particular customs officer who was "a noisy and clamourous reviler" of the president.

Adams balked. Most of the current customs officers around the country had been appointed by the previous secretary of the treasury, William Crawford, and Adams knew that the vast majority had favored their former boss in the recent election. To remove a single appointee on those grounds would create a precedent for removing almost all of them. Such a policy would promote "an invidious and inquisitorial scrutiny" into the personal convictions of public officers. It would kindle "selfish and sordid passions" among ambitious men and tempt them to seek political benefit as a reward for slander. Adams wanted none of it.[6]

So when he received credible reports of the disloyalty of his postmaster general, John McLean, the president overlooked his undeniable "political treachery." McLean had improved the efficiency of the mail service, Adams commented, and that was all that mattered. And when additional reports reached him of federal customs agents using "all the influences of their offices against us," he again refused to act. His policy was to punish "official misconduct" only, he reiterated to his diary. Otherwise, he would adhere to "the principle . . . of removing no public Officer, for merely preferring another Candidate for the Presidency."[7] It was a noble, virtuous, politically suicidal rule.

The stubbornly independent son of his stubbornly independent father, Adams brought an expansive vision of government to the presidency, but he wouldn't try to promote popular enthusiasm for such a controversial program, nor would he use patronage to build congressional support. He would simply recommend what he believed was best for the country and make the strongest argument in its favor that he could. He knew that "severe trials" would follow, and the outcome would be beyond his control, but wasn't that always the case

---

[5]Ibid., 2:124.
[6]Ibid., 2:102-4.
[7]Lynn Hudson Parsons, *The Birth of Modern Politics: Andrew Jackson, John Quincy Adams, and the Election of 1828* (New York: Oxford University Press, 2009), 141; Adams, *Diaries*, 2:185, 141.

in life? "It is not in man that walketh to direct his steps," the Old Testament prophet Jeremiah reminded him.[8]

Adams presented his vision to the nation at the end of 1825 in his first "annual message," what today we would call his State of the Union address. Today the State of the Union address has become an interminable, nationally televised infomercial for the president and his party. In the nineteenth century, the president's annual message was a *written* document sent to the Capitol for Congress to read. Article II, section 3 of the Constitution enjoins the executive to provide Congress "from time to time" with information on "the state of the union." With that end in mind, it was customary for the president to include detailed summaries of reports from each of the cabinet-level departments under his direction as part of his "message."

But the Constitution also encourages the executive to recommend to Congress "such measures as he shall judge necessary and expedient." At a time when sitting presidents made few public speeches, the annual message constituted a rare opportunity for both Congress and the nation to hear directly from their highest officer. The country paid attention, and in 1825 John Quincy Adams gave them their money's worth.

The theme of Adams's suggestions was *improvement*. The purpose of government is the improvement of the condition of the governed, he contended. "No government . . . can accomplish the lawful ends of its institution but in proportion as it improves the condition of those over whom it is established."[9] Toward this end, Adams called for the building of roads and canals, the establishment of a national university and national observatory, the expansion of the navy, and the creation of a new cabinet-level Department of the Interior. He concluded by challenging Congress to act boldly, proceeding in advance of, even in contradiction to, popular opinion. "Were we to slumber in indolence or fold up our arms and proclaim to the world that we are *palsied by the will of our constituents*," he asked rhetorically, "would it not be to cast away the bounties of Providence and doom ourselves to perpetual inferiority?"[10]

Jacksonians were aghast. To the sin of corruption, Adams was now adding the crime of "consolidation," openly calling on Congress to create an all-powerful,

---

[8]William J. Cooper, *The Lost Founding Father: John Quincy Adams and the Transformation of American Politics* (New York: W. W. Norton, 2017), 225; Jeremiah 10:23, King James Version.
[9]James D. Richardson, comp., *A Compilation of the Messages and Papers of the Presidents* (New York: Bureau of National Literature, 1897), 2:877.
[10]Ibid., 2:882, italics added.

centralized federal apparatus that would swallow up the prerogatives of the states. As night follows day, "despotism" would follow consolidation. Wasn't Adams already encouraging Congress to ignore the will of the people? Soon American liberty would be no more. That, at least, was what Andrew Jackson claimed to foresee. He professed to "shudder" after reading Adams's address and grouped the president among the "enemies of freedom."[11]

The Jacksonians in Congress successfully blocked almost all of Adams's proposals during his lone term in office, but the president's annual message was not without effect, for it helped to crystalize two emerging camps within the old Democratic-Republican Party. Adams's recommendations reflected a "positive . . . conception of liberty"—freedom *to*—that saw in government the potential to facilitate human initiative. Those who embraced his vision—primarily individuals who had voted for Adams or Clay in 1824—identified as the "friends of the administration," occasionally adopted the label "National Republicans" and in due time became the nucleus of the future Whig Party.[12]

Those who howled in protest at Adams's message tended toward a negative understanding of liberty—freedom *from*—and saw the limiting of government intrusion as the key to maximizing liberty. Voters who shared such views—typically the followers of John C. Calhoun, William C. Crawford, and above all, Andrew Jackson—gradually made common cause against Adams. In 1828 they would simply call themselves "Jackson men" or "friends of Jackson." Eventually they would call themselves "Democrats."

Over time, these differing conceptions of liberty would become integral to the politics of antebellum America and to what historians label the Second Party System. That was in the long run. In 1828, nothing much would matter but the contested character of the candidates and their affinity with a virtuous people.

It would be premature to say that the legions of supporters who rallied around John Quincy Adams and Andrew Jackson had coalesced into formal, permanent political parties by 1828, but they were taking significant strides in that direction. Both candidates continued to play the role of the Mute Tribune in public, but a corps of professional politicians on both sides mobilized to build party organizations, raise

---

[11]Jackson, *Papers of Andrew Jackson*, 6:142-43, 187.

[12]John M. Sacher, "The Elections of 1824 and 1828 and the Birth of Modern Politics," in *A Companion to the Era of Andrew Jackson*, ed. Sean Patrick Adams (Oxford, UK: Blackwell Publishing Ltd., 2013), 288; Howe, *What Hath God Wrought*, 253.

money, and generate popular enthusiasm from the top down. The Jacksonians took to this more naturally and were better at it than the Adams men, but both sides waged campaigns that were far more aggressive, more coordinated, more expensive, and more polarizing than anything the nation had seen before.

There were numerous critical issues confronting the country in 1828—disagreements about banking, tariffs, territorial expansion, international trade, and the place of Native Americans and African Americans in American life, to name the most important—but none of these loomed large in the election of that year. The presidential election of 1828 focused on the candidates themselves, pure and simple.

That said, thoughtful discussion of either candidate was in short supply. In its place were ward meetings, state and local conventions, barbecues and banquets, street rallies and parades. There were also campaign buttons, songs, jokes, puns, and cartoons as well as commemorative bandanas, snuffboxes, plates, whiskey flasks, and goblets. Substance was scarce, but slogans and symbols abounded.

So did slander. One historian of the election concluded that it "splattered more filth in more different directions and upon more innocent people than any other in American history."[13] If this was true—some modern observers would claim that honor for more recent campaigns—it was due largely to the countless party newspapers that now dotted the landscape. There had been only ninety newspapers in the country when George Washington took his first oath of office in 1789. By 1828 there were eight hundred, and the vast majority were openly, bitterly partisan. In most instances they owed their survival to income from one faction or the other.

Politicians and parties supported newspapers in a variety of ways. They steered government printing contracts toward loyal editors, encouraged supporters to subscribe to their chosen paper, and subsidized the ventures directly with seed money and equipment. The price for such support was unflagging adherence to the party line, and the party papers delivered. There was nothing hypocritical in this. This was still generations before the rise of journalism as a professional discipline with aspirations of objectivity, and few papers tried to hide their partisan ties. Nor is it at all clear that readers even wanted objective coverage. Most readers chose a paper in the 1820s for much the same reason that we tend to choose a cable news channel or internet site today: to affirm our political biases and abuse the other side.

---

[13]Robert V. Remini, *The Election of Andrew Jackson* (Philadelphia: J. B. Lippincott, 1963), 118.

And make no mistake: abuse was rampant in 1828. A pro-Adams newspaper—the ironically named *Truth's Advocate*—announced with calculated astonishment (and a lot of capital letters and exclamation points) that "General Jackson's mother was a COMMON PROSTITUTE brought to this country by the British soldiers! She afterwards married a MULATTO MAN, with whom she had several children, of which number General JACKSON IS ONE! ! !"

Jackson papers shot back with their dispassionate discovery that Adams had served as a "pimp" for Czar Nicholas during his tenure as ambassador to Russia. He had also filled the White House with "gaming tables and gambling furniture," his wife had been born out of wedlock, she and Adams had had sex before marriage, and the president harbored a secret fondness for silk underwear.[14]

These ludicrous charges were widely believed. As Adams lamented to his diary, in the heat of the contest, even individuals of intelligence and integrity "surrender themselves up to their Passions—Believe every thing, with, without, or even against Evidence, according as it suits their own wishes."[15] Certainly, the party papers did nothing to challenge readers to think deeply, weigh competing evidence and arguments, or take seriously opinions other than their own. Whatever the question, your chosen news source could spin the issue to support your preferred candidate or party. Sound familiar?

If the mudslinging followed a scattergun approach in which no allegation was too irrelevant or too salacious to pass up, beneath the slander both factions offered voters a central, coherent, overarching message—about Andrew Jackson. Jackson was *the* central issue of the campaign. But there was always a related issue intertwined with that of Jackson's character and qualifications—namely, the character and competence of the voters. Just how reliable was popular judgment? Would "the people" be able to distinguish between a savior and a scoundrel?

For their part, the "friends of the administration" labored to prove that Jackson was wholly unqualified to hold the nation's highest office. It was bad enough that Jackson did "not possess a single qualification, suitable for the office

---

[14]Parsons, *Birth of Modern Politics*, 143-44; Edwin A. Miles, "President Adams' Billiard Table," *New England Quarterly* 45 (1972): 34; Remini, *Election of Andrew Jackson*, 118.
[15]Adams, *Diaries*, 2:161.

of chief magistrate."[16] Far more troubling was that his *character* rendered him wholly unfit for such a responsibility. In making their case, they leveled more than forty separate charges of wrongdoing against the general. These included his multiple duels, extensive land speculation, and high-stakes horse racing as well as allegations of slave trading, malfeasance while negotiating Native American treaties, and misuse of funds while in the government's service.

Two charges stood out above all others. The first involved Jackson's marriage. When Jackson first met his future wife on the Tennessee frontier, Rachel Donelson Robards was separated from her husband and living with her mother, who happened to be Jackson's new landlady. Nearly four decades later, when the matter came under scrutiny as the election drew near, the Jackson central campaign committee in Nashville circulated a pamphlet contending that "Mr. Robards separated from his wife, applied for a divorce, obtained it, and General Jackson married her."[17] End of story.

This was false. The Adams press insisted, and most historians now agree, that Jackson and Rachel ran away together, probably during the winter of 1789–1790, well *before* Rachel's husband brought suit for divorce in his home state of Kentucky. This may have been an innocent mistake—with the couple wrongly believing that Robards had sued for and been granted a divorce—but it's at least as likely that they eloped fully knowing that Rachel was still married.

In the late eighteenth century, it was almost impossible for a *wife* to sue successfully for divorce. By eloping, the couple may have also hoped to force Rachel's husband to stop dragging his feet by handing him the only grounds for divorce that courts in the 1790s would reliably accept: his wife's adultery. If that was their goal they succeeded, for the Kentucky court that eventually granted Lewis Robards's divorce petition ruled that "the defendant, Rachel Robards, hath deserted the plaintiff . . . and hath and doth still live in adultery with another man."[18]

The Adams press contended that the decades-old offense was relevant to "the National character, the National interest, and the National morals," and they

---

[16]*An Address to the People of the United States on the Subject of the Presidential Election: With a Special Reference to the Nomination of Andrew Jackson, Containing Sketches of His Public and Private Character, by a Citizen of the United States* (New York, 1828), 28.

[17]*A Letter from the Jackson Committee of Nashville in Answer to One from a Similar Committee at Cincinnati upon the Subject of General Jackson's Marriage* (Nashville: Hall & Fitzgerald, 1827), 4.

[18]*View of General Jackson's Domestic Relations in Reference to His Fitness for the Presidency* (Cincinnati, 1828), 14; Norma Basch, "Marriage, Morals, and Politics in the Election of 1828," *Journal of American History* 80 (1993): 891; H. W. Brands, *Andrew Jackson: His Life and Times* (New York: Anchor Books, 2005), 64.

cautioned that "the immorality of nations has, generally, been produced by the vices of their rulers." Perhaps so, but they exaggerated egregiously in portraying Jackson as a sexual predator who "tore from a husband the wife of his bosom."[19]

More compelling was their charge that Jackson had a long track record of defying authority and disregarding the rule of law. Building on Henry Clay's

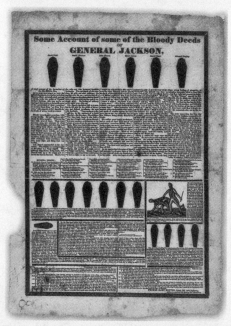

critique of Jackson as a "military chieftain," they warned that the general's election would be "dangerous to our liberties." An Adams meeting in New York charged Jackson with abusing power whenever he wielded it, exhibiting "anti-republican principles" in addition to "vindictiveness and cruelty." His "impetuous temper," "irritability," and "repeated acts of violence" proved definitively that he "cannot be intrusted with any power, either civil or military."[20]

Focusing on Jackson's imposition of martial law at New Orleans, an Ohio editor thundered that the Tennessean had "set at naught the Constitution and laws of his country, and trampled under his feet the rights of his fellow-citizens, with a lawless disregard of everything but his own will."

"Some Account of Some of the Bloody Deeds of General Jackson." This is one of a series of "coffin hand bills" produced by anti-Jackson newspaper editor John Binns during the 1828 presidential campaign. The coffins at the top represent six militiamen Jackson had ordered executed shortly after the battle of New Orleans. The text of the broadside provides a detailed account of that and other alleged atrocities attributed to the general.

Throughout his military career, echoed a Virginia convention, the general had shown a penchant for "disobeying the orders of his superiors" and making "his own arbitrary will the rule of his conduct."[21]

---

[19] View of General Jackson's Domestic Relations, 1, 17; Basch, "Marriage, Morals, and Politics," 897.

[20] A History of the Life and Public Services of Major General Andrew Jackson, Impartially Compiled from the Most Authentic Sources (n.p., 1828), 31; Address to the People of the United States, 6-7; Truth's Advocate and Monthly Anti-Jackson Expositor (Cincinnati: Lodge, L'Hommedieu, and Hammond, Printers, January 1828), 36.

[21] Truth's Advocate and Monthly Anti-Jackson Expositor, (January 1828), 36; Republican Party (NY), To the People of the State of New York (n.p., n.d., but probably 1828), 11.

The Adams press hammered away at Jackson's execution of innocent militiamen, his unauthorized invasion of Spanish territory, and the "cold-blooded massacre" at the Horse-Shoe, where Jackson had pledged to "exterminate" the Creek warriors allied with the British. In sum, Jackson's critics asked, what did these episodes reveal, if not a "moral depravity" that greater power would only magnify? "What trait in his character does not denote him the haughty, fierce and arbitrary tyrant?"[22]

The Jacksonians responded by lauding a hero of such stern and unimpeachable integrity that "corruption trembles at his name." A New Hampshire meeting extolled the general as "an honest man, an inflexible patriot and republican, a man of sound and ripe judgment, of excellent discrimination, and of practical knowledge of the genius and spirit of our free institutions."[23]

As they had done in 1824, Jackson's supporters lauded the general's "great services and deeds of devotion" to the country. This was the theme of his life: from the American Revolution, when "he poured out his youthful blood" for independence; to the Battle of Horseshoe Bend, when he annihilated the "savage invaders"; to his glorious victory at New Orleans, when he reversed the tide of the War of 1812 and "light broke in upon the darkness." As a rally at New Orleans proclaimed, Andrew Jackson was nothing less than "the Saviour of His Country."[24] A theologian might call this idolatry or blasphemy. In 1828, Jacksonians called it effective.

But overshadowing every other claim was the insistence that the general was the people's choice and champion. "Andrew Jackson is the *candidate of the People*," Jacksonian editor Duff Green told readers in almost every issue of his Washington, DC, newspaper, the *United States Telegraph*. (Green would break with Jackson within a few years.) "He has always been found upon the side of the People," a Jackson committee in New York City echoed, and "the People" have always been for him.[25]

---

[22]*Address to the People of the United States*, 16; *A Review of the Battle of the Horse Shoe, and of the Facts Relating to the Killing of Sixteen Indians on the Morning After the Battle by the Orders of Gen. Andrew Jackson* (n.p., n.d.), Tennessee State Library and Archives, 4, 5; *The Principles and Acts of Mr. Adams' Administration* (Concord: Office of *The New Hampshire Journal*, 1828), 32.
[23]*Address of the Republican General Committee of Young Men of the City and County of New York Friendly to the Election of Gen. Andrew Jackson to the Presidency, to the Republican Electors of the State of New York* (New York: Alexander Ming, printer, 1828), 38.
[24][Henry Lee], *Vindication of the Character and Public Services of Andrew Jackson* (Boston: True and Greene, 1828), 3; *Address of the Republican General Committee*, 43, 36-37; Robert V. Remini, *Andrew Jackson and the Course of American Freedom, 1822–1832* (New York: Harper & Row, 1981), 132.
[25]Remini, *Election of Andrew Jackson*, 102; *Address of the Republican General Committee*, 43.

Andrew Jackson, equestrian print. This popular print captures a theme prominent in all three of Jackson's presidential campaigns: the portrayal of the general as a military hero who had saved his country on the battlefield.

The general was not only for the people, his supporters stressed. They increasingly contended that he was one of the people as well. They drove home the point primarily with unflattering comparisons to Adams. The contest, they told unwitting voters, pitted the "ploughman" versus the "professor." Jackson owned more than a hundred slaves by 1828, and he hadn't spent time behind the business end of a plow horse in decades, but his savvy campaign managers referred to him ceaselessly as the "farmer soldier" or the "Farmer of Tennessee." Jackson was a "plain cultivator of the soil," a man of *practical* experience, *native* intellect, and *common* sense "unclouded by the visionary speculation of the academician."[26]

In contrast, the college-educated Adams had received "a princely education in and near the despotic courts of foreign governments." Any potential he might have had for genuine wisdom had been corrupted by exposure to intellectuals and Europeans. It might look impressive to some, but his book-learning had primarily equipped him to feed from the public trough while sneering at the plain folk he claimed to serve. It had also whetted his appetite for luxury and decadence. The "Farmer of Tennessee" was a man of simplicity and cordial hospitality, "not raised in the lap of luxury and wealth." The effete Adams had been "reared on sweetmeats from the tables of kings and princes." As president he had surrounded himself with "royal extravagances" and "kingly pomp and splendor."[27]

If much of this sounded familiar, there was a darker, harder edge to Jacksonian rhetoric than ever before. At the heart of the Jacksonians' appeal to the voters in 1828 was not a set of specific policy proposals or a careful comparison of the candidates' qualifications. Above all, they offered the voters a larger *story* in which to situate their lives. Its central themes were grievance, conflict, corruption, and conspiracy. Even as the Jackson campaign lauded the "good sense" of the "honest yeomanry," the Jackson press invited voters not to think but to feel, not to consider policy proposals but to nurture fear and outrage.

History revealed a perpetual struggle between two great political parties, Jacksonians maintained: "the aristocracy" and "the people." It was a battle of might against right, a relentless struggle in which "power is always stealing from the many to the few." The 1828 election was simply an extension of this age-old war. The choice was between "Jackson and Adams, democracy and aristocracy," and the outcome would determine whether the government or the people would rule. "We are contending in the cause of freedom," Jacksonians declared before cheering audiences. "The second 'REIGN OF TERROR'" would follow should they fail. "Every thing . . . dear to freemen is at stake."[28]

---

[26]John William Ward, *Andrew Jackson: Symbol for an Age* (New York: Oxford University Press, 1953), 44, 46.

[27]*Proceedings, and Address of the New Hampshire Republican State Convention of Delegates Friendly to the Election of Andrew Jackson to the next Presidency of the United States, Assembled at Concord, June 11 and 12, 1828* (Concord, NH: Printed at the Patriot Office, 1828), 24; Ward, *Andrew Jackson*, 66, 71; Remini, *Election of Andrew Jackson*, 102.

[28]*Proceedings, and Address of the New Hampshire Republican State Convention*, 8; Remini, *Jackson and the Course of American Freedom*, 130; *Address of the Republican General Committee*, 4, 44; Jackson, *Papers of Andrew Jackson*, 6:460.

More than anything else, the unholy alliance between Adams and Henry Clay in 1825 had proven just how far the "well-born" were willing to go to subvert the people's liberty. There was no more evidence for the "Corrupt Bargain" in 1828 than there had been in 1825, but this didn't stop the Jacksonians from leveling the charge relentlessly. In public, Adams's friends rightly alerted voters that the president's assailants "take for granted what they cannot prove." In private, Adams thought it "highly probable" that the "infamous slander" would succeed. "When suspicion has been kindled into popular delusion," he reflected in his diary, "truth and reason and justice" proved slender reeds.[29]

The lack of evidence notwithstanding, the charge of a "Corrupt Bargain" offered a campaign narrative that was simply too good to pass up, and it left an indelible stamp on the 1828 election. It increased sympathy for Jackson, making him "now both hero and *victim*." It transformed Adams into an unprincipled pretender whose very presidency was illegitimate. Above all, it persuaded the general's followers that the previous election hadn't been lost. It had been *stolen*. In 1824 a corrupt cabal had subverted the Constitution in order to thwart the rightful victory of "the Nation's Hero and the People's Friend."[30] To reward these enemies of the people by reelecting their leader would signal the final demise of American liberty.

There was one other major issue embedded in the partisan rhetoric of 1828, and in the long run it eclipsed all else in importance. Inseparable from the argument about Andrew Jackson was a corresponding debate about the character and judgment of the electorate. In 1828 the voters, not the state legislatures, would now choose the electors in all but two of the twenty-four states in the Union. (Delaware and South Carolina were the lone holdouts.) Restrictions on the franchise had declined to the point that something approaching universal white male suffrage would obtain across the country. A debate about the virtue and discernment of the voters shaded into a debate about human nature and, by implication, about democracy itself.

Two years earlier the historian and orator George Bancroft had proclaimed at a Fourth of July celebration that the United States was "a determined,

---

[29]*Principles and Acts of Mr. Adams' Administration*, 17; Adams, *Diaries*, 2:162.
[30]James C. Curtis, *Andrew Jackson and the Search for Vindication* (Boston: Little, Brown and Company, 1976), 84, italics added; David S. Reynolds, *Waking Giant: America in the Age of Jackson* (New York: Harper Perennial, 2008), 39.

uncompromising democracy." It was on that occasion that he had famously observed that, for Americans, "the popular voice" was the very "voice of God."[31] But the truth is that Bancroft overstated the case. A confirmed Jacksonian in his politics, he spoke primarily for Jacksonians in his tribute to the people. Jackson's opponents could be ambivalent, even downright skeptical about the voters' judgment.

More often than not, the Adams press tried to have it both ways. They repeatedly challenged the dogma that Jackson had been the favorite of the majority of voters in 1824. But even if that were true, they went on to argue, there was absolutely nothing unconstitutional about Adams's election. The members of the House were in no way legally obligated to reflect the preferences of their constituents. "It will be recollected," a pro-Adams pamphlet reminded the nation, "that the freemen, individually, have heretofore had no agency in choosing a president." Instead, they had traditionally trusted "in the wisdom and discretion of those to whom they had delegated that power."[32]

Looking ahead to the election, the supporters of John Quincy Adams expressed the hope that "there is yet a redeeming power in a great majority of the people," that they would exhibit "enough of reflection and consideration" not to cast their ballots for a designing demagogue who would ultimately endanger their freedom. They called on the people to "awake to their duty," to "arise in the majesty of their virtue and guard every avenue to the citadel of our liberties."[33] That seems optimistic enough.

But there was always an undercurrent of doubt. Noting the widespread support for a candidate who "has made his own arbitrary will the rule of his conduct," an Adams convention in Richmond confessed that "nothing has occurred in the history of our country, so much calculated to shake our confidence in the capacity of the people for self-government." If the majority should insist on electing a man such as Andrew Jackson, then "indeed it may be said of us that political delusion has triumphed over reason and truth."[34]

As supporters of an incumbent president who had received only a third of the popular vote in the last election, it is not surprising that many in the Adams camp may have anticipated defeat. What is significant is how they explained that prospect,

---

[31] Robert Wiebe, *Self-Rule: A Cultural History of American Democracy* (Chicago: University of Chicago Press, 1995), 55, 38.

[32] *Address to the People of the United States*, 30.

[33] Ibid., 22.

[34] *To the People of the State of New York*, 9; *Address to the People of the United States*, 38.

for it underscores just how different their mental universe was from ours. American politics was becoming ever more democratic, but one of the two major factions had yet to internalize fully the democratic mindset that we take for granted.

Our modern democratic ethos presupposes that we are individually good as well as collectively wise in our political choices. From this it logically follows that losing candidates *deserve* to lose, at least when the system is functioning as it should. If the electorate is both virtuous and discerning, then losing candidates face one of two options: either acknowledge that their opponents genuinely deserved to win or point to real or alleged abuses of the system that prevented the voice of the majority from being accurately registered. What they *can't* do—unless they're bent on political suicide—is blame the majority for making a bad decision.

To make this more concrete, I would suggest that this is one way to make sense of Donald Trump's strategy in both 2016 and 2020. As opinion polls repeatedly predicted his defeat in the run-up to both elections, Trump proactively exonerated himself by claiming (in 2016) that the Electoral College was "rigged" against him, or by insisting (in 2020) that voting by mail would facilitate widespread fraud. In both campaigns, critics charged him with recklessly undermining popular faith in the democratic process—a valid point—but we must see that there was also something quintessentially "democratic" about his strategy. In a democratic culture, losing candidates can either graciously concede or they can claim that the election was unfair. What they cannot do—without contradicting democracy's cardinal assumption—is impugn the character or the discernment of the electorate.

Two centuries ago, the supporters of John Quincy Adams felt no such hesitation. In 1828 they not only questioned the wisdom of the majority; they did so extensively *in advance* of the election. At times, they openly ridiculed the kinds of voters drawn to Jackson "worship." One editor, for example, griped that the typical Jackson rally attracted "the dissolute, the noisy, the discontented, and designing of society."[35] This was not an unguarded reference behind closed doors, as when Democratic presidential candidate Hillary Clinton was caught on tape at a private fundraiser in 2016 referring to Republican voters as a "basket of deplorables."[36] It was a public condemnation of the virtue and discernment of Jackson's "base."

---

[35]*Truth's Advocate*, February 1828, 49; Remini, *Election of Andrew Jackson*, 116.
[36]David Brody and Scott Lamb, *The Faith of Donald J. Trump: A Spiritual Biography* (New York: HarperCollins, 2018), 242.

More broadly, the friends of the administration observed that, while the consent of the governed is foundational to a republic and thus nonnegotiable, it simply isn't true that the majority is always wise. If this sounds condescending to our democratic ears, we should recall that this was precisely the view that the Framers of the Constitution espoused. And what is especially notable about these more general observations is how closely they echoed comments in support of the Constitution from the late 1780s.

Like the Framers, Adams supporters questioned whether the majority of voters could be trusted to exercise discernment in their political decisions. Recent trends suggested that they were more easily impressed by military exploits than by "the profoundest display of wisdom." They also doubted that the typical voter was well informed. An Adams pamphlet observed that "too many of our citizens are destitute of that information, which might enable them to detect the arts of intrigue and deception with which they are continually assailed by designing men." Nor were they reliably guided by reason. The ongoing campaign revealed all too clearly an inclination among the people "to place a blind confidence in their favorites."[37]

These were limitations of judgment, but the Adams camp also had doubts about the voters' character. "The *People* love to be flattered," argued a Cincinnati editor and supporter of the administration. They bristle at the impertinence of the public figure who fails to praise them, and they are easy marks for the unscrupulous schemer who deals in honeyed allusions to "*the people's rights, the people's intelligence, and the people's power.*"[38]

History showed that flattery was the stock-in-trade of the demagogue and the path to power of the despot. An Adams pamphlet cautioned that "the most abandoned tyrants that have heretofore consigned republican liberty to the dominion of despotism have owed their elevation to *the people.*" This was essentially a paraphrase of *Federalist* no. 1, in which Publius had warned Americans "that of those who have overturned the liberties of republics the greatest number have begun their career, by paying an obsequious court to the people."[39] In sum, popularity isn't equivalent to merit. From Nero to Napoleon, some of the greatest villains of history have won popular acclaim.

---

[37]*Address to the People of the United States*, 19, 28, 22.

[38]*Truth's Advocate*, February 1828, 70.

[39]*An Address to the People of the United States*, 27, italics added; Alexander Hamilton, *Federalist* #1, in Alexander Hamilton, James Madison, and John Jay, *The Federalist*, ed. J. R. Pole (Indianapolis: Hackett, 2005), 3.

To all of which the Jacksonians replied, "Nonsense!" (or something considerably stronger). If the Adams campaign wondered out loud whether the majority could be trusted, the Jackson campaign offered an unceasing ode to their virtue and wisdom. "Our strength is in the spirit and intelligence of the American people," Jackson orators proclaimed. The general would inevitably triumph because he is "sustained by the strength of an enlightened and virtuous people." "The intelligence and virtue of the people" constitute the "stamina" of the American constitutional system. "The cause of the people . . . WILL PREVAIL" because "the great mass of the people cannot be corrupted."[40]

These tributes to popular intelligence, enlightenment, and virtue echoed the refrain emanating from the Hermitage itself. While in public Jackson largely stuck to his scripted role as Mute Tribune, indifferent to politics and above the fray, in private he sustained a detailed correspondence with some forty or so political lieutenants and advisers and kept a close watch over the campaign. And to these, his mantra was relentless: his defeat in 1824 had been a victory of corruption over virtue, but the people were now aroused, and precisely because they were virtuous, they (and he) would be victorious in the next campaign.

"I can assure you I have too much confidence in the *virtue* of the people," Jackson wrote to the governor of Kentucky, "to believe that an attachment to designing Demagogues can wean them from those principles which secure all our rights as freemen." As attacks on his service and character mounted, he fantasized about killing the instigators, but at the same time he reassured concerned correspondents that he had "too much faith in the *virtue* of our people to believe that they could be influenced by such vile acts."[41]

John Quincy Adams was bent on leading the country down a path of consolidation and despotism, he warned a senator from North Carolina, "yet, I have great confidence in the intelligence, and *virtue*, of the great body of the American people; they will never abandon the constitutional ship." His hope rested in "the *virtuous* yeomanry of the country," he informed his running mate, John C. Calhoun. The impending election was a "struggle between the *virtue* of the people & executive patronage," he explained to a New York ally. "I for one do not despair of the republic; I have great confidence in the *virtue* of a great majority of the people, and I cannot fear the result."[42]

---

[40] *Address of the Republican General Committee*, 3, 35; *Proceedings, and Address of the New Hampshire Republican State Convention*, 27.

[41] Jackson, *Papers of Andrew Jackson*, 6:87, 132, italics added.

[42] Ibid., 6:143, 187, 477, italics added.

There was no single election day in 1828. In keeping with established tradition, the states scheduled presidential elections individually, with the result that voters went to the polls over a span of two weeks or so, beginning with Pennsylvania and Ohio at the end of October and concluding with Tennessee in mid-November. The outcome was decisive. Jackson took nearly 56 percent of the popular vote (up from 40 percent in 1824), and he won the Electoral College by more than 2:1, 178-83.

Equally important, the number of individuals taking part in the election had skyrocketed, more than tripling the 360,000 voters casting ballots in 1824. This was partly because four more states had switched to the popular election of presidential electors since 1824 (including New York, with roughly one seventh of the country's population). Even so, voter turnout as a percentage of eligible voters had more than doubled in four short years, from 27 percent to nearly 58 percent. Voter turnout had frequently approached or even exceeded such levels in state elections prior to 1828, but no previous presidential election had come close to stimulating such widespread involvement.

In Jackson's mind, this all added up to one unmistakable conclusion. "The virtue of the people became aroused," he observed to a Kentucky senator. "In the majesty of their strength" they had pronounced a righteous verdict. As he observed modestly to a sympathetic editor, his election reflected "a triumph of the virtue of the people."[43] And that, Jackson would go on to announce in his first annual message, was precisely what the Framers of the Constitution had always intended.

As had often been the case with his predecessors, Jackson's inaugural address in March 1829 was a brief, vague, formulaic statement. There had been no time to produce anything else, even if he had been so inclined. Three days before Christmas, his wife Rachel had died from a heart attack, and for months thereafter he would be in mourning, his heart "nearly broke" by the loss of his "dear companion."[44]

By December, Jackson was ready to sketch his vision for the government, and, like John Quincy Adams before him, he chose his first annual message as the venue for a series of major policy proposals. The most important aimed squarely

[43]Ibid., 6:545, 535.
[44]Ibid., 7:13, 7.

at preventing a repeat of the travesty of 1824. It was imperative, Jackson maintained, that the Congress introduce a constitutional amendment to eliminate the Electoral College.

Predictably, Jackson condemned the Electoral College in part because it was undemocratic. Under its auspices, the will of the people was too easily thwarted. But his argument was also historical: the Electoral College was a defect that the Framers had mistakenly inserted, Jackson suggested, because it so obviously contradicted another constitutional principle that Jackson was certain they espoused—namely, that "to the people belongs the right of electing their chief magistrate." The Framers "had never designed that their choice should in any case be defeated," he explained, "either by the intervention of electoral colleges or by the agency confided, under certain contingencies, to the House of Representatives."[45]

This was garbage, or to use a more scholarly term, hogwash. As we have seen, probably no more than a tenth of the delegates at Philadelphia had supported giving the selection of the executive to the people. Most had scorned the idea. Of all the options on the table, popular election was "worst of all." It ensured that "the worst possible choice will be made." They would sooner "refer a trial of colors to a blind man." The Framers had insisted that the people act directly in electing members of the House of Representatives, but otherwise they had opted for a complicated system in which intermediaries would "refine and enlarge" the popular voice in the selection of senators, justices, and the executive.[46]

This doesn't mean that Jackson was wrong to recommend the abolition of the Electoral College. His argument for doing so was actually pretty compelling. As we have seen as recently as 2016, one of the occasional functions of the Electoral College is to award the presidency to a candidate who loses the popular vote, and as Jackson suggested, such a candidate necessarily enters office lacking the confidence of the majority of voters. In a democratic culture, this can be a crippling liability.

Not anticipating the development of a permanent *two*-party system, Jackson also anticipated that the pattern of the 1824 election, in which no candidate wins a majority in the Electoral College, would be regularly repeated. By throwing such elections to the House, the process mandated by the Constitution creates a situation in which the potential for corruption is enormous. Influential congressmen might exchange support for future favors.

---

[45]Richardson, *Messages and Papers of the Presidents*, 3:1010.
[46]Edward J. Larson and Michael P. Winship, *The Constitutional Convention: A Narrative History from the Notes of James Madison* (New York: Modern Library, 2005), 99, 110, 93; James Madison, *Federalist* #10, 52.

The problem, then, was not that Jackson recommended an amendment to the Constitution. The problem was that he justified his proposal in the name of the Constitution's Framers. G. K. Chesterton once commented on the frequency with which "the boldest plans for the future invoke the authority of the past." The result, Chesterton observed, is that "even a revolutionary seeks to satisfy himself that he is also a reactionary."[47] This seems to describe Jackson's overture to a tee. By enlisting the Framers as his supposed allies, by invoking their authority, Jackson obscured the degree to which he was encouraging the country to repudiate their values.

Again, Jackson's offense was not in disagreeing with the Framers per se. He had every right to make the suggestions that he did. As I have already cautioned, the Framers were not infallible, and even to hint that they were is idolatry. But in falsely claiming that the Framers would have agreed with him, Jackson made it even harder for his contemporaries to think deeply about the mindset they were adopting. This is always the case, by the way, when we exaggerate the similarity of the present to the past: we actually see *both* less clearly.

In 1829, Andrew Jackson reassured Americans that democracy was not a rejection but a fulfillment of values inherited from the Founders, most particularly their faith in the innate virtue of the people. This meant that the triumph of democracy should be celebrated, not questioned. Yet all the while, "the People's President" was justifying a new democratic mindset by appealing to an understanding of human nature that the Framers roundly rejected and Christian teaching had long contradicted. It was a deceptively conservative argument for a revolutionary break with the past.

To the majority of white Americans, however, the good news of Jackson's democratic gospel was as appealing as it was simple. James Madison was wrong. We really *are* angels. Or as a wise philosopher once put it, "America is great because she is good."

---

[47]G. K. Chesterton, *The Everlasting Man* (New York: Dodd, Mead & Company, 1925), 62.

The Trail of Tears, 1838. The forced removal of some eighteen thousand Cherokees from the state of Georgia was one of the top priorities of Andrew Jackson's presidency, a popular policy initiated by Jackson but executed after he left office. Approximately one-fourth of the Cherokees died during their journey to present-day Oklahoma.

PART THREE

"SERVITUDE OR LIBERTY"

Jacksonian Democracy in Action

"THE AMERICANS ARE NOT A VIRTUOUS PEOPLE," he mused to himself, "and yet they are free."[1] The year was 1831, Andrew Jackson was president of the United States, and the European visitor who scribbled this comment in a tiny pocket notebook was none other than Alexis de Tocqueville. Yes, the same French aristocrat we've imagined attributing the "genius and greatness" of the United States to our oh-so-admirable goodness.

Tocqueville had traveled to America propelled by two assumptions. He was convinced that democracy represented the wave of the future, that his native France would inevitably follow the example of the United States in becoming ever more democratic. He was equally certain that the United States was perched atop the crest of that wave, that there was no nation on earth where the trend toward democracy was further advanced. And so he crossed the ocean with the modest goal of understanding what the rise of democracy meant for the Western world.

To an amazing degree, he succeeded. His classic *Democracy in America* is rightly appraised as "the best book ever written on democracy and the best book ever written on America."[2] We'll devote part four of this book to getting to know Alexis de Tocqueville and listening carefully to him, but here are a couple of

[1] Arthur Schlesinger Jr., "Individualism and Apathy in Tocqueville's Democracy," in *Reconsidering Tocqueville's Democracy in America*, ed. Abraham S. Eisenstadt (New Brunswick, NJ: Rutgers University Press, 1991), 96.
[2] Harvey C. Mansfield and Delba Winthrop, "Editors' Introduction," in Alexis de Tocqueville, *Democracy in America*, trans. and ed. Harvey C. Mansfield and Delba Winthrop (Chicago: University of Chicago Press, 2000), xvii.

things I'd like you to know even now. First, Tocqueville's tour of the United States didn't convince him that Jacksonian America was unusually *good*, but rather that it was extraordinarily *democratic*. Second, whereas we tend to conflate those terms, Tocqueville did not. I'm going to challenge you to follow his example as you read the next two chapters.

Our focus to this point has been on changes in rhetoric and belief. In what it declared about human nature, Jacksonian democracy flatly contradicted the convictions of the Founding Fathers, even while paying them homage. In the process, it proclaimed an American gospel in conflict with centuries of Christian orthodoxy and the precepts of Scripture. If it has troubled you to hear this—or offended you, even—I get it. Keep reading. I'll say it again: my goal isn't to build a case against democracy but rather to help us rediscover the only "true ground" on which democracy can flourish. To do that, we have to think more deeply about it.

Toward that end, it will help to observe Jacksonian democracy in action. In chapters five and six we'll revisit two key episodes of Andrew Jackson's presidency: the removal of the Cherokee Nation and the struggle over the Second Bank of the United States, a conflict typically remembered as "the Bank War." I'm not suggesting that these episodes somehow defined Jacksonian democracy. They were hugely significant at the time, however, and embedded in each is a warning to *us* today.

But whether we have ears to hear the warning will depend on how we approach these events. This is where Tocqueville's mindset can make all the difference. In the opening pages of *Democracy in America*, the author tells us that he came to the United States "looking for lessons." His goal wasn't to condemn or to defend America. He wanted to understand democracy, to see more clearly "its inclinations, character, prejudices, and passions."[3]

It's not just that Tocqueville was teachable and fair-minded, although he was, and we should strive to be. More crucially, he evaluated American democracy with a *democratic philosophy* rather than with *democratic faith*. Do you remember these concepts from the introduction? As defined by the late Irving Kristol, we apply a democratic philosophy when we draw from a more fundamental set of moral convictions to assess democracy's strengths and weaknesses. We adopt a democratic faith when we think of democracy as intrinsically just and assume that "all the ills of democracy can be cured by more democracy."[4]

---

[3]Alexis de Tocqueville, *Democracy in America*, ed. Olivier Zunz (New York: Literary Classics of the United States, 2004), 14.

[4]Irving Kristol, *On the Democratic Idea in America* (New York: Harper & Row, 1972), 66.

The latter is our default mode. Democratic faith was already well developed in the United States when Tocqueville visited two centuries ago, and it's only grown in the American mind since. In common parlance, we think of *democratic* as a synonym for *good* or *just*. We use *democracy* as a catch-all term for "whatever we like," the embodiment of a creed that we venerate but hesitate to define.[5]

Not Tocqueville. "I have only one passion," Tocqueville confessed to a correspondent while he was working on *Democracy in America*: the "love of liberty and human dignity. To me, all forms of government are merely more or less perfect means of satisfying this sacred and legitimate human passion."[6]

Tocqueville's American tour quickly confirmed his supposition that democracy was far advanced in the United States. Nowhere was the ideal of majority rule more lauded. Nowhere was the moral authority of the majority more universally acclaimed. "The people reign over the American political world as God reigns over the universe," he marveled. "They are the cause and end of all things; everything proceeds from them, and to them everything returns."[7]

And so the question that Tocqueville wrestled with was never whether Jacksonian America was democratic. The one big question that preoccupied him stemmed from the "one passion" that possessed him: what impact would the rise of democracy have on liberty and human dignity? "I wanted to become familiar with democracy," he explains in the introduction to *Democracy in America*, "if only to find out what we had to hope from it, or to fear." In the end, he found grounds for both. Democracy, he ultimately concluded, can result in "servitude *or* liberty, enlightenment *or* barbarism, prosperity *or* misery."[8]

Applying a democratic philosophy doesn't require that we accept Tocqueville's conclusion. Nor does it require that we agree that his "one passion" was the proper one, that a commitment to liberty and human dignity should be our highest priority. As a Christian, for example, I'm inclined to agree with Jonathan Leeman that our preeminent political value should be justice.[9] "For the LORD loves justice," declares the psalmist. "Let justice run down like water," echoes the prophet Amos.[10]

---

[5]Robert Wiebe, *Self-Rule: A Cultural History of American Democracy* (Chicago: University of Chicago Press, 1995), 1.
[6]Olivier Zunz, ed., *Alexis de Tocqueville and Gustave de Beaumont in America: Their Friendship and Their Travels*, trans. Arthur Goldhammer (Charlottesville: University of Virginia Press, 2010), 573.
[7]Tocqueville, *Democracy in America*, 65.
[8]Ibid., 834, 15, italics added.
[9]Jonathan Leeman, *How the Nations Rage: Rethinking Faith and Politics in a Divided Age* (Nashville: Nelson Books, 2018), chapter 8.
[10]Psalm 37:28; Amos 5:24.

The more important point, for now, is that it was Tocqueville's lack of democratic faith that enabled him to see democracy so clearly. Tocqueville didn't think about democracy as an end in itself, but as a means to a higher end. Committed to a particular moral principle, he was uncertain whether democracy would promote or detract from it, and he was determined to find out. It's a good approach for us to imitate.

In part four, we'll converse with Tocqueville at length, listen to his conclusions, and invite him to explain his reasoning. For now, I'll encourage you to keep his democratic philosophy in mind as we revisit the Jackson presidency. After returning to France, Tocqueville rejoiced that his visit to Jacksonian America had "vividly illuminated" his understanding.[11] May that be true for us as well.

---

[11]Zunz, *Tocqueville and Gustave de Beaumont in America*, 563.

— 5 —

"BY PERMISSION OF THE
GREAT SPIRIT ABOVE, AND
THE VOICE OF THE PEOPLE"

Given that we're products of a culture steeped in democratic faith, it's no easy task to adopt a democratic philosophy on the turn of a dime. That's especially true when we're asked to apply it to such a morally charged topic as the focus of this chapter: the Jacksonian program of "removing"—forcibly dispossessing and relocating—all Native Americans east of the Mississippi River. Everything within us cries out that the policy was undemocratic. But what we really mean is that we find it morally repugnant (as we should), and because we reflexively equate "democratic" with *good* and "undemocratic" with *bad*, we have no doubt which label to apply.

This is the approach of democratic faith. The conclusion is understandable but it doesn't help us very much. It rests on the unspoken premise—unproved and unprovable—that a "pure" democracy is morally flawless. Democratic faith allows us to critique particular societies and frameworks of government but never to think critically about democracy per se, since true democracy is actually the standard by which all else is judged. As the expression of an aspirational goal it may be inspiring, but in practice its primary effect is to muddle our thinking.

So how can we proceed differently? I'd suggest that we start with a distinction offered a generation ago by the historian Robert Wiebe, who observed two basic ways to conceive of democracy: in terms of "output" or in terms of "input."[1] In the first instance, we define democracy in terms of socially desirable outcomes.

---

[1]Robert Wiebe, *Self-Rule: A Cultural History of American Democracy* (Chicago: University of Chicago Press, 1995), chapter 1.

Some broad examples might include a society characterized by liberty, justice, equality, opportunity, security, or order. To the extent that these or other desired qualities prevail, we say that a given society is more or less democratic. In the second instance, we conceive of democracy not in terms of outcomes but in terms of process—namely, the political process of governance. To the degree that a particular process abides by the rules that we think should govern it, we deem it to be democratic.

As you've probably already guessed, democratic faith tends to focus on democracy as output, vaguely equating "true" democracy with the Good Society. But there's more to it than that. To the degree that it thinks about democracy as input, democratic faith implicitly assumes that there is a democratic process that will reliably deliver ideal social outcomes. The most important assumption of democratic faith, in other words, is that the two conceptions of democracy can be perfectly reconciled.

Democratic philosophy, however, is more skeptical. It proceeds from the conviction that all frameworks of government, like human institutions more generally, are invariably imperfect, albeit to different degrees and in different ways. This means that democracy, like every other form of government under the sun, involves tradeoffs. It comes with advantages and disadvantages. It delivers benefits and it exacts costs. That's why Tocqueville peered into the democratic future with both "hope" and "fear."

Not imbued with democratic faith, Tocqueville naturally conceived of democracy in terms of input. By Tocqueville's reckoning, the long-term output of democracy was known only to God, but the input of democracy could not be more obvious. If Americans today were asked to list the defining features of democratic self-government, we'd likely start with majority rule and add a number of other criteria. For example, we'd maintain that a genuine democracy includes a universal franchise in which all citizens over a certain age are accorded the right to vote. We'd add that any democracy worthy of the name places certain restrictions on the prerogative of the majority in order to guarantee the civil liberties of its citizens and protect the rights of minorities within its midst. You can probably think of other features you would add to the list.[2]

Tocqueville's list, like ours, would begin with majority rule—but that's also where it would stop. Democracy as Tocqueville understood it encompasses far

---

[2]David T. Koyzis, *Political Visions and Illusions: A Survey and Christian Critique of Contemporary Ideologies*, 2nd ed. (Downers Grove, IL: InterVarsity Press, 2019), 122.

more than the realm of government, but the political expression of democracy is simple and straightforward: "The very essence of democratic government," Tocqueville tells us in *Democracy in America*, is that "the majority has absolute sway."[3] Period.

Among other things, this means that one of the prerogatives of the majority is to limit the franchise as it sees fit. As one scholar summarizes Tocqueville's position, as long as the majority remains in control, "it can also accept imperfections and inequalities if it wishes and still remain democratic."[4] The majority may also freely abuse their freedom by tyrannizing the minority or even forfeit their own freedom by submitting to an authoritarian leader. "Absolute sway" means absolute sway.

Tocqueville acknowledges that democracies sometimes include structural features designed to mitigate such abuses—for example, a court system empowered to strike down popular but unjust laws. Such safeguards may serve to protect liberty and promote justice, but Tocqueville forbids us to call anything that curbs the will of the majority democratic. On the contrary, he views such features as vestiges of an earlier, aristocratic age.

From across the centuries, Tocqueville challenges us to abandon the idea that democracy is *intrinsically* good, that it leads *inevitably* to morally desirable outcomes. It is more accurate, he believed, to think of democracy as morally indeterminate. As Tocqueville reckoned it, the output of a purely democratic process would simply be whatever the majority advocates, condones, or tolerates, and precisely because we are *not* naturally virtuous, the range of possible outcomes is vast.

Although it was scarcely mentioned during the 1828 presidential campaign, Andrew Jackson entered the White House determined to relocate the nearly one hundred thousand Native Americans in the eastern United States to lands west of the Mississippi River. "Indian removal" was priority number one on Jackson's domestic policy agenda, and he acted immediately and aggressively to bring it about. Martin Van Buren later credited Jackson's "indomitable vigour and unresting activity" for the success of the "great work." In the mind of Jackson's

---

[3] Alexis de Tocqueville, *Democracy in America*, ed. Olivier Zunz (New York: Literary Classics of the United States, 2004), 283.

[4] Harvey C. Mansfield, "What We Neglect in Tocqueville," *National Review*, December 3, 2020, www.nationalreview.com/magazine/2020/12/17/what-we-neglect-in-tocqueville/.

confidante and handpicked successor, "There was no measure in the whole course of his administration of which he was more exclusively the author."[5]

Like so much of Jackson's presidency, his policy toward Native Americans differed drastically from that of the Founders whom he claimed to revere. Federal policy had always aimed at acquiring the bulk of Native American lands; that much was a constant from the beginning. But prior to the general's election, the official strategy for facilitating this acquisition was framed by four attendant goals or assumptions that Jackson would either modify beyond recognition or reject entirely.

First, since the presidency of George Washington, federal policymakers had consistently worked toward the "civilization" of Native American tribes. In the new nation as they conceived it, there was "no place for Indians as Indians."[6] They would labor to alter their primary institutions, practices, and beliefs to re-semble more closely those of the surrounding white majority. As Native Americans became civilized, they would give up their traditional way of life for a settled agriculture, live in nuclear families on individual farms, learn to read and write in English, adopt European styles of dress, convert to Christianity, and learn to govern themselves according to republican principles.

Second, policymakers anticipated that civilization would lead naturally to *assimilation*. From our twenty-first-century perspective, the federal govern-ment's emphasis on civilizing Native Americans was ethnocentric and conde-scending, but it's crucial not to lose sight of its underlying optimism: policy-makers believed the strategy could succeed. And as Native Americans became increasingly capitalist, Christian, and republican, they would successfully as-similate individually into the majority culture, literally blending in with the Eu-ropean Americans then rapidly flooding into the trans-Appalachian frontier.[7]

Third, until this process was complete, federal policymakers, in theory at least, believed that they were obligated to *respect the tribes' sovereignty* and *recognize their property rights*. In contrast to a fair number of state lawmakers and frontier settlers, no high-ranking federal official had ever publicly advocated that the government simply take the lands it wanted. Writing only two months after the

---

[5]John C. Fitzpatrick, ed., *The Autobiography of Martin Van Buren* (1920; repr., New York: De Capo Press, 1973), 295.

[6]Anthony F. C. Wallace, *Jefferson and the Indians: The Tragic Fate of the First Americans* (Cambridge, MA: Harvard University Press, 1999), 11, quoted in Andrew K. Frank, "Native American Re-moval," in *A Companion to the Era of Andrew Jackson*, ed. Sean Patrick Adams (Oxford: Blackwell, 2013), 394.

[7]Mary Young, "The Cherokee Nation: Mirror of the Republic," *American Quarterly* 33 (1981): 504.

inauguration of government under the Constitution, Secretary of War Henry Knox laid down the axiom in a report to President Washington. "The Indians being the prior occupants, possess the right to soil," Knox observed. "It cannot be taken from them unless by their free consent." To wrest their lands by brute force "would be a gross violation of the fundamental laws of nature, and of that . . . justice which is the glory of a nation."[8]

Finally, the insistence on "free consent" meant that Native American lands could be legally acquired only through treaties with the various tribes, and during the first three decades of the nineteenth century the United States negotiated a slew of them, ninety-one to be exact. The result was a largely uncoordinated "dispossession by degrees."[9]

Most land transactions resulted from a monotonous pattern: disregarding existing treaties, white settlers would squat on tribal land and then pressure the government to come to their aid. Sometimes violent conflict between squatters and Native Americans led to outright war. More frequently, in the desire to avoid a bloody conflict and minimize cost, the government would negotiate a treaty with the relevant tribe, agreeing to acquire all or part of their domain in exchange for cash or goods. After the Louisiana Purchase of 1803, it also became common to pay for Native American lands by exchanging them for territory west of the Mississippi, an appealingly cheap solution for the cash-strapped government in Washington.

With an average of three such transactions per year in the early 1800s, the incremental acquisition of Native American land had become routine long before "the virtue of the people" elevated Andrew Jackson to the presidency. It was accompanied so often by relocation to the west that government-directed "removal" was also becoming commonplace. Yet much changed with the election of "the People's candidate." The pace of the process accelerated, for one thing; during the next decade more than eighty thousand Native Americans would be removed west of the Mississippi. The overarching vision of federal policy was transformed as well. Even as late as the 1820s, it was possible to conceive of relocation as a byproduct of the more fundamental goal of acquiring Native

---

[8]Daniel Blake Smith, *American Betrayal: Cherokee Patriots and the Trail of Tears* (New York: Henry Holt & Company, 2011), 11.

[9]Stuart Banner, *How the Indians Lost Their Land: Law and Power on the Frontier* (Cambridge, MA: Belknap Press, 2005), 146; Jean O'Brien, *Dispossession by Degrees: Indian Land and Identity in Natick, Massachusetts, 1650–1790* (New York: Cambridge University Press, 1997), 212, quoted in Frank, "Native American Removal," 392.

American lands in order to facilitate white expansion. Under Andrew Jackson removal became an end in itself.

Equally important, with Jackson's encouragement the United States government rejected the subsidiary goals of civilization and assimilation and repudiated tribal claims of sovereignty and property rights. Thanks in part to Jackson himself, federal policy became politically supercharged, and during his presidency the matter "received more attention from Congress, the Supreme Court, and the public than at any time before or since."[10] The controversy that ensued was important to contemporaries because of the moral, political, and constitutional questions that it raised. It speaks to us still today by shedding light on the nature of democracy, both then and now.

When Andrew Jackson took office in 1829, the bulk of the Native American population east of the Mississippi River was concentrated in what was then known as the southwestern United States. An 1825 War Department report put the total number of Native Americans in the country at 129,000, a rough guess at best. Nearly half of these lived within the borders of Tennessee, Georgia, Alabama, and Mississippi.

North of Tennessee, most tribes were now located in western areas that had not yet been organized as states. With the exception of New York, the Native American population residing within existing northern states was negligible. If there was an "Indian problem" when Jackson became president, its epicenter was further south—in the region most responsible for Jackson's election—where tribes such as the Creek, Cherokee, Choctaw, and Chickasaw lay claim to tens of millions of acres coveted by whites.

Although federal policy would affect each of these tribes in all of these states, for a variety of reasons the country's attention would come to focus primarily on Georgia and the Cherokees. They were neither the most populous of the southern tribes nor did they control the most land, but the Cherokees were definitely the most resistant to removal. They were also arguably the most "civilized" of the southern tribes, a trait that increased popular sympathy for their plight. Finally, the discovery of gold on Cherokee lands in the summer of 1829 raised the stakes for all concerned and further captivated the popular imagination.

---

[10]Banner, *How the Indians Lost Their Land*, 192.

As early as 1820, a northern missionary organization reported that the Cherokees were "rapidly adopting the laws and manners of the whites."[11] Although the tribe owned its land corporately, by the mid-1820s the typical Cherokee family farmed a specific plot, raised domesticated livestock, and tilled the soil with the aid of a plow. Just under a tenth of families owned black slaves. Approximately the same fraction had converted to Christianity. Roughly a third could read and write in English—thanks to some nineteen missionary schools—but they were also the only Native American tribe with their own written language, thanks to the development of a syllabary by the Cherokee scholar Sequoyah.[12]

In 1827, the tribe went so far as to adopt a written constitution based extensively on the US Constitution. The following year the first Native American newspaper, the *Cherokee Phoenix*, opened for business at the tribal capital at New Echota. Its first issue featured, among other things, the Lord's Prayer and the text of the new constitution. As one study of the tribe concludes, "If the effort to remodel Native American culture after the collective self-image of Jackson's generation worked anywhere, it worked among the Cherokee."[13]

If the Cherokees were the most "civilized" of the southern tribes when Andrew Jackson took office, the government of Georgia was the most aggressive and the least patient of the southern states with large indigenous populations. At the conclusion of the American Revolution, Georgia had appealed to its original colonial charter to lay claim to a domain stretching all the way to the Mississippi River. After years of resistance, in 1802 the state finally ceded to the United States the western two-thirds of this vast region (lands that would eventually become the states of Alabama and Mississippi). In return, the state extracted a commitment from the federal government to "extinguish" all tribal land claims within its newly constricted borders as soon as that could be accomplished "peaceably" and "on reasonable terms."[14]

A quarter-century later, the state was fed up with waiting. By the mid-1820s, white Georgians believed that they had been badly used, and the politicians

---

[11]Smith, *American Betrayal*, 69.

[12]William G. McLoughlin and Walter H. Conser Jr., "The Cherokees in Transition: A Statistical Analysis of the Federal Cherokee Census of 1835," *Journal of American History*, 64 (1977): 695; Theda Perdue and Michael D. Green, *The Cherokee Nation and the Trail of Tears* (New York: Penguin, 2007), 33.

[13]Steve Inskeep, *Jacksonland: President Andrew Jackson, Cherokee Chief John Ross, and a Great American Land Grab* (New York: Penguin, 2015), 121; Smith, *American Betrayal*, 82; Young, "Cherokee Nation," 504.

[14]Perdue and Green, *Cherokee Nation and the Trail of Tears*, 55.

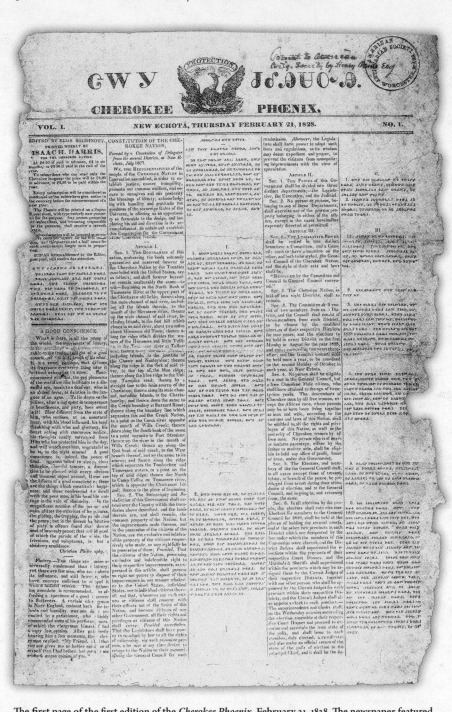

The first page of the first edition of the *Cherokee Phoenix*, February 21, 1828. The newspaper featured parallel columns in English and in the Cherokee script devised by Sequoyah.

seeking their votes routinely told them that *they*, not Native Americans, were the real victims of federal policy.

At issue was how to interpret the so-called Compact of 1802. In Washington, government policymakers understood the agreement in light of the decades-old commitment to "free consent." The pledge to acquire tribal lands "peaceably" and "on reasonable terms" ruled out coercion. In 1823, President James Monroe made this explicit, informing Congress that "there is no obligation on the United States to remove the Indians by force." But down in Georgia, public figures like Congressman Wilson Lumpkin denounced such "pettifogging quibbles" as a lame excuse for violating a solemn pledge.[15] The US government was guilty of bad faith. The time had come to force its hand.

The ink was scarcely dry on the Cherokees' constitution when the Georgia legislature responded with a resolution declaring the Cherokees to be "tenants at will" who occupied their lands as a privilege granted by the state of Georgia. Disregarding decades of precedent, federal laws passed in 1790 and 1802, and innumerable treaties, the Georgia Assembly asserted that the state had the right unilaterally to evict the Cherokees "at any time she pleases." Then came a pointed threat: Not wanting to disturb "the public tranquility," the state would refrain from "violence until all other means of redress fail." But if the United States refused to redeem "her pledged honor," there would be consequences. "The lands in question *belong* to Georgia," the resolution concluded. "She *must* and she *will* have them."[16]

A year later the Georgia Assembly ratcheted up the pressure. In December of 1828 it enacted a measure that unilaterally abrogated the Cherokee constitution, declared all the tribes' laws null and void, and proclaimed the Cherokee to be subject to the laws of the state of Georgia, effective June 1, 1830. (In a matter of months, the legislatures of Alabama and Mississippi followed suit, formally imposing state law over the tribes within their borders. Tennessee would do so four years later.) Over the next three years, Georgia continued to tighten the screws, enacting laws that disqualified Native Americans from voting and from testifying in court against whites, prohibited the Cherokee council from convening, and ordered an immediate survey of Cherokee lands in anticipation of the tribe's removal.

---

[15]Ibid., 56; Louis Filler and Allen Guttmann, eds., *The Removal of the Cherokee Nation: Manifest Destiny or National Dishonor?* (New York: Krieger Publishing, 1977), 32.

[16]Theda Perdue and Michael D. Green, eds., *The Cherokee Removal: A Brief History with Documents*, 2nd ed. (Boston: Bedford/St. Martins, 2005), 75.

In 1832, the Georgia Assembly capped off its campaign against the Cherokees by initiating a statewide lottery in which nearly every white household head in the state would qualify for a chance at winning a free homestead on Cherokee land. Overnight, the legislature gave the entire white population of Georgia a concrete incentive to advocate removal. The prospect of such a windfall led to the popular ditty, "All I want in this creation / Is a pretty little wife and a big plantation / Way up north in the Cherokee Nation."[17] Although a federal treaty signed as recently as 1819 pledged to respect the Cherokees' rights to occupy their ancestral homeland, white squatters would soon begin to pour into the contested lands.

In all this Georgia had honored its pledge to refrain from violence, but it seemed more than willing to provoke both a national showdown and a constitutional crisis if necessary to have its way. If it didn't come to that, it was because the country's new president not only acquiesced but affirmed the state's repudiation of existing laws and treaties. And this was precisely what the state had expected. As a future governor of Georgia observed at the time, white Georgians had a "special confidence" in the new administration.[18] It was not misplaced.

It's hard to nail down exactly why Andrew Jackson was such an ardent advocate of removal, an objective he pursued so relentlessly that a sympathetic biographer likens it to an "obsession."[19] He certainly saw Native Americans as inferior—*Indian* and *savage* were synonyms in his vocabulary—but then so did the vast majority of white Americans in the Jacksonian era.[20] Having earlier speculated extensively in Alabama lands acquired from the Creeks (by means of a treaty he himself had negotiated), Jackson also keenly appreciated the economic opportunities that removal presented to whites. That said, there's no evidence he expected to profit personally from the policy he pursued as president.

By all appearances, Jackson genuinely believed that removal would enhance national security by strengthening the country's southern border, although that

---

[17]Ibid., 95.

[18]George Gilmer, *Sketches of Some of the First Settlers of Upper Georgia, of the Cherokees, and the Author* (Americus, GA: Americus Book Company, 1926), 267.

[19]Robert V. Remini, *The Legacy of Andrew Jackson: Essays on Democracy, Indian Removal, and Slavery* (Baton Rouge: Louisiana State University Press, 1988), 54.

[20]See, for example, Jackson's 1830 annual message to Congress, in James D. Richardson, comp., *A Compilation of the Messages and Papers of the Presidents* (New York: Bureau of National Literature, 1897), 3:1083, 1084, 1085.

potential benefit applied more to the Creek and Choctaw lands closer to the Gulf of Mexico than to the Cherokee lands in northern Georgia. He also recognized that expeditious removal would please the southern states with large Native American populations and head off a likely clash over the boundaries of federal and state authority. (As time passed, this factor would grow in importance when the South Carolina legislature began to challenge the legitimacy of federal tariffs and threaten to "nullify" them.) And over time he increasingly insisted, apparently sincerely, that removal would be in the best interest of the tribes themselves. Each of these beliefs likely factored into his thinking. Each pointed toward the same conclusion.

Whatever his motives, this much is clear: Jackson had never seen negotiating treaties with Indian tribes as anything but preposterous. If no major national official had publicly suggested that the government simply take the lands it wanted, Jackson had pointedly argued for just such a policy in private.

In 1817 he had written to James Monroe to offer the newly inaugurated president some free advice. "I have long viewed treaties with the Indians an absurdity," he divulged to Monroe. Native Americans were "subjects" of the United States— that's all there was to it—and it was ridiculous for the sovereign to negotiate with the subject. The United States could define the boundaries of a tribe's land "at pleasure," and any time that the national interest would be served by acquiring it, the government had "the right to take it and dispose of it."[21]

Still reeling from Rachel's recent death, Jackson devoted little attention to Native Americans in his brief inaugural address of March 1829. In the emptiest of platitudes, the new president promised "a humane and considerate attention to the rights . . . of the Indian tribes," being careful to leave those rights undefined. Behind the scenes, however, he was already committed to a strategy that would make removal on a massive scale almost inevitable.[22]

Three weeks into his term, Jackson made a formal response to a protest from the Creek Nation after the state of Alabama had acted to extend its laws over the tribe. "By permission of the Great Spirit above, and the voice of the people," Jackson began, "I have been made president of the United States, and now speak to you as your father and friend." Jackson assured the Creeks that he loved his "red children" and that they could trust him. He then explained that they had only

---

[21]Remini, *Legacy of Andrew Jackson*, 48.
[22]Andrew Jackson, in *The Papers of Andrew Jackson*, ed. Sam B. Smith, Harriet Chappell Owsley, Harold D. Moser, et al., 10 vols. (Knoxville: University of Tennessee Press, 1980–2016), 7:79.

two choices: submit to the state of Alabama or relocate to a distant land their "father" had reserved for them.[23]

A couple of weeks later, Jackson instructed Secretary of War John Eaton—his close friend and former campaign manager—to respond to a similar protest from the Cherokees in Georgia. If they were willing to "remove" beyond the Mississippi, Eaton informed a Cherokee delegation, the United States would assure the tribe "protection and peace." The federal government would guarantee them that "the soil shall be yours while the trees grow, or the streams run." But if they insisted on remaining on their ancestral homeland, then the government would be largely powerless to protect them.

The state of Georgia owned the Cherokee lands, Eaton told his stunned audience. In "forbearance" it had permitted the Cherokees to remain until now, but it had every right to extend its laws over the tribe. It was unconscionable to call on the president to interfere with the constitutional act of a sovereign state, Eaton lectured the delegation. "This can never be done," he insisted. "The President cannot, and will not, beguile you with such an expectation."[24]

When a new Congress convened that December, Jackson informed them that the Constitution prohibited the government from recognizing the sovereignty of any Native American tribe situated within a state. In effect, he was pronouncing the government's policy of the last forty years to be unconstitutional. It would not be the last time that he asserted the president's right to interpret the Constitution unilaterally.

Affirming Georgia's unlimited authority over the Native Americans within her borders, the president then invited Congress to craft legislation that would set apart "an ample district west of the Mississippi," beyond the borders of any existing state, "to be guaranteed to the Indian tribes as long as they shall occupy it." It was absolutely imperative that any emigration be voluntary, Jackson insisted, "for it would be as cruel as unjust to compel the aborigines to abandon the graves of their fathers and seek a home in a distant land." But should any tribe choose to remain, Jackson wanted it "distinctly" understood that they must submit to the laws of the surrounding white majority.[25]

This was the very first legislative initiative that Andrew Jackson proposed as president, and the Jacksonian majority in Congress quickly went to work. By

---

[23]Ibid., 7:112.
[24]David S. Heidler and Jeanne T. Heidler, *Indian Removal* (New York: W. W. Norton, 2007), 128, 129.
[25]Richardson, *Messages and Papers of the Presidents*, 3:1021-22.

February 1830, the Senate Committee on Indian Affairs had reported a bill to the general's liking. Three months later the Indian Removal Act became law, signed by the president after passing comfortably in the Senate, 28-19, and narrowly in the House, 102-97.

The measure authorized the president to offer land west of the Mississippi to tribes willing to relinquish their claims to eastern lands. It also appropriated funds to compensate individual Native Americans for their improvements (houses, barns, etc.), cover the costs of relocation, and provide for their subsistence for a year. The act did not mandate removal or authorize the use of force, but to the Cherokees and the other southern tribes it offered only the most dismal of options: they could relinquish their identity as a self-governing people and live at the mercy of a white majority that viewed them as savage, or they could relocate.

For the next five years, Andrew Jackson and the Georgia Assembly worked in tandem to force the Cherokees to "choose" removal as the lesser of evils. Although Jackson rarely showed respect for laws that stood in his way, he would begin by acknowledging meekly that the Constitution prevented him from helping the Cherokees. Given the green light, Georgia would then increase the pressure on the tribe, doing their best to make it intolerable for them to stay. Letting Georgia do the dirty work, Jackson could then claim the mantle of magnanimity, offering to rescue the Cherokees by facilitating their removal. The solution, Jackson happily observed, was "just," "humane," "liberal," "generous," and "kind."[26]

Not everyone agreed. The Cherokees, for one, were less than persuaded. Georgia's abrogation of all Cherokee law was in direct "defiance of the laws of the United States, and the most solemn treaties," a delegation informed the secretary of war early in 1829. The following year a memorial from the nation to the US government mocked President Jackson's insistence that "all his illustrious predecessors . . . had made promises of vital importance to us, which could not be fulfilled." The Cherokees' "wish to remain on the land of our fathers," the memorial asserted, was grounded in a right long "acknowledged and guaranteed by the United States."[27] They were absolutely, indisputably correct.

---

[26]Jackson, *Papers of Andrew Jackson,* 7:491, 9:99, 10:89; Richardson, *Messages and Papers of the Presidents,* 3:1085.

[27]Heidler and Heidler, eds., *Indian Removal,* 126; Filler and Guttmann, eds., *Removal of the Cherokee Nation,* 47.

From its offices at New Echota, the *Cherokee Phoenix* kept up a withering critique of the new policy. Editor Elias Boudinot reviewed the tribe's impressive progress toward "civilization." Instead of hunters the Cherokees "have become the cultivators of the soil," Boudinot wrote. "Instead of wild and ferocious savages, thirsting for blood, they have become the mild 'citizens,' the friends and brothers of the white man. Instead of the superstitious heathens, many of them have become the worshippers of the true God." Such progress led to one logical conclusion: "cupidity and self-interest" were driving the new policy. "A desire to *possess* the Indian land is paramount to a desire to see him *established* on the soil as a *civilized* man."[28]

As far as law and logic go, these were strong arguments, but in a democratic republic, it's popular opinion that matters most.

Here the Cherokees were less successful. On the positive side, they won the sympathy of numerous northern churches and religious organizations. Long before the removal bill was introduced, organizations like the American Board of Commissioners for Foreign Missions were calling on Christians across the country to "be exerting themselves to save a persecuted and defenseless people."[29]

In the summer of 1829, the board's corresponding secretary, a Congregational missionary named Jeremiah Evarts, began denouncing removal in a series of twenty-four essays in the Washington *National Intelligencer*. Writing under the pseudonym William Penn, Evarts warned complacent Americans to expect "the wrath of heaven" should they persist in promoting "cruelty and oppression" at the expense of "the poor and defenseless."[30]

That Christmas, Connecticut schoolteacher Catherine Beecher authored a circular letter asking "benevolent ladies of the United States" to help "avert the calamity of removal." Beecher, the daughter of one of the foremost Protestant ministers of the era, urged women to petition Congress and otherwise do all within their power on behalf of the Cherokee. "These people are to have their lands torn from them, and to be driven into western wilds and to final annihilation, unless the feelings of a humane and Christian nation shall be aroused," she informed her readers. Then followed the pointed reminder: "There is a Being who avenges the wrongs of the oppressed."[31]

---

[28]Perdue and Green, *Cherokee Removal*, 144-45.
[29]Mary Hershberger, "Mobilizing Women, Anticipating Abolition: The Struggle Against Indian Removal in the 1830s," *Journal of American History* 86 (1999): 21.
[30]Perdue and Green, *Cherokee Removal*, 110.
[31]Hershberger, "Mobilizing Women," 26; Perdue and Green, *Cherokee Removal*, 111, 113.

The Cherokees could also count on a number of champions in Congress. When Jackson's removal bill came up for debate in 1830, opponents of the administration (soon to be known as Whigs) mounted a staunch resistance. Martin Van Buren dismissed them as "partisan agitators" bent on crippling the administration "at the expense of the highest interests of the Country." The president, true to form, took it personally, attributing criticism of the measure to the "machinations" of his "enemies." They would "overturn heaven & earth, to prostrate me," he complained to an old friend.[32]

There was a measure of calculated opportunism, to be sure. Henry Clay, for example, would condemn removal after his return to the Senate in 1831, declaring that it "threatens to bring a foul and lasting stain upon the good faith, humanity, and character of the nation." In private he considered Native Americans "essentially inferior to the Anglo-Saxon race" and "did not think them as a race, worth preserving."[33]

And when the Whigs were strong enough to put their own man in the White House a few years later, they chose as their banner carrier an "Indian fighter" of their own, the hero of the Battle of Tippecanoe, General William Henry Harrison. "Old Tip" promptly named as his secretary of war one of the primary authors of the Indian Removal Act, congressman John Bell of Tennessee. In sum, the Whigs embraced criticism of removal as "a wonderful political weapon" while they were out of power. When on top, they "continued Jackson's policy without pause."[34]

But there were also principled voices among the partisan posturing. Theodore Frelinghuysen, a deeply religious senator from New Jersey, lambasted the Removal Bill for six hours over the course of three days. White Americans were rapidly becoming "traitors to our principles," the future president of the American Bible Society cautioned his colleagues. "Do the obligations of justice change with the color of the skin?" he asked. "Is it one of the prerogatives of the white man, that he may disregard the dictates of moral principles, when an Indian shall be concerned?"[35]

Over in the House, New York representative Henry Storrs mocked Democrats' insistence that removal would be voluntary. Follow the "plain path of

---

[32]Fitzpatrick, *Autobiography of Martin Van Buren*, 284, 288; Jackson, *Papers of Andrew Jackson*, 10:225.

[33]Alfred A. Cave, "Abuse of Power: Andrew Jackson and the Indian Removal Act of 1830," *Historian* 65 (2003): 1347; John Quincy Adams, *Diaries*, ed. David Waldstreicher (New York: Library of America, 2017), 2:122.

[34]Remini, *Legacy of Andrew Jackson*, 81.

[35]Filler and Guttmann, *Removal of the Cherokee Nation*, 24, 25.

honor," he pleaded. "Retrace your steps. Acknowledge your treaties. Confess your obligations. Execute your laws. Let the president revise his opinions. It is never too late to be just." Isaac Bates of Massachusetts similarly ridiculed the contention that the Constitution forbade the government to prevent the injustice that Georgia was inflicting on the Cherokee. "It will be in vain you tell the world you did not set fire to the city, when you saw it burning, and would not put it out, though you were its hired patrol and watch."[36]

In the end, these pleas fell short. If "the law was . . . on the side of the Indians," as a leading legal scholar concludes, popular opinion favored removal.[37]

Supporters of the policy unleashed a barrage of diverse arguments to shore up this support. For those who were uneasy with the administration's apparent willingness to disregard existing treaties, Jacksonians offered a range of justifications. At times they were openly contemptuous of past agreements. It had always been ludicrous to suggest that treaties genuinely accorded sovereignty to "savages and half-breeds," a cabinet member noted. Such agreements were at best an elaborate charade, explained a member of the House Committee on Indian Affairs. They might seem to acknowledge tribal sovereignty, but this was never more than an "empty gesture" to satisfy Native Americans' "vanity." These treaties shouldn't be read *literally*.[38]

On a more sophisticated level, the Jacksonians reiterated the president's assertion that all prior treaties with tribes within state borders had violated the Constitution's prohibition of erecting a state within a state. They were thus null and void from the beginning. It was regrettable that this had left Native Americans with a load of solemn promises that the government was powerless to honor, but "that step can not be retraced," as Jackson philosophically put it. And while the pledges made to the various tribes had been unconstitutional, in 1802 the United States had entered into an agreement with the state of Georgia that *was* legally binding. "The strongest human obligations" constrained the government to relieve long-suffering white Georgians from their "Indian perplexities" and advance their "peace, happiness, and prosperity."[39]

---

[36]Inskeep, *Jacksonland*, 235; Banner, *How the Indians Lost Their Land*, 216.
[37]Banner, *How the Indians Lost Their Land*, 205.
[38]Fitzpatrick, *Autobiography of Martin Van Buren*, 283; Cave, "Abuse of Power," 1333.
[39]Richardson, *Messages and Papers of the Presidents*, 3:1021; Filler and Guttmann, *Removal of the Cherokee Nation*, 32.

While pledging to honor their long-deferred commitment to the state of Georgia, the Jacksonians also insisted indignantly that they never once "contemplated a removal of the tribes against their will."[40] If at first blush this seemed at odds with their solemn pledge to white Georgians, they resolved the apparent contradiction by the happy discovery that coercion would be unnecessary. Despite appearances to the contrary, the Cherokees actually *wanted* to relocate.

"The masses of these people would be glad to emigrate," Secretary of War John Eaton insisted, except that they "are kept from this exercise of their choice by their Chiefs." But when skeptics in the Senate sought to amend the removal bill to ensure a fair referendum and require the government to enforce the tribes' sovereignty and property rights until such time that they freely chose to relocate, advocates of removal voted down the amendment. (Privately, Van Buren conceded that "no one would for a moment believe that any of the tribes would remove as long as the power of Congress stood pledged to support them.")[41]

Adopting the philosophy that the best defense is a good offense, pro-removal politicians also engaged in an 1830s version of "whataboutism." Sneering, they noted that "great sympathy was evinced for Native Americans by the people of those States in which there were none." In the Northeast, a combination of white expansion, war, disease, and migration had long ago resulted in the disappearance of the indigenous population. Now New Englanders were crying crocodile tears for the southern tribes, salving their guilty consciences without jeopardizing their material interests.[42] Critics of removal were all hypocrites, defenders of the policy charged, either unprincipled politicians, money-loving Yankees determined to cripple the South, or "religious fanatics" with a gift for "intermeddling with other people's concerns."[43]

The moral high ground belonged entirely to the advocates of removal, or so they said. Of all feasible options, removal is "the wisest and best for the Indians," the secretary of state maintained. "The cause of humanity requires it," intoned the governor of Georgia. It is the path of "humanity and justice," declared the US Commissioner of Indian Affairs.[44] As with Whigs' condemnation of the policy, a healthy measure of self-interest lurked beneath the praise of removal,

---

[40]Fitzpatrick, *Autobiography of Martin Van Buren*, 277.

[41]Ibid., 288; McLoughlin and Conser, "Cherokees in Transition," 679.

[42]Gilmer, *Sketches*, 318.

[43]Ibid., 313; Carl J. Vipperman, "The 'Particular Mission' of Wilson Lumpkin," *Georgia Historical Quarterly* 66 (1982): 295-316.

[44]Fitzpatrick, *Autobiography of Martin Van Buren*, 293; Gilmer, *Sketches*, 258; Banner, *How the Indians Lost Their Land*, 208.

and some portion of the Jacksonians' rhetoric surely rationalized a less elevated agenda. Yet it is equally certain that many who defended removal on humanitarian grounds believed what they were saying.

Whether cynical or sincere, it had become logically possible to defend removal as benevolent because of two assumptions that were rapidly becoming Jacksonian dogma: First, the government's decades-long efforts to civilize Native Americans had failed abysmally. Second, the policy hadn't succeeded because it *couldn't* succeed, and it couldn't succeed because of traits intrinsic to Native Americans.

From Georgia, Governor George Gilmer reminded religious critics of removal that "Aboriginal people" are "ignorant, thoughtless, and improvident." When surrounded by whites, they "continue to disappear, until they become extinct." In Washington, Secretary of State Martin Van Buren agreed that when Native Americans lived in proximity to whites it "tended to hasten their demoralization and extinction," while the Commissioner of Indian Affairs informed Congress that in such instances an immutable "law of nature" decreed that the Native Americans "*must perish.*" One of Andrew Jackson's Tennessee correspondents put it more bluntly. If the southern tribes insisted on remaining "in the vicinity of the white man," he wrote the president, "they may begin to dig their graves and prepare to die."[45]

This was preaching to the choir. In his first annual message, the president had already postulated that no Native American tribe could long survive in proximity to whites. "Weakness and decay" were inevitable. Extinction was likely. It followed that "humanity and national honor" demanded removal. For the rest of his presidency, Jackson asserted the "established fact" that Native Americans "can not live in contact with a civilized community and prosper." This made removal their only hope. It was the only policy that could "possibly perpetuate their race."[46]

As a rule, white Americans had always deemed Native Americans inferior, but for decades federal policymakers had attributed this to ignorance, not to race. Official government policy assumed that education would lead relatively quickly to "civilization," and civilization would lead to assimilation and equality.

---

[45]Gilmer, *Sketches*, 296, 258; Fitzpatrick, *Autobiography of Martin Van Buren*, 276; Banner, *How the Indians Lost Their Land*, 208; Jackson, *Papers of Andrew Jackson*, 8:20.

[46]Richardson, *Messages and Papers of the Presidents*, 3:1021, 1390; Jackson, *Papers of Andrew Jackson*, 7:492.

This assumption was dead wrong, Jacksonians now proclaimed. At their most optimistic, they intimated that removal might allow Native Americans to adopt civilized ways in a protective isolation, at their own glacial pace. In his farewell address, President Jackson congratulated his countrymen for adopting a policy toward the "aborigines" that would save them from "degradation and destruction." Once settled in their new and distant homes, "we may well hope that they will share in the blessings of civilization."[47] ("Where have we an example in the whole history of man," the *Cherokee Phoenix* asked, of a people being driven from a civilized land *"in order to be civilized?"*[48])

Increasingly though, advocates of removal denied that the civilization project could *ever* succeed. "An Indian will still be an Indian" was their mantra, and not even the "cant and fanaticism" of so-called philanthropists could alter this immutable truth. Outsiders who insisted that the Cherokees were becoming civilized were either deceivers or deceived. After the passage of the Removal Act, for example, a group of missionaries working among the tribe had issued a public statement that the Cherokees were soon to be "nearly on a level with their white brethren." Of course they would assert such a falsehood, advocates of removal replied. The missionaries were making a comfortable living off of the tribe and didn't want to lose it.[49]

Others who exaggerated the Cherokees' capabilities had been fooled by the modest steps toward civilization among "half-breeds." The "real" Cherokees—those without white blood flowing in their veins—"had remained ignorant savages, notwithstanding the constant efforts to change them into better beings." As Governor Gilmer of Georgia summed up, "The unmixed Indians have remained what they ever were, *and will ever be*." On the floor of Congress, Georgia representative John Forsyth underscored this assessment. The Cherokees were a "useless and burdensome" people, the future secretary of state asserted, a "race not admitted to be equal" and "probably never to be entitled to equal civil and political rights."[50]

In 1831, these views became the official position of the US government when President Jackson named Lewis Cass as his new head of the War Department,

---

[47]Richardson, *Messages and Papers of the Presidents*, 3:1513.

[48]Banner, *How the Indians Lost Their Land*, 211.

[49]Perdue and Green, *Cherokee Removal*, 143; Filler and Guttmann, *Removal of the Cherokee Nation*, 32, 60; Jackson, *Papers of Andrew Jackson*, 7:652.

[50]Gilmer, *Sketches*, 246-48, emphasis added; Perdue and Green, *Cherokee Nation and the Trail of Tears*, 63.

the cabinet position most responsible for the oversight and direction of Native American affairs. Cass came to the position as a highly regarded expert who regarded the civilization policy as "a total failure." "What tribe has been civilized by all this expenditure of treasure, labor, and care?" Cass inquired in a widely circulated article in the *North American Review*. None had, he answered, but the failure of the experiment had nothing to do with the "qualifications, or conduct, of those who have directed it." Rather, the fault lay in "some insurmountable obstacle in the habits or temperament of the Indians."[51]

And what about the so-called civilization of the Cherokees? Cass informed his readers that whatever progress they may have demonstrated was limited "to some of the *half-breeds* and their immediate connexions." As for the rest of the tribe, "We doubt whether there is, upon the face of the globe, a more wretched race." As long as they remained in proximity to more civilized whites, they would "decline in numbers, morals, and happiness."[52] Removal was the Cherokees' best hope.

Cass knew this not because of any firsthand interaction with Cherokees but because of his experience with other tribes while serving as governor of the Michigan Territory, a thousand miles to the north. He could speak authoritatively about the Cherokees because of the "general resemblance" they bore to "the other cognate branches of the great aboriginal stock."[53] The conclusion was straightforward because the axiom was unequivocal: since "insurmountable obstacles" in the traits of all Native Americans prevented their civilization, it was inconceivable that full-blooded Cherokees could demonstrate genuine progress.

By the 1830s, hardly anyone could deny that removal would serve the material interests of the country's white majority. Away from the frontier, hardly any white Americans wanted to think of themselves as conquerors who simply took what they wanted. In this setting, advocates of removal marshaled a range of arguments to make the policy more palatable: It violated no *valid* treaties. It fulfilled a long-deferred obligation to Georgia. It would never be implemented by force. What is more, the majority of Native Americans desired it, it was genuinely for their good, and the only whites who thought otherwise were wild-eyed fanatics or conniving politicians. And the growing conviction that Native Americans were wholly *other*—that they "were, and will ever be" intrinsically inferior—undergirded each of these arguments and made them easier to believe.

---

[51]Perdue and Green, *Cherokee Removal*, 116.
[52]Ibid., 117, 119.
[53]Ibid., 117.

With the passage of the Indian Removal Act and President Jackson's indication that he sided with the state of Georgia, the Cherokees desperately needed a way to protect themselves from a hostile majority. Their efforts to reshape public opinion had had some effect, but not enough. Given the disparity in power and numbers, going to war to defend their rights was out of the question. And so, in the ultimate demonstration of their acculturation, they chose to take the state of Georgia to court.

To do so, they turned for help to William Wirt of Maryland, one of the nation's foremost lawyers and formerly attorney general of the United States under two administrations. President Jackson was livid upon learning that Wirt had agreed to represent the tribe. He was "truly wicked" for doing so, Jackson complained to a friend. His "wicked" course would lead "the poor ignorant Indians" on a path to "annihilation."[54]

In the summer of 1830, Wirt wrote to Governor Gilmer of Georgia to suggest that the difficulties between Georgia and the Cherokees could be impartially settled by the Supreme Court. Gilmer replied that even to hint as much was "disrespectful to the Government of the State." Declaring uncontestable what the Cherokees were in fact contesting, Gilmer informed Wirt that the Cherokees residing in Georgia were wholly subject to state authority and that the federal courts had no right whatsoever to intervene.[55]

Half a year later, when the Supreme Court ordered the state to appear before it as a defendant being sued by the Cherokees, Gilmer remained true to his word and refused to send counsel. To do so would be to submit to federal usurpation, he told the state legislature. It would lead inexorably to "the utter annihilation of the State government."[56]

The suit that Wirt instigated would become *Cherokee Nation v. Georgia*. Through it, the lawyer sought an unequivocal ruling that Georgia's aggressive statutes affecting the Cherokees were in violation of federal treaties and thus null and void. All he actually obtained was the court's sympathy.

Wirt had initiated the suit in the Supreme Court on the basis of Article III, section 2 of the Constitution, which gives federal courts jurisdiction in controversies between "a state . . . and foreign states." But the Cherokees were not a

---

[54]Jackson, *Papers of Andrew Jackson*, 8:501.
[55]Gilmer, *Sketches*, 274.
[56]Ibid., 291.

foreign state, Chief Justice John Marshall announced in the spring of 1831. They were better categorized as a "domestic dependent nation," their relationship to the United States akin to "that of a ward to his guardian." Marshall acknowledged that "a case better calculated to excite" the court's sympathies could "scarcely be imagined." Unfortunately, the Cherokees lacked the constitutional standing to bring suit before the court.[57]

A year later Wirt tried again, this time with a different plaintiff. Among its numerous measures aimed at making life miserable for the Cherokees, in late 1830 the Georgia legislature had passed an act mandating that all whites living among the tribe obtain a license from the state and swear an oath promising to obey all state laws. This effectively required anyone interacting with the Cherokees to acknowledge the state's authority over the tribe. When eleven Christian missionaries working among the Cherokees defied the law, the governor had ordered them arrested, and in short order a state court had sentenced the desperate outlaws to four years in the penitentiary.

This was a public relations disaster for the state of Georgia, even among sympathetic southerners. "If we introduce a minister of the Gospel to preach to us the way of life," the *Cherokee Phoenix* trumpeted, "here is a law of Georgia . . . ready to seize him and send him to the penitentiary." Hoping to make the fiasco go away, the governor offered pardons to the missionaries in exchange for their promise either to take the oath or leave the state, but two of the group, Samuel Worcester and Elizur Butler, refused and opted for prison instead. Georgia's governor denounced them as "a living monument to fanaticism."[58] William Wirt welcomed them as potential plaintiffs who would have standing before the Supreme Court.

The resulting case was *Worcester v. Georgia*. Speaking for a 6-1 majority, Chief Justice Marshall observed that, since the birth of the republic, the federal government had passed acts and negotiated treaties with the various tribes "which treat them as nations, respect their rights, and manifest a firm purpose to afford that protection which treaties stipulate." Regarding the Cherokee Nation specifically, Marshall concluded that the tribe constituted "a distinct community, occupying its own territory, with boundaries accurately described, in which the laws of Georgia can have no force, and which the citizens of Georgia have no

[57]Filler and Guttmann, *Removal of the Cherokee Nation*, 61, 63.
[58]Perdue and Green, *Cherokee Removal*, 143; Gilmer, *Sketches*, 342.

right to enter, but with the assent of the Cherokees themselves."[59] It followed that the Georgia law leading to Worcester's arrest was unconstitutional and that Worcester should be released.

Technically, the only parties in the case were the state of Georgia and a single Christian missionary, and once the Jackson administration had discretely persuaded Georgia's governor to pardon Worcester, the court's ruling was moot. But more broadly construed, the implications of Marshall's ruling threatened to eviscerate Jacksonian policy. As a leading expert on the case concludes, *Worcester v. Georgia* "vindicated the Cherokees' position on virtually every point."[60]

On hearing the decision, the *Cherokee Phoenix* exulted that the court had "forever settled . . . who is right and who is wrong." It was "a great triumph on the part of the Cherokees." Cherokee diplomat John Ridge was on a speaking tour in Boston when news of the ruling arrived. Ridge reported to his cousin that he felt "newly revived—a new man," although he conceded that "the contest is not over."[61]

Ridge was right to show caution. As Alexander Hamilton had observed long before, the judicial branch has "neither FORCE nor WILL."[62] For the court's ruling to accomplish anything beyond Worcester's release, either Georgia would have to back down and revoke its unconstitutional laws or Andrew Jackson would have to wield federal power in support of a ruling that he abhorred. Neither was going to happen.

As with the *Cherokee Nation* case, Georgia had refused even to take part in *Worcester*, and the state wasn't about to acknowledge the legitimacy of the Supreme Court's decision. Georgia senator George Troup condemned the ruling as "flagrantly violative" of the state's "sovereign rights." The state's new governor, Wilson Lumpkin, accused all who supported it as "traitors" conspiring to "exterminate civil liberty from the earth." He denounced the decision and promised "to meet this usurpation of federal power with the most prompt and determined resistance."[63]

Lumpkin's threats were unnecessary. As the leading scholars of removal observe, Georgia's aggressive legislation against the Cherokees "could not have pleased President Andrew Jackson more if he had written the laws

---

[59]Filler and Guttmann, *Removal of the Cherokee Nation*, 74, 77.
[60]Banner, *How the Indians Lost Their Land*, 220.
[61]H. David Williams, "Gambling Away the Inheritance: The Cherokee Nation and Georgia's Gold and Land Lotteries of 1832–33," *Georgia Historical Quarterly* 73 (1989): 522; Perdue and Green, *Cherokee Nation and the Trail of Tears*, 94.
[62]Alexander Hamilton, *Federalist* #78, 412.
[63]Filler and Guttmann, *Removal of the Cherokee Nation*, 79, 80; Vipperman, "'Particular Mission' of Wilson Lumpkin," 306.

himself."[64] If anything, the laws were integral to the success of his policy. And so Jackson did nothing.

Decades later, journalist Horace Greeley circulated a colorful story of how President Jackson greeted reports of the Supreme Court's decision with characteristic defiance: "John Marshall has made his decision: *now let him enforce it!*"[65] Jackson may not have uttered those exact words, but they accurately captured his response. Within days of the decision, newspapers from around the country were reporting rumors from the capital that the president would do nothing to enforce the court's decision. Before the month was out, the Cherokees knew unmistakably that this was true.

From Boston, John Ridge rushed to Washington to join a Cherokee delegation waiting for an audience with the president. In a meeting in the White House, Jackson broke the news to Ridge in person. Afterward, the general wrote to his close friend and relative by marriage, John Coffee, and gloated that "the decision of the Supreme Court has fell still born." Ridge and the other Cherokee representatives had learned that the court "cannot coerce Georgia to yield to its mandate."[66]

Ridge's report was more colorful. "The Chicken Snake General Jackson" had chosen to "crawl and hide in the luxuriant grass of his nefarious hypocrisy." The *Cherokee Phoenix*, which had so recently celebrated *Worcester* as a "great triumph," now asked in despair, "What sort of hope have we then from a President who feels himself under no obligation *to execute*, but has an inclination *to disregard* the laws and treaties?"[67]

What sort of hope. In the aftermath of the *Worcester* decision and Jackson's nonresponse, even the Cherokees' strongest white advocates tended to give up the fight and encourage the Cherokees to do the same. They had played their last card and come up short, and now the wisest course was to make the best deal that they could and head west. A tiny minority of the Cherokees themselves arrived at the same conclusion, including both John Ridge and *Cherokee Phoenix* editor Elias Boudinot.

---

[64]Perdue and Green, *Cherokee Nation and the Trail of Tears*, 93.
[65]Horace Greeley, *The American Conflict: A History of the Great Rebellion in the United States of America, 1860–1864* (Hartford, CT: O. D. Case & Company, 1864), 1:106.
[66]Jackson, *Papers of Andrew Jackson*, 10:226.
[67]Smith, *American Betrayal*, 141.

But the vast majority of the tribe renewed their determination to stay put. Led by Principal Chief John Ross (who had fought under Jackson twenty years earlier at the Battle of Horseshoe Bend), they persisted in their appeals to northern benefactors, US congressmen, and even to the "Chicken Snake" in the White House. They sent a stream of letters and memorials to the capital, claiming rights long "recognized and established by the laws and treaties of the United States."[68]

More broadly, they reminded the country that they had learned "the lessons of civilization and peace" from the "humane and christian policy" of previous administrations. They expressed confidence in "the *justice, good faith, and magnanimity of the United States.*" They informed the Senate that "our cause is your own. It is the cause of liberty and justice. It is based upon your own principles which we have learned from yourselves."[69]

These pleas were unavailing, but so, for a time, were Jackson's efforts to force the Cherokees to accept removal. Down south, the state of Georgia was still doing its part. Lottery winners poured onto Cherokee lands to claim their prizes. White settlers harassed the rank and file of Cherokees. (Tribe members were being "robbed & whipped by the whites almost every day," John Ridge reported to John Ross.) The state guard evicted Ross from his home and arrested him twice, the second time on the ludicrous grounds that the slaveholding Ross was plotting to incite a slave insurrection. In the spring of 1834, Georgia's Governor Lumpkin published an

Cherokee chief John Ross

open letter suggesting that "before the close of the year it may become necessary to remove every Cherokee from the limits of Georgia, peaceably if we can, forcibly if we must."[70]

---

[68]Walter Conser Jr., "John Ross and the Cherokee Resistance Campaign," *Journal of Southern History* 44 (1978): 198.

[69]Ibid., 199-200; Perdue and Green, *Cherokee Removal*, 92.

[70]Perdue and Green, *Cherokee Nation and the Trail of Tears*, 101, 104.

From Jackson's perspective, the chief political obstacle was that most Americans —white Georgians and frontier squatters excepted—still believed that Native American lands should be acquired by treaty only. In the end, the shortest way out of his predicament was through fraud.

In the summer of 1835, the administration entered into negotiations with the leaders of a minority faction of Cherokees known as the Treaty Party. They weren't authorized to represent the tribe, and they spoke for a miniscule fraction, but no matter. The government ordered a popular referendum on the proposed treaty to be held that December at the traditional Cherokee capital of New Echota, and it announced that non-participation in the referendum would be considered equivalent to approval. Even so, perhaps 15/16 of the tribe boycotted the referendum, with the remnant approving the tribe's removal to the new Indian Territory by a miniscule vote of 79-7.

The Cherokee Council submitted a formal letter of protest, declaring the Treaty of New Echota "a fraud upon the government of the United States and an act of oppression on the Cherokee people." President Jackson returned the letter as "disrespectful" and ordered that the treaty be enforced "without modification." Even as the "People's President" was refusing to consider their protest, Chief Ross insisted in a pamphlet, "I still strongly hope we shall find ultimate justice from the good sense of the administration and of the people of the United States."[71]

Two years later—after the United States Army had invaded the Cherokee Nation, rounded up some eighteen thousand Cherokees at gunpoint, and herded them into detention camps—Ross bowed to the inevitable and led his people west. One fourth died along the way. Among the dead was his wife, Qatie.

So what are we to make of this episode in American history? Surely, there were some principled white voices on both sides of the debate. Many, perhaps most, of the advocates of removal simply wanted the Cherokees out of the way, but others were genuinely persuaded that, in a realistic scenario with no good options, removal was the only path that might conceivably allow the Cherokees to survive as a distinct, self-governing people, perhaps even to survive at all.

At the same time, it would be an abuse of language to consider the Cherokees' removal voluntary. The state of Georgia blatantly violated federal treaties and

---

[71]Inskeep, *Jacksonland*, 303-4; Perdue and Green, *Cherokee Removal*, 158.

enacted legislation aimed at driving the Cherokees from their ancestral home. The party in power in Washington clucked its tongue and cheerfully acquiesced. Both hid behind the fig leaf of a new treaty that they knew to be fraudulent. And in the end, after repeated pledges never to resort to coercion, the United States government evicted the Cherokees with rifle and bayonet, leading to untold suffering and death. It was a classic example of what Alexis de Tocqueville would label "the tyranny of the majority."

Tocqueville arrived in the United States a year after the passage of the Indian Removal Act, and he returned to France more than six years before the Cherokees' "Trail of Tears." He encountered numerous Native Americans along his journey, however, and he even shared a Mississippi River steamboat with a large contingent of Choctaws being forcefully relocated from Alabama to the Indian Territory. It was an unusually frigid December—ice blocked navigation on the Mississippi north of Memphis—and Tocqueville watched in horror as the young and old, sick and maimed trudged on board carrying all their worldly possessions in bundles on their backs.

"The whole spectacle had an air of ruin and destruction," Tocqueville wrote to his mother that Christmas night in 1831 while still aboard ship. Three years later the memory of the "truly lamentable scene" still haunted him, and as he recounted the episode in *Democracy in America*, he was not tempted to rhapsodize that "America is great, because she is good."[72]

Modern scholars who condemn the removal of Native Americans typically describe it as a "contradiction of democracy" or a "betrayal of democracy."[73] This would have mystified Tocqueville. Remember, as Tocqueville understood it, the "output" of democracy is whatever the majority in a democratic society advocates, condones, or tolerates—good or bad, wise or unwise, just or unjust. By Tocqueville's reasoning, any act of government that commands the support of the majority is by definition "democratic." To suggest otherwise would be illogical.

There were no opinion polls two centuries ago, of course, but we can be almost certain that a comfortable majority of white Americans in the 1830s, both male and female, either supported removal or comfortably acquiesced to it, while an overwhelming majority harbored the feelings of racial superiority that

---

[72]Alexis de Tocqueville, *Letters from America*, ed. Frederick Brown (New Haven, CT: Yale University Press, 2010), 256, 255.

[73]Perdue and Green, *Cherokee Nation and the Trail of Tears*, xvi; Smith, *American Betrayal*, 2.

helped make the policy acceptable. We mustn't be fooled by the narrow vote in the House of Representatives in favor of the Indian Removal Act. Pro-removal congressmen were surely correct that much of the opposition in the House was fueled more by partisan politics than principled concern. As we've noted, most Whig congressmen fully supported removal once their party was in power, and it was a challenge to find significant white opposition to removal in any region where Native Americans actually lived.

The view that removal was a *contradiction* of democracy is the response of democratic faith. Tocqueville's democratic philosophy persuaded him that, among fallen people, injustice is always a possible *expression* of democracy. This was the case with Native American removal as it unfolded in the 1830s. It was a democratic policy, prompted by democratic desires, fueled by democratic sentiments. It was also, as Tocqueville described it to his mother that Christmas night, an "abomination."[74]

---

[74]Tocqueville, *Letters from America*, 255.

— 6 —

"THE PEOPLE ARE
INCAPABLE OF PROTECTING
THEMSELVES"

*E*ven as he was pressuring the Cherokees to head west, the People's President was confronting a different kind of challenge on the people's behalf. The people were in danger—although they didn't know it yet—and the republic itself was in peril. In 1815, Andrew Jackson had saved his country from a foreign foe. Now a domestic enemy threatened American liberty, and Jackson again must be his country's savior. In a spate of letters in the spring of 1832, the president alerted correspondents to "that *monster*" which was "winding its way into all the ramifications of our Government" and "corrupting every branch of it." The "monster" had to be "put down," he warned, before it "destroys the virtue & morality of our country, and with that, our present happy form of Government."[1]

Monster was one of Jackson's rarer epithets, and he seems to have reserved it for enemies who were not only ambitious and unprincipled, but evil incarnate. A generation earlier he had employed it against false friends who accused him of speculating in land acquired by treaty from the Creeks after the Battle of Horseshoe Bend. "I can scarcely believe," he fumed to John Coffee—his friend and fellow land speculator—"that I have hugged such monsters to my boosom."[2]

Toward the beginning of his presidency, he hurled the charge at those who questioned the virtue of Peggy Eaton, the wife of his former campaign manager

---

[1]Andrew Jackson, in *The Papers of Andrew Jackson*, ed. Sam B. Smith, Harriet Chappell Owsley, Harold D. Moser, et al., 10 vols. (Knoxville: University of Tennessee Press, 1980–2016), 10:270.
[2]Steve Inskeep, *Jacksonland: President Andrew Jackson, Cherokee Chief John Ross, and a Great American Land Grab* (New York: Penguin, 2015), 78.

and now secretary of war. The rumors were "unholy wicked & unjust," Jackson thundered. Those who circulated them were "political monsters" willing to destroy a chaste maiden for partisan gain. Their real goal, Jackson was certain, was to embarrass *him*.[3]

Toward the end of his second term, he resurrected the epithet to denounce northern abolitionists who were trying to flood southern post offices with antislavery tracts. He was sure that these "monsters" were trying to incite slave rebellion, the slaveholding Jackson informed the postmaster general. They deserved "to atone for this wicked attempt with their lives."[4]

But in 1832 Jackson aimed his indignation not at individuals but at an institution, not against "monsters" but against "*the* monster": the Second Bank of the United States, a corporation chartered by act of Congress and headquartered in Philadelphia. In a struggle historians remember as "the Bank War," Jackson would battle against the bank and its congressional defenders for the next two years.

Economic historians study the Bank War to explore its impact on the country's financial system and its possible relation to a major recession that began at the end of Jackson's presidency. We'll revisit it with an eye not to its consequences but to how it was waged. In his struggle against "the monster," Andrew Jackson pioneered and perfected a political strategy that flourishes in the twenty-first century. In his war against the bank, Jackson emerged as the nation's first, and until recently, its only *populist* president.

In recent years you've likely heard countless references to the "populism" that propelled Donald Trump to the presidency in 2016 as well as to "populist" movements gaining momentum in Britain, Europe, and Latin America. Depending on the source, you may have learned that this was cause for hope or reason for alarm. That's because much about the concept is ambiguous. Populism can be a movement of the left or of the right. (In both 2016 and 2020, the two leading populists were Donald Trump and Bernie Sanders.) It can champion a precise set of policies or stand for nothing beyond enthusiasm for a charismatic leader. It can promote the expansion of liberty or facilitate the concentration of power. Yet there are enough persistent traits in populism to make the term, and the concept, coherent.

---

[3]Jackson, *Papers of Andrew Jackson*, 8:579.
[4]Daniel Walker Howe, *What Hath God Wrought: The Transformation of America, 1815–1848* (New York: Oxford University Press, 2007), 429.

For our purposes, it's best to think of populism as a kind of rhetorical political strategy, "a specific way of competing for and exercising political power."[5] Populists see the world (or claim to see it) as a struggle between "the people"—always clothed in robes of righteousness—and some insidious threat to the people, typically a corrupt elite who would subvert the people's welfare for selfish gain. Among a list of usual suspects, the threat may stem from bankers, industrialists, racial or ethnic minorities, leaders of rival parties, or even from the government itself—perhaps especially from the government itself.

As the central heroes in this perpetual war, populist leaders serve several key functions. They *identify the enemy* of the people, focusing the attention and energy of the movement. They *speak for* the people, channeling the imputed moral authority of the masses. They *defend* the people, often assuming considerable power in doing so. Finally, they *define* the "true" people, separating sheep from goats.

A word here about terminology: When populist politicians in Jacksonian America referred to "the people," they almost never had in mind all of the inhabitants of the United States. They meant native-born white males—not African Americans, not Native Americans, often not the recent immigrants from Europe who were arriving in ever-increasing numbers on American shores. But this was less a populist trait than a near universal assumption of the day. When office seekers paid tribute to "the people" as the foundation of American democracy, they reflexively thought in terms of voters, of the citizens assumed to be entitled to a voice in political affairs.

Where populists stood out was in their further winnowing of the white male citizenry. Because at the heart of populism is a "celebration of the virtue of ordinary people," populist logic dictates that those who oppose the movement can't genuinely be a part of the people, regardless of their race or ethnicity.[6] When populist leaders pay tribute to "the people," who they really have in mind are the folks who agree with them. Everyone else is an enemy.

Ever since the election of 1824, Andrew Jackson had fallen naturally into this way of thinking. The "Corrupt Bargain" and the alleged thwarting of the will of the majority had convinced him that America's greatest enemies were internal and that he alone could defeat them. When the central villains in the travesty of '24

---

[5]Kurt Weyland, "Clarifying a Contested Concept: Populism in the Study of Latin American Politics," *Comparative Politics* 34 (2001): 11.

[6]George H. Nash, "How Should Conservatives Respond to the Populist Challenge?," *The New Criterion* 35, no. 5 (January 2018): 7.

emerged as key supporters of the Second Bank of the United States, the general instinctively framed the debate over the bank's future in populist terms. No episode of his presidency better illustrates Jackson's populism than the Bank War, and none more starkly reveals the danger awaiting us today when we ground our support for democracy in an unqualified faith in human nature.

The descendant of an institution originally proposed by Alexander Hamilton in 1790, the Second Bank of the United States had been established by Congress in 1816 with broad bipartisan support. According to the terms of its charter, which was to last for twenty years, the federal government would subscribe one-fifth of the bank's stock and appoint one-fifth of the members of its board of directors. The charter authorized the bank to issue paper currency up to the amount of its stock, and it required it to redeem its paper dollars in gold or silver at face value upon demand.

In return, the federal government committed to employ the bank as its exclusive agent and to accept the bank's currency at face value, for example when it was tendered in payment of taxes or for the purchase of public lands. Apart from its minority representation on the board, however, the government would have no direct control over the bank's actions. Its primary leverage over the institution would consist in its right not to renew its charter when it expired and,

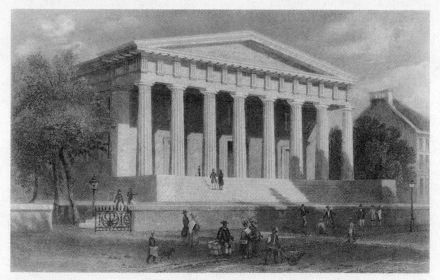

Second Bank of the United States, Philadelphia, Pennsylvania

in the most extraordinary circumstances, to withdraw all federal monies from the bank's coffers.

Neither fish nor fowl, the Bank of the United States (BUS) was an odd creature. Technically, it was a "mixed public-private corporation."[7] (Although strange to us today, both the Bank of England and Bank of France were organized on similar lines until shortly after World War II.) In its private capacity, the BUS functioned as a typical commercial bank, extending loans to individuals and businesses and trying to earn the best rate of return that it could for its four thousand stockholders. In its public capacity, the bank functioned as an agent of the federal government with a responsibility to promote the welfare of the entire country.

Supporters of the bank's original charter envisioned numerous ways that it could benefit the public. To begin with, it would serve as the sole depository for the federal government's money and facilitate its transactions. Second, because its reserves would be vast and its notes were guaranteed not to depreciate, the bank could also provide a far more reliable circulating medium for the nation than would exist otherwise. The quantity of "hard money" available—gold and silver coins—was inadequate to the needs of the economy, but the circulation of paper dollars by hundreds of unconnected, independent banks was nothing short of chaotic. Ideally, the BUS would bring some much needed order.

By 1830, the country's more than three hundred banks each issued their own distinct currencies—often vastly in excess of what they could redeem in gold or silver—and the torrent of paper money in circulation fluctuated widely and erratically in value. In the nineteenth century, all paper dollars were supposed to be "redeemable" in hard money. If a businessman received a paper dollar issued by a local bank in payment of a debt, he would be willing to accept it at face value as long as he was confident that, if he wished to do so, he could submit the paper note to the cashier of the local bank and receive a dollar coin in return.

But if he was offered paper currency issued by a distant bank, perhaps one he knew nothing about, he might insist on "discounting" the note; that is, he would credit his customer only a percentage of the note's face value. In sum, this was a system in which the real value of paper currency was constantly in doubt and subject to negotiation between debtor and creditor. The conspicuous exception would be the notes of the Bank of the United States.

Finally, its supporters also hoped that, because of its comparatively enormous resources, the BUS could extend loans to private banks during hard times and

---

[7]Howe, *What Hath God Wrought*, 376.

help them weather the storm, reducing the frequency of bankruptcy and miti-
gating economic fluctuations. By presenting the currency of private banks for
redemption, it could also discourage "wildcat banks" from irresponsibly over-
extending their reserves. In the best case scenario, the bank's policies would bring
greater stability and soundness to the country's often turbulent financial sector.

In the 1830s, defenders of the BUS maintained that it was fulfilling these ob-
jectives admirably, and modern-day historians have generally agreed. Yet the
contemporary critics of the bank also had a point: it wielded enormous economic power with precious little accountability to the government.

By the time that Andrew Jackson took office, the BUS was easily the largest
corporation in America. It had expanded from its base in Philadelphia to include
twenty-nine branches across the country, handled roughly a fifth of all bank
loans, issued a fifth of all circulating bank notes, and held fully a third of all bank
deposits. Its capitalization of $35 million might not sound like much today, but
in the 1830s it was more than double the annual federal budget. For its day, the
Bank of the United States was "a financial colossus."[8]

It's worth noting as well that the bank's president, Nicholas Biddle, did little
to alleviate fears about the power of the institution he directed. A polymath who
graduated from Princeton at age fifteen, by his early thirties Biddle had already
served as secretary to the American ambassador to Great Britain, practiced law,
and edited a literary journal. Only then did he take up banking, but in no time
he had risen to the presidency of the largest bank in America. Biddle managed
the BUS far more effectively than any of his predecessors, and in 1832 he probably
knew more about banking than anyone else in the country. His Achilles' heel
was that he was aware of this.

Like the president of the United States, the president of the Bank of the United
States was supremely confident in his own judgment and impatient with authority.
In Biddle's view, apart from the appointment of the five government directors, "no
officer of the Government, from the president downwards, has the least right, the
least authority, the least pretense, for interference in the concerns of the bank."[9]

To Biddle's credit, on the whole he seems to have managed the bank with
integrity and with the stability and efficiency of the country's financial sector
in mind. But he was not a politician, and playing the role of the humble public
servant seems never to have occurred to him. His education, expertise, and

---

[8]Robert Remini, *Andrew Jackson and the Bank War* (New York: W. W. Norton, 1967), 39.
[9]Sean Wilentz, *Andrew Jackson* (New York: Times Books, 2005), 78.

arrogance made him the perfect foil for the bank's critics, who would soon find it effective to portray the BUS as the resurrection of Old World aristocracy.

For his part, Andrew Jackson had been suspicious of banks in general for much of his adult life, but he didn't immediately declare war on the bank upon taking office. He devoted a mere three sentences of his first annual message to the bank, vaguely observing that "a large portion of our fellow-citizens" questioned both its con-

Nicholas Biddle

stitutionality and its "expediency" and urging the Congress to "deliberate consideration" of the institution before its charter expired. As late as 1831, Jackson's secretary of the treasury recommended rechartering the BUS in his annual report, and Jackson hinted that he would be willing to sign off on whatever modifications to the bank that Congress could agree on.[10]

Then two crucial things happened. At the end of 1831, one hundred and fifty "National Republican" delegates gathered in Baltimore, nominated Henry Clay for president, and publicly endorsed the Bank of the United States. A few weeks later, Clay and other congressional supporters of the BUS persuaded Nicholas Biddle to apply to Congress for an extension of the bank's charter during the current legislative session.

Even though the charter wouldn't expire for another four years, Clay and company made the case that an immediate request for renewal would maximize the likelihood of success. Jackson would hesitate to veto the measure in advance of the upcoming presidential election, they reasoned, given the bank's popularity in Pennsylvania and that state's enormous weight in the Electoral College. If the general proved them wrong and blocked the renewal, then a popular backlash would lead to Jackson's defeat, and with President Clay in the White House, the BUS would still be renewed in the end.

---

[10]James D. Richardson, comp., *A Compilation of the Messages and Papers of the Presidents* (New York: Bureau of National Literature, 1897), 3:1025.

From this point on, it became impossible for Jackson to separate his suspicion of the bank from his loathing of Clay, the "Judas" who had betrayed the people and sold out their savior. Nor did it help that other vocal supporters of the BUS included John Quincy Adams, who had supposedly paid Clay his thirty pieces of silver for the presidency, and Vice President John C. Calhoun, whom Jackson now also heartily despised. (The trigger had been Jackson's discovery that, back in 1819, Calhoun had wanted him court-martialed for his unauthorized invasion of Florida. By 1832, the president of the United States no longer spoke to the vice president of the United States, whom he denounced as "one of the most base hypocritical & unprincipled villains in the United States."[11])

The decision to press for renewal in advance of the election further convinced Jackson that the real objective of the bank's advocates didn't concern the bank at all: what they primarily wanted was to thwart his reelection. As was so often the case with Jackson, a difference of opinion became personal, transforming a debate over policy into "a war to defend his own reputation and honor." As Jackson famously put it to his trusted ally, Martin Van Buren, "The bank, Mr. Van Buren, is trying to kill me, *but I will kill it.*"[12]

Much to Jackson's displeasure, in early July Congress approved a bill to extend the life of the BUS for another fifteen years, despite Jacksonian majorities in both chambers. The vote had been close: 107-85 in the House and 28-20 in the Senate. In neither house did the president's supporters and critics line up neatly for or against the bank, a pattern that mirrored the larger electorate. As a careful student of the period observes, in 1832 "the public as a whole was not sharply divided into pro- and anti-Bank factions." Andrew Jackson was about to change that. He would veto the bill to renew the bank's charter, and by doing so, a member of his inner circle predicted, he would ensure "that whoever is in favor of that Bank will be against Old Hickory."[13]

For help in crafting his veto message, Jackson turned to a newspaperman named Amos Kendall. Like modern-day presidents, the general routinely had help on all his major state papers, but unlike latter-day executives, he didn't have

[11]Jackson, *Papers of Andrew Jackson*, 10:37.

[12]Wilentz, *Andrew Jackson*, 75; John C. Fitzpatrick, ed., *The Autobiography of Martin Van Buren* (1920; repr., New York: De Capo Press, 1973), 625.

[13]Howe, *What Hath God Wrought*, 376; Charles Sellers, *The Market Revolution* (New York: Oxford University Press, 1991), 322-23.

a corps of White House speechwriters to draw from. Jackson often enlisted the help of the cabinet with his addresses, but the only member of his cabinet who actually opposed the Bank of the United States was Roger Taney, and the attorney general's prose was as dry as dust. That wouldn't do. Jackson wanted to reach an audience far beyond the other lawyers on Capitol Hill. He wanted to speak directly to the American people.

And so Jackson enlisted Kendall. A master of "vulgar" prose, the New England–born Kentuckian had been one of the general's most ruthless journalistic advocates during the 1828 campaign. Among other sensational charges, he had gleefully condemned the "Corrupt Bargain" and trumpeted the salacious claim that the puritanical Adams had procured a young American blonde as a sexual companion for the czar of Russia.

After gaining the White House, an appreciative Jackson had rewarded Kendall with a well-paying but undemanding job in the Treasury Department—a post for which he had no particular qualifications or relevant experience. ("The labor is very light," Kendall reported to his wife, while the salary would enable them to live "comfortably and genteelly."[14]) In his more than ample spare time, Kendall would be free to write editorials for the pro-Jackson Washington *Globe* and craft occasional messages for the president.

Kendall was an ideal choice for the veto message, in part because of his flair for earthy prose, in part because he hated the bank as much as Jackson himself and could channel the president's views with delight. And make no mistake: if the final wording was Kendall's, the sentiments were wholly the president's. It was the perfect marriage of man and mouthpiece. Jackson's rejection of the renewal bill, returned to Congress on July 10, 1832, was very possibly "the most important presidential veto in American history." His veto *message* was arguably even more important. It was a "masterstroke" of populist propaganda.[15]

This was no mean feat, given the likelihood that a majority of the electorate, like Congress, actually favored renewal of the bank's charter. The day after the veto, Massachusetts senator Daniel Webster told his colleagues that "a great majority of the people are satisfied with the bank."[16] Webster was a staunch supporter of the BUS and had an incentive to exaggerate, but his assessment was probably correct.

---

[14]William Stickney, ed., *Autobiography of Amos Kendall* (Boston: Lee and Shepard, 1872), 290, 293.
[15]Remini, *Jackson and the Bank War*, 82; Howe, *What Hath God Wrought*, 380.
[16]George Rogers Taylor, ed., *Jackson Versus Biddle: The Struggle over the Second Bank of the United States* (Boston: D. C. Heath and Company, 1949), 24.

There were no opinion polls to back him up, of course, but during the next congressional session the Senate would receive 243 petitions in support of the BUS, signed by more than 128,000 individuals. (Proportional to the population, that would be like more than four million individuals today.) During the same period, opponents of the bank would send in 55 resolutions bearing some 17,000 signatures.

If support of the bank was better organized, which is likely, these figures overstate the disparity between supporters and opponents of renewal. But even a very conservative estimate, proffered by one of Jackson's most sympathetic biographers, holds that "a substantial majority" of Americans supported the bank on the eve of the veto. This means that Jackson's veto message, in which he would position himself as the defender of the people, was designed to shape popular opinion, not reflect it.[17]

At first glance, the general's argument against the bank seems to lack focus. It has an everything-but-the-kitchen-sink feel to it, pinballing from diatribe against foreign influence to assertion of executive prerogative to criticism of congressional process to warning about power to insinuation about motive to tendentious constitutional interpretation. And although he was striking down the most important economic institution in the country, the president had nothing to say about how the bank actually conducted its business or affected the economy. Nor, for that matter, did he so much as hint at what would replace the bank after it had been eliminated.

The key to comprehending Jackson's veto message is in recognizing that it was first and foremost a political statement and, more precisely, a populist manifesto. The crux of its argument—the assertion on which all else hinges—is Jackson's populist claim that the drive to extend the life of the bank had been engineered by elite enemies of the people.

"It is to be regretted that the rich and powerful too often bend the acts of government to their selfish purposes," Jackson laments in one of the message's most frequently quoted lines. The true goal of the renewal bill was "to make the rich richer and the potent more powerful." It would prostitute the government "to the advancement of the few at the expense of the many." The victims would be the "humble members of society—the farmers, mechanics, and laborers—who have neither the time nor the means of securing like favors to themselves."[18]

---

[17]Remini, *Jackson and the Bank War*, 41.
[18]Richardson, *Messages and Papers of the Presidents*, 3:1140, 1153.

Let's stop and think about this before we go on. It may have been rhetorically effective, but Jackson's melodrama of villains and victims bore little resemblance to reality. If historians are correct that a "substantial majority" of the electorate was pro-bank on the eve of the Bank War, then it's not remotely possible that support of the bank was limited to the country's upper class. In numerical terms, the typical advocate of the bank had to be one of "the humble members of society" Jackson claimed to be defending from the bank.

Similarly, critics of the BUS included many of "the rich and powerful." Although you'd never know it from the veto message, the bank's opponents "were a diverse group from all walks of life." They objected to it for a variety of reasons. Many were suspicious of paper money, concerned about the bank's power, or doubtful of its constitutionality. But a sizable portion of the bank's opponents were bankers who had to compete against the BUS, as well as aspiring entrepreneurs and businessmen who desired a more liberal credit market than the conservative bank promoted. It was this realization that prompted one congressman to blame opposition to the bank on "the selfish feelings of the capitalists and speculators who have kindled the fire to consume it."[19]

Nicholas Biddle oversimplified things when he characterized the Bank War as a contest "between Chestnut St and Wall St"—that is, a battle between wealthy bankers in Philadelphia and wealthy bankers in New York City to see which city would become the nation's financial capital.[20] Jackson oversimplified just as grossly in casting the conflict as a class war between rich and poor. History is complicated, and a closer look invariably explodes crude dichotomies. Populist rhetoric thrives on them.

A recent assessment of populism observes that "populists are dividers, not uniters."[21] That's true, but it's more accurate to say that populists are dichotomizers. They divide society into precisely *two* groups. And so in framing a complex problem concerning the unprecedented financial needs of a dynamically growing economy, Jackson portrayed "the people" as an undifferentiated mass with identical interests, all of whom would suffer if "the Monster" triumphed.

The Framers of the Constitution would have been horrified. In *Federalist* nos. 10 and 51, James Madison had argued that the only way to protect minority

---

[19]Remini, *Jackson and the Bank War*, 40; Harry N. Scheiber, "Some Documents on Jackson's Bank War," *Pennsylvania History* 30 (January 1963): 51.

[20]Scheiber, "Some Documents on Jackson's Bank War," 46.

[21]Uri Friedman, "What Is a Populist?," *The Atlantic*, February 27, 2017, www.theatlantic.com/international/archive/2017/02/what-is-populist-trump/516525.

groups in a republic was to hope that the society would be so diverse and the number of distinct interest groups so large that majority coalitions would rarely emerge. Do you remember why? Because whenever "a majority be united by a common interest, the rights of the minority will be insecure." This led Madison to conclude that, in a free society, the primary "security for civil rights" would be the people's "multiplicity of interests."[22]

Predictably, Jackson concluded his veto message with a tribute to "the sages of the Revolution and the fathers of our Union," but this was just one more example of his habit of honoring the Founders while repudiating their values.[23] Far from promoting a "multiplicity of interests" in order to discourage the development of a majority coalition, Jackson sought to understate real differences of interest in order to build the largest, most powerful majority possible. In the Bank War, Jackson's goal would be Madison's nightmare.

When we read the entire veto message in the context of its populist framework, its disparate arguments crystallize into a coherent whole. One of Jackson's first allegations concerned the degree of foreign influence in the affairs of the bank. Appealing to national pride (and nativist fears), the president informed the country that foreign investors owned fully a fourth of the bank's stock. It was bad enough that this made Americans "debtors to aliens." Jackson hinted darkly that, in the event of war, these foreign agents could transform the bank into a hostile weapon "more formidable and dangerous than the naval and military power of the enemy."[24]

This was ridiculous. The bank's charter expressly denied foreign investors the right to vote in shareholders' meetings. Every officer of the bank was expressly required to be a US citizen. Ditto for every member of the board of directors. That a small minority of voteless shareholders residing thousands of miles away could somehow transform the BUS into a traitorous fifth column was far-fetched, to put it politely. No one who had actually read the bank's charter could take the warning seriously.

But in the president's defense, he wasn't addressing that kind of voter. Jackson's veto message was never intended for readers who knew the fine points of

[22]James Madison, *Federalist #51*, in Alexander Hamilton, James Madison, and John Jay, *The Federalist*, ed. J. R. Pole (Indianapolis: Hackett, 2005), 283.

[23]Richardson, *Messages and Papers of the Presidents*, 3:1153.

[24]Ibid., 3:1143, 1144.

the bank's charter or had an accurate understanding of how the bank functioned. His target audience was the legion of loyal supporters who would listen if the Hero of New Orleans warned them that they were in danger. And when the general revealed that the secret instigators of the bank bill were "rich and powerful" Americans at war with the country's "humble" majority, they would find it plausible that the people's domestic enemies might conspire with their enemies abroad.

Read in its populist context, Jackson's caution about foreign influence over the bank becomes another way of indicting the wealthy Americans who were scheming to extend its life. In perpetuating an institution supposedly vulnerable to foreign intrigue, the members of a corrupt elite were sacrificing national security for personal profit. They were failing to put America first.

Jackson was on more solid ground in calling attention to the bank's inordinate power and the absence of effective government oversight. It undeniably wielded enormous influence, and it's just as undeniable that it operated independently of government control. Even many of the bank's supporters conceded that its charter could be modified to protect the public interest more effectively.

The president was also correct in suggesting that the BUS owed much of its frightful potential to its unique relationship with the US government. The bank's advantage over its competitors was "artificial," Jackson stressed repeatedly. It didn't result from market forces but from "exclusive privileges" bestowed by Congress. (Kendall, who desperately needed a thesaurus, used the adjective *exclusive* eighteen times.) In sum, the government had foolishly created a behemoth that could just as easily abuse the public interest as promote it. "Great evils to our country and its institutions might flow from such a concentration of power in the hands of a few men irresponsible to the people," Jackson warned. "Is there no danger to our liberty and independence in a bank that in its nature has so little to bind it to our country?"[25]

It was a good question. But if Jackson's diagnosis in this respect was sound—the bank did exercise inordinate influence with limited accountability—his prescribed solution was classically populist. *He* would save the people from the Monster that threatened them. *He* would save the people from a government that wouldn't defend them.

In justifying his veto of the renewal bill, Jackson suggested that Congress had erred by not seeking his input *before* considering the measure. "Neither upon the

---

[25]Ibid., 3:1144.

propriety of present action nor upon the provisions of this act was the Executive consulted," he admonished them. "It [i.e., the president] has had no opportunity to say that it neither needs nor wants an agent clothed with such powers."[26]

Think about what Jackson was saying. The day after the veto, an incredulous Daniel Webster marveled to his fellow senators that the president of the United States "claims to divide with Congress the power of originating statutes."[27] In our day, Congressional leaders often decline to take up legislation that the president is known to oppose, so the implications of Jackson's objection may be lost on us. Two centuries ago, congressmen generally held to the view that the constitutionally prescribed role of the *executive* is to *execute* the law, not to make it. Jackson, however, was staking his claim to a central role in the legislative process.

After demanding a role in making the law, the general then asserted that it was his job to interpret the law. Measured by the number of words devoted to the question, the paramount argument in the veto message was Jackson's insistence that the BUS was unconstitutional.

This wasn't an easy argument to make. Congress had repeatedly approved the institution. It had chartered the First Bank of the United States in 1791. It had created its successor, the Second Bank of the United States, in 1816. It had voted to extend the life of the latter in 1832. What is more, the Supreme Court had twice explicitly upheld the constitutionality of such a bank—in *McCullough v. Maryland* in 1819 and again in *Osborn v. the Bank of the United States* five years later. Supporters of the bank thought that this surely decided the matter.

They were wrong, Jackson announced. The prior acts of Congress were in no way authoritative. "Mere precedent is a dangerous source of authority," he contended. "Questions of constitutional power" always remain open until the opinion of "the people and the States can be considered as well settled." That hadn't happened yet, the president announced. And as for the Supreme Court's rulings on the subject? "Each public officer who takes an oath to support the Constitution swears that he will support it as *he* understands it," Jackson explained, "not as it is understood by others."[28]

---

[26]Ibid., 3:1152-53.
[27]Taylor, *Jackson Versus Biddle*, 30.
[28]Richardson, *Message and Papers of the President*, 3:1144-45, italics added.

This was a novel reading of the Constitution, to say the least. In Jackson's view, the legislative and executive branches each had as much right to determine the constitutionality of legislation as the judicial branch. The opinion of the Supreme Court, he explained, "has no more authority over Congress than the opinion of Congress over the judges, and on that point the president is independent of both."[29] In determining the constitutionality of the Bank of the United States, Jackson was simply exercising his constitutional duty to uphold the Constitution—as *he* unilaterally interpreted it.

A recent uncritical biography of Jackson would have us believe that the general was merely taking steps to elevate the executive branch to a level of true equality with the other branches of government. "Jackson never would have allowed" the swollen executive power that characterizes today's presidency, the author insists. "He just wanted it to have an equal say."[30]

Possibly. But bear in mind two things: First, the Framers of the Constitution never spoke of the three branches of the federal government as equal. Rather, they made clear that the legislative branch was preeminent. The input of the people and of the states was to be expressed through that channel alone, and once Congress had acted on that input, it would be the job of the president, among other things, to execute the laws that resulted.

The Framers did speak of the two houses of Congress as "co-equal," and they alluded to the "co-equal" taxing powers of the state and federal governments, but they did not speak of the three branches of the federal government in such language.[31] Although our contemporary legislative branch has progressively forfeited much of its responsibilities to an imperial presidency, this was never what the Framers envisioned. If all Jackson wanted was an "equal say," then this was just another example of his extensive ignorance of the constitutional order he had sworn to uphold.

But note also that the Constitution explicitly clothes the executive branch with the unique responsibility to "take care that the laws be faithfully executed." If each branch of the federal government has an equal right to determine the constitutionality of laws, but only the president has the authority to execute the laws, then it's the president's understanding of the Constitution that matters

---

[29]Ibid.

[30]Bradley J. Birzer, *In Defense of Andrew Jackson* (Washington, DC: Regnery History, 2018), 145.

[31]Danielle Allen, "The Impeachment Memo Returns to Questions at the Roots of Our Democracy," *Washington Post*, December 13, 2019, www.washingtonpost.com/opinions/2019/12/13/house-judiciary-memo-returns-roots-our-democracy/.

most. You could almost say that it's *only* the president's understanding that matters *at all*.

If you have doubts on this point, just ask yourself what their victory in *Worcester v. Georgia* had accomplished for the Cherokee Nation four months earlier. Some sympathy, perhaps, but not a particle of legal relief. The Supreme Court's decision "fell still born," as Jackson exulted, precisely because he disagreed with the ruling and wouldn't lift a finger to enforce it.[32]

Boiled down, Jackson's dictum that every officer of the government is duty bound to uphold the Constitution "as *he* understands it" means that, when it comes to the enforcement of the law, the Constitution means what the president says it means. Whatever his intentions, the general was claiming powers for the presidency that none of his predecessors had even dared to imagine.

And remember why he was doing this: to defend the people from concentrated power. If this was more than a little ironic, it was not as contradictory as it might seem at first. Like Jackson's warning about foreign influence, his assertion of presidential prerogative is best understood in light of the veto message's overarching populism. In the same address in which he asserted a dramatic expansion of executive power, the president concluded by implying that neither of the other branches of government could be trusted.

There was a double punch to Jackson's lament that "the rich and powerful too often bend the acts of government to their selfish purposes." In classical populist terms, he was defining the debate over the bank as a death struggle between the people and the people's enemies. But he was also telling his followers that the enemies of the people had co-opted much of the government. Whether as willing accomplices or witless pawns, both the Congress and the Supreme Court had functioned repeatedly as instruments of "the rich and powerful." If the "humble members of society" had a reliable champion in Washington, it was the People's President, and him alone. No officeholder who disagreed with him could be trusted.

With Jackson's veto the Bank War began in earnest. The first phase involved a public referendum like the country hadn't seen before. In pushing for an early recharter of the BUS, Henry Clay had anticipated that a presidential veto would make the bank the central issue of the 1832 presidential campaign. Far from

---

[32]Jackson, *Papers of Andrew Jackson*, 10:226.

cowed, Andrew Jackson had welcomed the challenge and couched his veto as a call to arms, an invitation to Jacksonians around the country to sustain their champion against the machinations of the Monster. For really the first time in US history, the president of the United States had taken a clear stand on a divisive issue and invited the electorate to ratify his position.

In the campaign that followed, pro-Jackson journalists and politicians echoed the populist themes of the veto message. An Ohio editor depicted the veto as the "triumph of the people over avarice" and exulted that the general had "cast off a yoke even more dangerous than British domination." A pro-Jackson rally praised it as "the final decision of the President between the Aristocracy and the People." A North Carolinian marveled at Jackson's courage in confronting a "corrupt Aristocracy."[33]

In like manner, Kentuckians thanked the general for saving the country's "free institutions" by destroying "that Giant of Aristocracy." The Vermont *Patriot* applauded Jackson for defending "the interests of the WHOLE PEOPLE" and proclaimed that his only opponents were "the rich—the powerful—the men who grind the faces of the poor and rob them of their hard earnings." And in the capital, the Washington *Globe* summarized "the Jackson cause" as "the cause of democracy and the people, against a corrupt and abandoned aristocracy."[34]

In reply, Henry Clay's "National Republicans" decried Jackson's ham-handed efforts to "inflame the poor against the rich." It reeked of the French Revolution, they said. "The spirit of Jacksonism is JACOBINISM," a Boston newspaper declared, referring to the French political faction responsible for instituting the Terror of 1793–1794.[35]

A New England editor agreed that the veto message was "the most wholly *radical* . . . document that ever emanated from any Administration, in any country." For "falsely and wickedly" fomenting a war of rich against poor, the president "deserves the execration of all who love their country." Another editor reminded voters that despots from Caesar to Cromwell had begun by "pretending to be the sole friends of the People and often by denouncing the rich."[36]

If there was a real threat to Americans' liberties, the National Republicans warned, it was not the Bank of the United States but the would-be tyrant in the White House. "The affairs of the country are approaching an important and

---

[33]Jackson, *Papers of Andrew Jackson*, 10:420; Wilentz, *Andrew Jackson*, 86.
[34]Jackson, *Papers of Andrew Jackson*, 10:524; Remini, *Jackson and the Bank War*, 100.
[35]Taylor, *Jackson Versus Biddle*, 30; Wilentz, *Andrew Jackson*, 85.
[36]Taylor, *Jackson Versus Biddle*, 31, 32.

dangerous crisis," Daniel Webster announced on the floor of the Senate. Even as Jackson pretended to perceive a threat to the people's liberty, their supposed defender was laying claim "to powers heretofore unknown and unheard of."[37]

Jackson's abuse of power became the central theme of the National Republican campaign. If Jackson were reelected, a Clay editor predicted, then "the time is near when the iron hand of despotism has swept our fair land." Less hopeful, another newspaper announced that that time had already arrived. "The Constitution is gone!" the Washington *National Intelligencer* announced. "It is a dead letter, and the will of a DICTATOR is the Supreme Law!" The danger to the country was not aristocracy but monarchy. "King Andrew I," not the BUS, was the prime threat to American liberty.[38]

Behind the scenes, Nicholas Biddle was doing everything he could to turn Jackson out of office. He contributed heavily to the Clay campaign, using the bank's resources to subsidize National Republican newspapers and to fund the publication of pro-bank pamphlets. He even paid for the circulation of thirty thousand copies of Jackson's veto message—believing that it strengthened the case for the bank by exposing Jacksonian radicalism—until he discovered that too many readers swallowed its arguments.

To be clear, this was long before conflict-of-interest statutes or campaign finance regulations. Nothing that Biddle did was illegal. At roughly the same time, Jackson was encouraging his department heads to steer lucrative printing contracts to the Washington *Globe*. Although the general didn't see it this way, he was effectively arranging for taxpayer dollars to subsidize his own reelection campaign.

Even so, Biddle's involvement in the election backfired, as rumors of the bank's efforts to sway the outcome seemed to vindicate Jacksonian warnings about its power. If "a mere monied corporation" can alter the course of an American election, the *Globe* lamented, then "nothing remains of our boasted freedom."[39]

In the end, "the People's Candidate" won reelection handily, sweeping to a decisive victory in a three-candidate race with National Republican Henry Clay and a minor third-party candidate, William Wirt (the former attorney general who had "wickedly" represented the Cherokee Nation before the Supreme Court). That said, it's unclear exactly how to interpret the results. Granted, Jackson's

---

[37]Ibid., 21, 30; Paul F. Boller Jr., *Presidential Campaigns: From George Washington to George W. Bush*, 2nd rev. ed. (New York: Oxford University Press, 2004), 55.

[38]Taylor, *Jackson Versus Biddle*, 31; Remini, *Jackson and the Bank War*, 101; Boller, *Presidential Campaigns*, 55.

[39]Remini, *Jackson and the Bank War*, 99.

"King Andrew I." This anti-Jackson caricature was likely crafted in response to Andrew Jackson's controversial decision to order the removal of federal deposits from the Second Bank of the United States. The artist portrays Jackson standing on a tattered copy of the Constitution, arrayed in regal robes and holding a scepter in one hand and a veto message in the other.

margin in both the electoral and popular votes was sizable. He swept the Electoral College with 219 votes to Clay's 49 and Wirt's 7. He received a comfortable majority of the popular vote as well: more than 54 percent of the more than 1.2 million ballots cast. Shouldn't we interpret this as a popular mandate in support of the bank veto?

It's not quite that straightforward. To begin with, the general's percentage of the popular vote had actually fallen slightly from four years earlier. Jackson remains the only president in US history to be reelected to a second term while suffering a decline in popular support. What is more, pro-administration candidates fared comparatively poorly in Congressional races. The Jacksonian majority in the House fell by thirteen, in comparison to 1828, while the party lost control of the Senate entirely. It's possible that the bank veto *hurt* the Jackson coalition more than it helped it, and it's far from clear that a majority of American voters actually approved of Jackson's action. A leading authority on the Bank War goes so far as to suggest the possibility that the country reelected the general "in spite of his Bank stand."[40] He may be right.

Yet if historians see the question as up for debate, Andrew Jackson did not. The meaning of his reelection was unequivocal, and he would brook no disagreement. In a formal communication to his cabinet, Jackson derided "the allegation that the question was not decided by the people. . . . Whatever may be the opinion of others," he continued, "the President considers his reelection as a decision of the people against the bank." Period. And now that "a just people" had rendered their verdict, he informed the cabinet, it was his duty to "effect their decision so far as it depends on him."[41]

Jackson's reelection in 1832 triggered the Bank War's next phase. The bill to extend the life of the BUS was dead, for now, but its current charter wasn't scheduled to expire until 1836, and that gave the "mamoth of corruption" another four years to assault democracy and threaten liberty.[42] The solution, Jackson came to believe, was to withdraw all government deposits from the bank immediately, depriving it of the lion's share of its resources and vastly reducing, if not eliminating, its potential for mischief.

---

[40]Ibid., 45.

[41]Richardson, *Messages and Papers of the Presidents*, 3:1226.

[42]John Spencer Bassett, ed., *Correspondence of Andrew Jackson* (Washington, DC: Carnegie Institution of Washington, 1931), 5:159.

This meant acting while Congress was not in session. Believe it or not, in the nineteenth century it was customary in odd-numbered years for Congress to adjourn from early spring until early December. In 1833, this meant that Congressmen headed for home shortly after Jackson's second inauguration on the fourth of March. Jackson was determined to present them with a fait accompli when they returned at the end of the year.

His reason for acting quickly is clear. The BUS was "buy[ing] up members of Congress by the Dozzen," the general told a Tennessee confidant that April.[43] Jackson knew this less from evidence than from intuition—his intuition that no one of integrity could persist in disagreeing with him once he had made his opinion known. Hadn't Congress endorsed the "Monster" only the year before? If that wasn't proof enough, over the winter the House had ordered an investigation of the bank's operations, and just prior to adjourning it had passed a resolution (by the decisive margin of 109-46) that the government's money was safe where it was.

This was a telltale sign that countless congressmen were on the take. How else to explain their stubborn support of such a dangerous institution? Given enough time, Jackson informed another correspondent, the BUS would gain complete control of the legislative branch. With a veto-proof majority, Congress could then extend the bank's charter despite his opposition. Unless Jackson acted quickly to destroy this "hydra of corruption," it would "rule the nation, and its charter will be perpetual and its corrupting influence destroy the liberty of our country."[44]

But not if Jackson could help it.

If Amos Kendall can be trusted, he and Washington *Globe* editor Francis Blair were the ones primarily urging haste in the president's ear. Decades later, Kendall remembered how he and Blair pressed Jackson to act quickly and promised that they would use the *Globe* to "bring up the people to sustain you." To hear Kendall tell it, this phase of the Bank War pitted Jackson, Blair, and Kendall against the world. "They were a Spartan band," he recalled modestly, "actuated by Spartan courage."[45]

Kendall was a self-promoter, and we might want to take his recollection with a few grains of salt. Even at the time, though, many opponents of the administration attributed Jackson's strategy to his "Kitchen Cabinet," an informal body of journalists, relatives, and longtime associates who had the president's

---

[43]Ibid., 66-67.
[44]Ibid., 53.
[45]Stickney, *Autobiography of Amos Kendall*, 376, 392.

confidence. Deriding a presidency under the sway of partisan hacks and hangers-on, the Washington *National Intelligencer* predicted that "the success of the Kitchen Cabinet . . . will be the downfall of the republic."[46]

Whatever the influence of Kendall and Blair (the nineteenth-century equivalent of cable news celebrities), this much is certain: in pushing for the rapid withdrawal of the federal deposits, Jackson ignored the opposition of Congress, of every member of his official cabinet save Taney, of his former campaign manager, his personal secretary, and his new vice president.

While Kendall and Blair pressed for the rapid removal of the deposits, Secretary of the Treasury Louis McLane offered the most cogent and comprehensive counter-argument in a lengthy memorandum to the president in May. Although McLane agreed that the BUS needed greater federal oversight, he opposed removal on four major grounds. The secretary began by flatly contradicting Jackson. The bank was undeniably constitutional. On that question he entertained "no doubt."[47]

Second, either the Bank of the United States or some similar institution was critical to the country's prosperity. The day was long past when the American economy could function solely with gold and silver as the medium of exchange. Paper currency was indispensable, and in the absence of a national bank it would come from "hundreds of different banks, acting without concert . . . and totally without controul and responsibility to Congress."[48]

Third, McLane was troubled by how federal monies would be handled if they were no longer deposited with the BUS. Echoing Kendall, Jackson had floated the suggestion that the government's money be distributed among a subset of approved state banks. McLane responded that state banks were typically less stable and less responsible than the BUS. They issued paper notes more aggressively, often far in excess of what they could actually redeem in gold or silver.

It followed that shifting the federal deposits to state banks would render the government's money less secure and the country's money supply less stable. McLane reminded Jackson that both a Treasury Department review in 1832 and the recently concluded House investigation had agreed that the government's money was secure in the BUS. Ignoring these findings would be hard to explain.

---

[46]Major L. Wilson, "The 'Country' Versus the 'Court': A Republican Consensus and Party Debate in the Bank War," *Journal of the Early Republic* 15 (1995): 620.
[47]Bassett, *Correspondence of Andrew Jackson*, 5:77.
[48]Ibid., 5:78.

Finally, although it was not an argument against removal per se, McLane reminded the president that, under the provisions of the 1816 act that created the Second Bank of the United States, only the secretary of the treasury was authorized to order the removal of the government's deposits. Any such decision, McLane added, ought to be "exercised in obedience to his sense of public duty, independently of the opinion of his colleagues."[49] McLane didn't connect the dots for the president, but Jackson understood him perfectly.

Nine days later Jackson reassigned McLane to the State Department. Historians disagree as to whether this was a calculated move to clear the path for removal, but at the very least it was convenient. As his replacement, Jackson chose William J. Duane, a prominent Jacksonian from Pennsylvania and an outspoken critic of the BUS. In contrast to McLane, Duane opposed the recharter of the bank and doubted that the institution was constitutional. Equally pertinent, he openly confessed to a "hereditary dislike of all privileged classes." Jackson didn't know Duane personally, but he concluded that he was a man marked by "purity of principle and politics." Translation: Duane agreed with him and would act accordingly.[50]

It didn't turn out that way. In late June, Jackson sent Duane a lengthy memorandum summarizing his position regarding the bank. Significantly, he began by explaining to the secretary the meaning of his recent reelection "by a decisive majority." It meant that "the people . . . approved the act of the President declaring the Bank to be both inexpedient and unconstitutional." Lest Duane miss the point, Jackson underscored that this was a decision "given by the *highest power known on earth*."[51]

In his veto message, Jackson had reserved the right to uphold the Constitution as *he* understood it in matters in which the opinion of "the people and the States" was not yet "well settled." Now he was asserting an exclusive prerogative to determine when the people had made up their minds. The people agreed with their president, Jackson insisted. Their opinion was now "well settled." It was the duty of all to "cheerfully submit."[52]

---

[49]Ibid., 81.
[50]William J. Duane, *Narrative and Correspondence Concerning the Removal of the Deposites, and Occurrences Connected Therewith* (Philadelphia, 1838), 82; Bassett, *Correspondence of Andrew Jackson*, 5:207.
[51]Bassett, *Correspondence of Andrew Jackson*, 5:113, italics added.
[52]Ibid.

Jackson concluded by sharing his opinion that it would be "just and wise" to order the removal of the government's deposits as rapidly as possible.[53] This was not a direct order, just the recommendation of the president of the United States in his role as the voice of "the highest power known on earth." Having made his position clear, Jackson surely assumed that his newest cabinet member would fall in line, and so he graciously ended his memorandum by assuring Duane that "it is not my intention to interfere with the independent exercise of the discretion committed to you by law over the subject."[54] He meant what he said, too—as long as Duane "independently" did what Jackson expected.

To Jackson's surprise, even though Duane was opposed to the recharter of the BUS, he was equally opposed to the removal of the government's deposits before the current charter expired. Like McLane before him, he worried that distributing the federal government's deposits among state banks would create new problems in the effort to solve others. Even worse for Jackson, Duane also took seriously the law's designation of the secretary of the treasury as the sole agent of the government who could order removal.

Should he do so, Duane knew that the law required the secretary of the treasury to explain his decision to Congress, and he realized that any rationale he might offer would be a lie. To order removal of the deposits "contrary to my own dispassionate conviction," Duane explained to Jackson, would be neither patriotic nor wise.[55] Surely the president would understand.

Jackson understood, all right. He understood that Duane's principles weren't as pure as he had reckoned. As he lamented to Vice President Martin Van Buren, he had inadvertently appointed a "secrete agent of the Bank" to his cabinet.[56] He wasn't kidding. Jackson had a gift for seeing conspiracies. He was willing to give Duane a little time to prove him wrong, but not much, and the secretary's persistent defiance convinced the president that Duane, too, had been bought up by the Monster.

In the end, Duane would have to be removed as well. Unwilling to wait any longer, on the eighteenth of September Jackson convened the cabinet and announced that it was time to remove the federal deposits from the bank. On the nineteenth he authorized the Washington *Globe* to announce the change in policy and dispatched an assistant to ask Duane if he was willing to comply. After

---

[53]Ibid., 115.
[54]Ibid., 113.
[55]Duane, *Narrative and Correspondence*, 81.
[56]Bassett, *Correspondence of Andrew Jackson*, 5:206.

a "long and occasionally animated" conversation with the general, an enraged Duane hand-delivered his formal refusal to the White House on the twenty-first. Among its many flaws, the secretary wrote, the president's order was "a breach of public trust" and appeared "vindictive and arbitrary."[57]

Jackson rested the next day, a Sunday, and then fired Duane on Monday morning. Shortly after breakfast he informed Duane by messenger that "your further services as Secretary of the Treasury are no longer required." Within minutes he had appointed Attorney General Taney as Duane's replacement. Within hours he was gloating in a letter to Van Buren that "the business of the Treasury is progressing as tho Mr. Duane had never been born."[58]

This time Jackson left nothing to chance. Taney was unequivocally a man of "sterling" character: he had pledged *in advance* to order the removal of the deposits if the president instructed him to do so.[59] The Senate would reject his formal appointment as Treasury secretary when they reconvened that winter, but not until after Taney, acting in an interim capacity, had fulfilled his one assigned task. Before leaving office, Jackson would reward his loyal subordinate by appointing him Chief Justice of the Supreme Court. We remember Taney today, if we remember him at all, as the architect of the most infamous judicial ruling in US history, *Dred Scott v. Sandford*.

Shortly after his abrupt dismissal from the cabinet, William Duane warned a correspondent that the president of the United States had "sanctioned the doctrine of the enemies of free government." Two tenets of this doctrine were key: "that the people are incapable of protecting themselves, and that their representatives have their prices." What followed, Duane maintained, was predictable: Jackson had concluded "that all virtue is in himself, and that without him the republic would perish."[60] Duane was understandably angry at Jackson at this point, but his assessment is not far off. To protect the people, Jackson sought to undermine popular confidence in the government and make the power of the president the paramount force in Washington.

This, too, is a classic characteristic of populism. Populist movements, by definition, are dissatisfied with the status quo, and this means that populist movements, by definition, are disenchanted with the current government. As a result, they are regularly drawn to strong leaders who promise to clean house and make

---

[57]Duane, *Narrative and Correspondence*, 101, 104-5.
[58]Bassett, *Correspondence of Andrew Jackson*, 5:206, 207.
[59]Ibid., 204.
[60]Duane, *Narrative and Correspondence*, 152.

the government more responsive to the people. While the Founders would teach us to be *suspicious* of power as a threat to liberty, populism teaches us to have *faith* in power, as long as it's exerted on behalf of the people by the champion of the people.[61] Knowing that he was virtuous, Andrew Jackson was willing to serve in that role.

Jackson's firing of Duane and removal of the deposits in opposition to Congress and the Treasury Department initiated the final phase of the Bank War. Until Congress reconvened, the main shots would be fired behind the scenes by Biddle and Jackson directly. Neither protagonist comes off looking noble.

Facing the likelihood that the BUS would soon lose its largest depositor, Biddle sharply curtailed the bank's loans, cutting back on new loans and calling in existing ones. Such a policy eventually would have been unavoidable, but it's clear that an angry Biddle acted quickly and aggressively in part to give the country a painful foretaste of life without the BUS. "Nothing but the evidence of suffering abroad will produce any effect in Congress," he explained to an ally, blind to how his strategy would only reinforce concerns about the bank's power.[62]

For his part, Jackson carried through with his determination to prove that neither the government nor the economy required a national bank. Resolved to have all federal monies out of the BUS before Congress reconvened, the president completed arrangements with a number of state banks to accept the government's deposits. Toward that end, in August he had sent Amos Kendall on a tour of eastern banks to identify institutions with both the willingness and the resources to accommodate a massive infusion of government funds.

At the time, Jackson had assured then-Secretary Duane that the selection of these "deposit banks," as they were officially known, would "be made without the slightest respect to persons or parties." In reality, the hyperpartisan Kendall openly admitted that he sought banks controlled by "politically friendly" financiers. Jackson either didn't know or didn't care.[63]

Critics ridiculed the deposit banks as "pet banks," and with good reason. Eventually, the number of deposit banks grew to over ninety, and almost every one was headed by a loyal "Democrat," the label pro-Jackson men were

[61]Nash, "How Should Conservatives Respond?," 8.
[62]Remini, *Jackson and the Bank War*, 127.
[63]Bassett, *Correspondence of Andrew Jackson*, 5:137; Remini, *Jackson and the Bank War*, 117.

increasingly adopting for themselves. In combating the supposed corruption of Congress by the Bank of the United States, Jackson had stumbled on a lucrative form of party patronage.

Even as the president was rewarding faithful Democrats, his handling of the removal of the deposits was propelling the formation of a rival political party. No single action did more to solidify opposition to his presidency. Around the country, anti-Jackson rallies condemned the general's "despotic influence" and disregard for the rule of law. They accused him of "presidential encroachment" and "executive usurpation." They charged him with encouraging his misguided followers to replace "love of liberty" with "devotion to a man."[64]

In the seventeenth century, English opponents of absolute monarchy had called themselves Whigs, and a century later American patriots who opposed George III had proudly taken the name as well. Now Jackson's critics could think of no more appropriate label for their new party. By designating themselves Whigs, the anti-Jackson coalition was charging the president with an abuse of power. They were warning the country that the greatest threat to their liberty was not the "Monster" in Philadelphia but the monarch in Washington.

After reconvening in December, Whigs in the Senate mounted a campaign to rebuke the president more formally. Henry Clay led the way. "We are in the midst of a revolution," Jackson's nemesis warned his fellow senators, "rapidly tending towards a total change of the pure republican character of our government, and to the concentration of all power in the hands of one man." (Jackson retorted that Clay was as "reckless and as full of fury as a drunken man in a brothel.")[65]

Clay mocked Jackson's claim that his reelection justified his highhanded tactics. Was it really true that whatever opinions Jackson had expressed before his reelection were now automatically the law of the land? "I had supposed that the Constitution and the laws were the sole source of executive authority," the senator observed. After extended debate, the Senate voted 28-20 to approve Clay's resolution that Jackson had exercised power over the federal monies "not granted to him by the Constitution and laws, and dangerous to the liberties of the people."[66] The resolution remains the only formal censure of the president by a house of Congress in history.

---

[64]Duane, *Narrative and Correspondence*, 139, 157, 159, 140.
[65]Remini, *Jackson and the Bank War*, 138; Bassett, *Correspondence of Andrew Jackson*, 5:249.
[66]Remini, *Jackson and the Bank War*, 138; Stickney, *Autobiography of Amos Kendall*, 394-95.

To no one's surprise, Jackson responded with a formal, blistering protest (written primarily by his new attorney general, New Yorker Benjamin F. Butler). In its twenty-five pages, Jackson condemned the Senate's action on three main grounds. To begin with, it was unconstitutional. The resolution of censure, nowhere formally authorized in the Constitution, was in fact tantamount to impeachment, yet the constitutionally stipulated procedure for impeachment had been ignored.

Second, Jackson insisted that his own actions had been eminently constitutional. It's not entirely clear what this was supposed to prove. Remember the rule Jackson had laid down in his bank veto message: "Each public officer who takes an oath to support the Constitution swears that he will support it as *he* understands it." For Jackson now to defend his withdrawal of the deposits as constitutional meant nothing more than that he had acted consistently with the Constitution as *he* chose to interpret it.

But by the same principle, the Senate had every right to view the president's actions as an abuse of power as *they* understood the Constitution. They were equally justified in maintaining that the Constitution, as *they* understood it, allowed them to pass a resolution of censure that was distinct from an act of impeachment. If Jackson understood the implications of his axiom, he ignored them, and it's hard to view his constitutional argument as anything but a convenient rationale for presidential prerogative.

Finally, and most importantly, Jackson condemned the Senate's actions as undemocratic. He began by repeating the mantra that his opposition to the bank had been affirmed by "the solemn decision of the American people." He noted further that four senators who supported his censure had disregarded instructions from their state legislatures to support removal. (He forgot to mention the flood of pro-BUS petitions the Senate had also received.) Above all, Jackson argued that no act of Congress should ever give a cabinet official authority independent of the president because of the president's unique relationship with the people. Unlike the cabinet secretaries, Jackson observed, "The President is *the direct representative of the American people.*"[67]

No US president had ever made such a claim before. As the Framers of the Constitution conceived it, the only segment of the government charged with representing the people directly was the House of *Representatives* (hence the name). They didn't assign this role to the Senate, nor to the judiciary, and

---

[67]Richardson, *Messages and Papers of the Presidents*, 3:1288, 1309.

emphatically not to the executive, whom they went to great pains to separate from popular influence. And implicit in Jackson's claims was a series of embedded implications. In making the claim that he was the direct representative of the whole people, he was above all reminding other federal officeholders that they were not. The president, and the president alone, would be the voice of "the highest power known on earth."

The Downfall of Mother Bank. Andrew Jackson holds aloft his decree requiring the removal of federal deposits from the Second Bank of the United States, while the bank's advocates—including Nicholas Biddle, shown with horns and cloven hooves—flee in terror.

So what are we to make of the Bank War? What might we learn from it?

To begin with the most obvious, it underscores the degree to which Jacksonian democracy upended the Framers' convictions about human nature and the dangers of power. Could they have read Jackson's veto message, they would have smelled a "demagogue" who manipulates public passions in order to build a personal following and gratify personal ambition. "Of those who have overturned the liberties of republics," Publius warned the country in the very first *Federalist* essay, "the greatest number have begun their career, by paying an obsequious court to the people, commencing demagogues and ending tyrants."[68]

---

[68]Alexander Hamilton, *Federalist* #1, 3.

Jackson would have denied the charge of demagoguery, of course—and threatened to shoot anyone who made it. I won't argue that he consciously manufactured popular outrage for selfish purposes, although he undoubtedly benefited from it. It's possible that deep down he was coldly calculating, but I'm inclined to think he was just thoughtlessly reckless. But however we assess Jackson's motives, this much is undeniable: In 1787, the Framers of the Constitution would have denounced Jackson's rhetoric as dangerous to liberty. In 1832, a comfortable majority of Americans reelected him president.

And what did they receive in return? The short-term results were not promising. If the Bank War teaches us anything, it's that successful populist leaders don't always bring more power to the people. Sometimes they just amass more power for themselves. Bluster aside, the dismantling of the BUS did nothing for the "humble members of society." However, it was a boon to countless bankers, to the fledgling Democratic Party, and to Andrew Jackson most of all.

Even as the People's President echoed the Founders' axiom that power is a threat to liberty, Jackson charted a strategy to defend liberty that led directly to an increasing concentration of power: his *own*. The Framers of the Constitution believed that power was a threat to liberty *regardless* of who wields it. Jackson invited the people to trust him—and only him—as he wielded unprecedented power on their behalf.

Old Hickory didn't proclaim that "I alone can fix it," as Donald Trump declared to the Republican National Convention in 2016.[69] But he did assert presidential prerogatives that threatened to demolish the separation of powers and checks and balances that the Framers wove into the Constitution to protect against tyranny. His example was the exception among executives until well into the twentieth century, but there's no question that our first populist president cast the mold for today's imperial presidency.

At the time, Whig leaders in Washington cautioned voters that the country was becoming an "elective monarchy" in which "the will of one man alone prevails."[70] Their warnings were probably overstated, and to some degree, they were surely politically motivated. But out west, an unknown state legislator would soon offer a more compelling critique.

Less than a year after Jackson left office, twenty-eight-year-old Abraham Lincoln spoke to the Young Men's Lyceum of Springfield, Illinois, on the topic

---

[69]"Full text: Donald Trump 2016 RNC Draft Speech Transcript," Politico, July 21, 2016, www.politico. com/story/2016/07/full-transcript-donald-trump-nomination-acceptance-speech-at-rnc-225974.
[70]Stickney, *Autobiography of Amos Kendall*, 396.

of "the perpetuation of our political institutions." The most serious threat to the American experiment in self-government did not come from a foreign invader, Lincoln told his small audience. "If destruction be our lot, we must ourselves be its author and finisher," Lincoln warned. "As a nation of freemen, we must live through all time, or die by suicide."[71]

The "strongest bulwark" of the constitutional framework bequeathed by the Framers is "the *attachment* of the People," Lincoln observed. Conversely, our free institutions are never more vulnerable than when the public has concluded that the government will neither protect them nor promote their interests. In such an environment, Lincoln cautioned, the majority may eventually conclude— recklessly, emotionally—that any change is better than no change since "they imagine they have nothing to lose."[72]

In the Bank War, Andrew Jackson told the American people that their government had been co-opted by the enemy—the Monster and its allies—and that he alone could be trusted to protect them from disaster. And then as he assaulted the constitutional checks and balances that the Framers had instituted to protect their liberty, a majority of the electorate applauded him as their champion and rewarded him with another term.

Both Lincoln and the Framers worried that the people might be susceptible to a demagogue. They didn't so much fear that a figure with "a thirst for distinction" and a contempt for the rule of law would stage a violent coup. Their real nightmare was that the people might voluntarily reward their perceived defender with ever more power, gradually but fatally forfeiting their own freedom.

Andrew Jackson didn't eventually crown himself king—although a Whig cartoonist famously portrayed him in royal robes—but he did convince a critical mass of the American people to be more accepting of concentrated executive power. Out on the prairie, Abraham Lincoln identified this as a threat to democracy. Across the Atlantic, Alexis de Tocqueville recognized it as a possible expression of democracy.

---

[71]Abraham Lincoln, *The Collected Works of Abraham Lincoln*, ed. Roy P. Basler, 8 vols. (New Brunswick, NJ: Rutgers University Press, 1953–1955), 1:108, 109.
[72]Ibid., 111.

Alexis de Tocqueville

PART FOUR

"I CANNOT REGARD YOU AS A VIRTUOUS PEOPLE"

A Conversation with Alexis de Tocqueville

WHEN ALEXIS DE TOCQUEVILLE ARRIVED in the United States, Andrew Jackson was beginning his third year in the White House, Congress had recently passed the Indian Removal Act, and the Bank War was just over the horizon. It was a dynamic time in early American democracy, and it was a determination to understand "democracy itself"—not America per se—that propelled the young Frenchman on a thirty-seven-day voyage from his homeland to the United States.[1] Tocqueville's insights aren't the last word, but the questions he posed are penetrating and his conclusions will challenge us if we're willing to listen to him.

"At its best," historian David Harlan writes, the study of the past can be "a conversation with the dead about what we should value and how we should live."

---

[1] Alexis de Tocqueville, *Democracy in America*, ed. Olivier Zunz (New York: Literary Classics of the United States, 2004), 15.

I love that metaphor of *conversation*. We peer into the past in order to see the present more clearly and to think about it more deeply, but we don't have to do our thinking alone. Part of the high cost of our present-mindedness is that it shuts out "the clean sea breeze of the centuries"—the best that has been thought and said across the ages.[2] History can serve as a mirror, helping us to see ourselves more clearly, but ideally it is also a form of conversation across time about the questions that endure. When it comes to thinking about democracy, it's hard to imagine a better conversation partner than Alexis de Tocqueville.

But listening to the dead requires that we read what they wrote, and that can be a sticking point where Tocqueville is concerned. The late journalist Russell Baker once judged Tocqueville the most frequently cited of the "great unread writers."[3] We relish quoting him—nothing adds more gravitas to a tweet—but actually slogging through *Democracy in America* is another matter.

Tocqueville's magnum opus is long, complicated, and demanding, written by a thinker who couldn't care less about entertaining us. No one reads Tocqueville for the jokes and anecdotes, trust me. The man reveled in complexity. He was obsessed with precision. He qualified every generalization that he offered. He packed his prose so densely that if our minds wander for a sentence, we miss something vital. And he did all this, relentlessly, for nearly nine hundred pages.

So we quote him without reading him, inventing a fictional Frenchman who gushed that "America is great, because she is good." And even when the quote is exposed as phony, we cling to its sentiment as the essence of Tocqueville's message. Popular writer Eric Metaxas, for example, acknowledges that the quote is bogus but insists that it remains a "brilliant summation" of *Democracy in America*. "The rest of the book," Metaxas maintains, shows that Tocqueville "saw clearly that it was the 'goodness' of America's people that made America work. For him it was inescapable: *The secret to American freedom was American virtue.*"[4]

It's hard to imagine a worse summation of *Democracy in America*.

Learning that Americans *weren't* virtuous was one of the most important discoveries Alexis de Tocqueville made while in the United States. There's no question he found much to admire. Within a month of arriving, he wrote to

---

[2]David Harlan, *The Degradation of American History* (Chicago: University of Chicago Press, 1997), xviii; C. S. Lewis, Introduction to Saint Athanasius, *On the Incarnation* (Crestwood, NY: St. Vladimir's Seminary Press, 1996), 5.

[3]Russell Baker, "Off the Top of de Tocq.," *New York Times*, November 26, 1976, 23.

[4]Eric Metaxas, *If You Can Keep It: The Forgotten Promise of American Liberty* (New York: Viking, 2016), 59.

his father that the population of the United States was "one of the happiest in the world." By "happy," Tocqueville didn't mean that Americans were content. Few of them were, in his opinion. What he meant was that (white) Americans were blessed in manifold ways: by unusual prosperity, social harmony, and extensive freedom.[5]

Over time he added to this list of the country's advantages. Few Americans were truly learned, but the rank and file were better educated than their counterparts in Europe. This made the American people, overall, "the most enlightened on earth." And although he determined that democracy "does not give the people the most skillful government," he found that it encourages widespread popular interest in politics and public policy. More broadly, "it spreads throughout society a restless activity, a superabundant strength, an energy that never exists without it."[6] These are positives.

But Tocqueville came to believe that none of these blessings had much to do with virtue. "I cannot regard you as a *virtuous* people," Tocqueville bluntly informed American diplomat Joel Poinsett, underlining "virtuous" to emphasize his point. Like the Framers of the Constitution, Tocqueville defined virtue as the sacrifice of personal interest in the service of the common good. Even though he consciously searched for it, he found little evidence of such self-denial during his stay.[7]

This puzzled him because he had come to the United States assuming that a republic required virtue to endure. What he encountered in America defied this law. "The Americans are not a virtuous people," he mused to himself, "and yet they are free." It would take years to make sense of this, but one implication seemed obvious right away. "Virtue," he scrawled in his notebook, "is not . . . the only thing that can maintain a republic."[8]

What intrigued Tocqueville most about the United States was always, then, this conundrum: Americans aren't virtuous, yet "the democratic republic in the United States continues to exist."[9] In the following two chapters we'll listen closely as he grapples with it.

---

[5]Alexis de Tocqueville, *Letters from America*, ed. Frederick Brown (New Haven, CT: Yale University Press, 2010), 53.

[6]Tocqueville, *Democracy in America*, 349, 280-81.

[7]Olivier Zunz, ed., *Alexis de Tocqueville and Gustave de Beaumont in America: Their Friendship and Their Travels*, trans. Arthur Goldhammer (Charlottesville: University of Virginia Press, 2010), 286.

[8]Arthur Schlesinger Jr., "Individualism and Apathy in Tocqueville's Democracy," in *Reconsidering Tocqueville's Democracy in America*, ed. Abraham S. Eisenstadt (New Brunswick, NJ: Rutgers University Press, 1991), 96; Zunz, *Tocqueville and Beaumont in America*, 354.

[9]Tocqueville, *Democracy in America*, 319.

As we do so, we'll need to remember Tocqueville's warning that "an idea that is clear and precise even though false will always have greater power in the world than an idea that is true but complex."[10] If that was the case in Tocqueville's day, how much more does it hold for our sound-bite culture with its ever-dwindling attention span? We demand simple answers to complicated questions. We "value confidence and aggression more than truth." We punish any public figure who doesn't play along.[11]

But you and I can choose a different path. In our angry, dogmatic, polarized present, one of the most patriotic things we can do for our country, one of the most loving things we can do for our neighbors, is to reject simplistic answers and pursue truth in all its complexity. Listening closely to Alexis de Tocqueville can be a good place to start, but don't expect him to praise our virtue. Far from an ode to American goodness, *Democracy in America* is an extended reflection on how *fallen* people can sustain a free government. That, more than any other reason, is why we desperately need to pay attention.

From across the centuries, Tocqueville reminds a present-minded people that democracy doesn't automatically produce moral outcomes. To a culture steeped in democratic faith, he insists that democracy can undermine liberty as well as expand it. And to a society given to idols, he calls on us to renounce *faith in* democracy and nurture *hope for* democracy instead.

---

[10]Ibid., 186.

[11]Ed Stetzer, *Christians in the Age of Outrage: How to Bring Our Best When the World Is at Its Worst* (Carol Stream, IL: Tyndale Momentum, 2018), 22.

PUNCTURING FAITH
IN DEMOCRACY

*I*t can be a daunting task to find the essence of Alexis de Tocqueville's message to us today. The scope of *Democracy in America* seems boundless. The author investigates the relationship between democracy and political institutions, civic culture, social justice, religious belief, family relations, individualism, educational practices, literature, theater, warfare, and oratory. He even assesses democracy's effect on popular attitudes about history. (It isn't good.) But always his greatest concern, the question that haunts and compels him, is the relationship between democracy and liberty. If democracy is the wave of the future, what will be the future of liberty and human dignity in a democratizing world?

Tocqueville's answer is one long, complicated, "It depends." If *Democracy in America* has a central thesis, I'd locate it in the book's final sentence, where the author tells us that democracy can result in "servitude or liberty, enlightenment or barbarism, prosperity or misery." But if our goal is to make sense of his ambivalent conclusion, a good place to start would be a few lines higher up on the page. "Having reached the end of my journey," Tocqueville writes, "I can now see, all at once but from afar, the various objects that I contemplated separately along the way, and I am full of fears and hopes."[1]

Full of fears and hopes. I'm convinced that this concise confession is the key to understanding *Democracy in America*. It captures Tocqueville's state of mind, and it summarizes how he hoped to affect *us*. So if our goal is to enter into conversation with him, to invite Tocqueville to talk with us about "what we

---

[1]Alexis de Tocqueville, *Democracy in America*, ed. Olivier Zunz (New York: Literary Classics of the United States, 2004), 834.

should value and how we should live," a simple way to frame our conversation would be to ask him two questions: With regard to democracy's impact on liberty and human dignity, what do we have to fear? With regard to democracy's impact on liberty and human dignity, what grounds do we have for hope? We'll pose the first of these questions in the current chapter and the second in the chapter to follow.

It's fitting that we begin with Tocqueville's fears. It's not a coincidence that he alludes to "fears and hopes" on the book's final page rather than "hopes and fears." His fears were stronger and he stressed them more. His premise, he tells us in the introduction to volume two, is that advocates of democracy will be quick to proclaim its benefits, "but few will dare warn of the perils that it holds in the offing. I have therefore focused primarily on those perils."[2] In the long run Tocqueville wants to encourage us, but first he is compelled to warn us.

His warnings are as timely today as when he first penned them.

Before we dive into *Democracy in America*, you should know a bit more about the author. It's possible, I suppose, to enter into a deep conversation with a total stranger, but I think it will help as you assess what you're hearing to have a sense of where he was coming from, why he was writing, and why his perspective might be valuable.

Let's start with the basics. His full name was Alexis Charles Henri Maurice Clerel de Tocqueville. He was twenty-five years old when he arrived in the United States, the third son of a French count, wealthy and well educated, privileged and precocious. A colleague remembered him as "a small, slight man with an agreeable, regular, but sickly face." His "mass of curly brown hair," which might otherwise have given him a youthful appearance, was offset by "sad, unanimated features" and a "livid pallor." He was reserved in public and hated chitchat. He loved to think, to observe, to ask questions, and then to think some more.[3]

Officially, he and colleague Gustave de Beaumont were on a mission from the French government to study American penitentiaries, but Tocqueville admitted afterward that "the penitentiary system was a pretext." Privately, he and

[2]Ibid., 480.

[3]Alexis de Tocqueville, *Letters from America*, ed. Frederick Brown (New Haven, CT: Yale University Press, 2010), 2; George Wilson Pierson, *Tocqueville in America* (Baltimore: Johns Hopkins University Press, 1938), 656.

Beaumont always envisioned a much grander project: to make sense of "a whole new world unfolding before our eyes."[4]

They began that work the moment their ship dropped anchor at Newport, Rhode Island, in early May 1831. For the next nine and a half months they were "the world's most ruthless questioners," Tocqueville boasted to his family back home. They visited seventeen states, slept in grand hotels and frontier cabins, collected reams of documents and books, and conducted interviews with over two hundred prominent and not-so-prominent Americans.[5]

The pair ended their American tour prematurely in February 1832, when the French government abruptly ordered them home. At that point Tocqueville left the penitentiary report to Beaumont and embarked on what historians sometimes call his "second voyage to America," a virtual one in which he revisited the country in his mind.[6] For nearly eight years he read voraciously, pored over his notebooks, and struggled to make sense of all that he had seen and heard. He finished volume one of *Democracy in America* in 1835 and the second volume five years later. Both were translated almost immediately into English, and the consolidated work has remained continuously in print ever since.

Beyond these rudimentary details, there are crucial aspects of Tocqueville's background and personality that you also need to know. To begin with the most obvious, the democratic culture he encountered in the United States was utterly foreign to him. The author of *Democracy in America* was neither American nor democratic. He was a French aristocrat, and in the pages of *Democracy in America* he speaks to us across chasms of time, place, and class. Tocqueville grew up in a villa with sixteen bedrooms, a mirrored drawing room, and a private theater, among other amenities, and his first thought upon landing in Newport was that the townspeople lived in houses "no larger than chicken coops."[7]

In other words, he speaks to us with an "outsider's perspective," and that's an advantage he has over us.[8] I noted in the introduction how difficult it is to think deeply about cultural values and patterns that haven't changed during our lifetimes. Because we see them as natural, we stop *seeing* them at all, and what we can't see, we can't think about carefully, much less Christianly. As an outsider to

---

[4]Olivier Zunz, ed., *Alexis de Tocqueville and Gustave de Beaumont in America: Their Friendship and Their Travels*, trans. Arthur Goldhammer (Charlottesville: University of Virginia Press, 2010), 563; Tocqueville, *Letters from America*, 53, 70.
[5]Tocqueville, *Letters from America*, 62.
[6]Leo Damrosch, *Tocqueville's Discovery of America* (New York: Farrar, Strauss, and Giroux, 2010), 194.
[7]Tocqueville, *Letters from America*, 18.
[8]Damrosch, *Tocqueville's Discovery of America*, 204.

the culture he was scrutinizing, Tocqueville saw a lot that Americans in his time, and ours, find invisible.

Even though Tocqueville wasn't one of "us," he always believed that he could learn from us, and this humility is another quality that commends him. When prominent Europeans visited Jacksonian America, they often came to gawk and sneer. Harriet Martineau and Charles Dickens wrote at length of how Americans butchered the English language, ate their meals like hogs at a trough, and showered "the floors of boarding-houses and the decks of steam-boats" with "tobacco-tinctured saliva." Fanny Trollope wrote a blistering condemnation of Americans in which she concluded, "I do not like them. I do not like their principles. I do not like their manners. I do not like their opinions."[9]

In contrast, Tocqueville came to the United States hungry for insights that might benefit his native France. Granted, he privately harbored much of the aversion to American manners that disgusted Trollope and company. He could never grow accustomed to "the casualness that prevails here," he confessed to a friend after watching an attorney pick his teeth while questioning a witness in court. He was "baffled by the sheer quantity of food that people somehow stuff down their gullets," and he could only describe the music at New York City soirees as "caterwauling." Being forced to listen to such racket was bad enough. Having to pretend to enjoy it was a form of "moral violence."[10]

What distinguished Tocqueville was the ease with which he looked past these features. They were "of superficial importance," he explained to his mother. What mattered was how much he could learn from these human beings who, for all their "unbuttoned" manners, weren't all that different from those on the other side of the Atlantic. "We are all eyes and ears," he told his family back home. "Our minds are constantly straining for the acquisition of useful knowledge."[11]

To this humility and zeal for knowledge, Tocqueville added a scrupulous fairness that is all the more remarkable because he was writing for a time and place as contentious as our own—namely, France of the 1830s. Since 1789, France had careened from absolute monarchy to democracy to dictatorship to a conservative constitutional monarchy to something marginally more democratic.

---

[9]Harriet Martineau, *Society in America*, edited, abridged, and with an introduction by Seymour Martin Lipset (New Brunswick, NJ: Transaction Publishers, 2005), 279; Charles Dickens, *American Notes for General Circulation* (London: Chapman & Hall, 1842), 65; Fanny Trollope, *Domestic Manners of the Americans* (1832; repr., New York: Penguin, 1997), 314.

[10]Tocqueville, *Letters from America*, 80, 24, 83.

[11]Ibid., 221, 27, 44.

The country was divided among radical democrats, arch royalists, and every shade of political conviction in between. To make things worse, the warring factions regularly alluded to the supposed strengths and weaknesses of American democracy to support their predetermined positions, and they looked to Tocqueville's assessment of America for vindication.

Tocqueville refused to oblige them. He wanted his analysis to be useful to his homeland—that was his primary motivation, actually—but he bristled at the prospect of his painstaking analysis being hijacked in the service of a particular political or religious faction. And so he refused to write as a partisan, fully realizing that many in his immediate audience would regard this as "the major defect of my book."[12]

Finally, you need to know that, although Alexis de Tocqueville was not "one of us," he was decidedly *for* us. One product of his tour of the United States was a heartfelt affinity for this strange, new democratic land. Fully twenty years after his visit, Tocqueville confided to an American friend that he considered himself "almost a citizen, so strong is my desire that your country prosper and become a great nation." Only two years before his death, he revealed to another, "I ardently wish that America's great experiment in self-government will not fail. If it were to fail, that would be the end of political liberty on this earth."[13]

But the American experiment *could* fail—that's precisely his point—which is why Tocqueville emphasized candor above compliments. "It is because I am not an enemy of democracy that I sought to deal with it in a sincere manner," he explains in the introduction to volume two. And so if Tocqueville was, by his own reckoning, "quite severely critical" of democracy in the United States, he was a *sympathetic* critic.[14]

Tocqueville opens *Democracy in America* by alerting his readers to a "great democratic revolution" sweeping across the West. For seven hundred years, he explains, "the Christian world" had been experiencing a slow but inexorable "universal leveling." The trend had begun with the decline of feudalism, and it was accelerating with the further weakening of monarchy and aristocracy. At its heart was "the gradual and progressive development of equality." Its culmination would be the triumph of "democracy."[15]

---

[12]Tocqueville, *Democracy in America*, 17.
[13]Zunz, *Tocqueville and Beaumont in America*, 603-4, 615.
[14]Tocqueville, *Democracy in America*, 480.
[15]Ibid., 3, 6, 5, 7.

Recognize that what Tocqueville labels democracy is much broader than a set of political practices that facilitate majority rule. Granted, he insists that "in a democracy nothing resists the majority," but democracy as he conceives it is always more all-encompassing than the process of self-government alone. The basic input of democracy is a "social state" characterized by comparative equality of condition and pervaded by a "passion for equality" in all facets of life.[16]

This is what Tocqueville found when he visited the United States, that country of all the countries in the world in which the democratic revolution was most advanced. "Among the new things that attracted my attention," he relates in the very first sentence of volume one, "none struck me more forcefully than the equality of conditions."[17]

A word of warning before we go on: From our twenty-first-century perspective, we may find Tocqueville's description of the United States bewildering, even offensive. Was it proper to characterize the United States as the most democratic nation on earth and to marvel at the country's level of equality when women lacked property rights and the vote, most blacks were enslaved, and Native Americans were being systematically driven from their ancestral homes?

Tocqueville was acutely aware of the condition of all three groups, and while he accepted the exclusion of white women from politics as natural and appropriate, he was unsparing in his condemnation both of slavery and of the removal of Native Americans, as we shall see. The key to making sense of Tocqueville's overall analysis is understanding that it is relentlessly comparative. Whether explicitly or (more often) implicitly, he was always measuring the United States against Europe, and compared with Europe, the distribution of property in the United States was broader, the range between rich and poor was narrower, and upward mobility was more common. Focusing on the country's free white population, Tocqueville goes so far as to assert that Americans in 1831 were "more equal in fortune and intelligence . . . than they are in any other country, or were at any other time in recorded history."[18]

And there was no denying that white men in Jacksonian America *loved* equality. Indeed, they *demanded* it—for themselves. The inhabitants of a less democratic society will accept hierarchy as natural, but white men recoiled from it in disgust. Equality was "the principal and constant object of their desire."[19] In

---

[16]Ibid., 283, 60.
[17]Ibid., 3.
[18]Ibid., 59.
[19]Ibid., 60.

contrast to the long-standing pattern in his homeland, in the United States white men *thought* of themselves as equal rather than assuming that some were naturally superior and born to rule.

By Tocqueville's reckoning, the vibrant political democracy of Jacksonian America—the exaltation of the will of the majority—was merely the logical extension of this mindset into the realm of politics. This is because democratic societies naturally extend their "theory of equality . . . to intelligence." In aristocratic societies—where inequality and deference are the norm—men and women "are naturally inclined to take the superior reason of a man or class as a guide for their opinions, while they are disinclined to recognize the infallibility of the masses." In democratic societies "the contrary is the case."[20]

In democracies, Tocqueville explains, citizens come to view deference to any individual as demeaning. They resent authority, devalue expertise, and scorn all individual claims of superior intelligence or wisdom. At the same time, they develop an "almost unlimited confidence in the judgment of the public" on the grounds that, "everyone being equally enlightened, truth should . . . lie with the greater number." This gives the majority "absolute sway" and makes majority rule "the very essence of democratic government."[21]

Tocqueville isn't just observing that in democratic societies the majority wields great power. He's stressing that the majority wields *moral* power. In a true democracy "nothing resists the majority," in large measure because in a true democracy the "moral ascendancy of the majority" is unchallenged. "We may anticipate that faith in common opinion will become a sort of religion," Tocqueville observes in volume two, "with the majority as its prophet."[22]

What is Tocqueville telling us here? He's predicting that democratic *faith* will be a standard feature of democratic societies. As we've observed more than once, this isn't inevitable. As C. S. Lewis reminded us, it's possible to advocate democracy on two very different grounds: because we have confidence in human nature or because we don't. Tocqueville is arguing that democratic societies will tend naturally to the former, to what Lewis called the "false, romantic doctrine of democracy."[23]

This is what Tocqueville claimed to find in the United States, at any rate, and it distressed him. We've invented a Frenchman who rhapsodized over American

---

[20]Ibid., 284, 491.
[21]Ibid., 491, 283.
[22]Ibid., 283, 285, 492.
[23]C. S. Lewis, "Membership," in *C. S. Lewis: Essay Collection and Other Short Pieces*, ed. Leslie Walmsley (London: HarperCollins, 2000), 336-37.

202 PART FOUR | "I CANNOT REGARD YOU AS A VIRTUOUS PEOPLE"

goodness. What Tocqueville actually discovered, and that almost immediately, was that Americans *thought* they were good. In part, this reflected a patriotism that refused to acknowledge national flaws. Americans "reckon themselves superior in many ways," Tocqueville reported in a letter home only five days after his arrival in the United States. "People here seem to reek of national pride."[24]

Tocqueville's initial impression that Americans tended to think too highly of themselves never faded. "For fifty years the inhabitants of the United States have been told repeatedly that they constitute the only people that is religious, enlightened, and free," he observes in *Democracy in America*. "They therefore have a very high opinion of themselves, and they are not far from believing that they constitute a distinct species within the human race."[25] (When's the last time you heard that in a campaign speech?)

But Americans' "perpetual self-adoration" also reflected a broader belief in human nature that Tocqueville found striking as well. In *Democracy in America*, Tocqueville reveals the key to the majority's moral authority: it was the near-universal assumption that human beings, when well informed, will "act justly and honestly." Its foundation was "a strong belief in human perfectibility."[26]

This, too, had been conspicuous from the beginning. Seven weeks into his tour of the United States, Tocqueville wrote a lengthy description of Americans' "beliefs" to a cousin back in France. Two stood out to him particularly. Along with an unshakable confidence in "the excellence of their government," Americans professed "faith in man's good sense and wisdom, faith in the doctrine of human perfectibility." Such views were so ubiquitous, he informed his cousin, that he was "hard pressed to find skeptics."[27]

But Tocqueville was one. He came to the United States without democratic faith and never converted. Aspects of his personal background and beliefs surely help to explain why. It is supremely relevant that he was not only *French* but a French *aristocrat*. "I did not write a single page without thinking of France," Tocqueville confided to a friend years afterward, "or without having France in a manner of speaking before my eyes."[28]

This vision reminded him daily that democracy could express "savage instincts." The French Revolution had begun as an assault on aristocracy and

[24]Tocqueville, *Letters from America*, 23-24.
[25]Tocqueville, *Democracy in America*, 432.
[26]Ibid., 295, 432.
[27]Tocqueville, *Letters from America*, 87, 88.
[28]Zunz, *Tocqueville and Beaumont in America*, 587.

monarchy, but it had ultimately demonstrated "how a people could organize an immense tyranny within even as they freed themselves from the authority of nobles and braved the power of all kings."[29] As the people had hoped, the first fruit of the Revolution had been liberty, but then liberty had been undermined by anarchy before being swallowed up by tyranny and terror. To full-throated cries of "*Liberté! Egalité! Fraternité!*" the guillotine had murdered thousands, and mob violence tens of thousands.

Tocqueville's family did not survive unscathed. Nine of his relatives, including both of his parents, were among those sent to fetid dungeons in the name of the citizens of France. Although his parents escaped the guillotine, five of his relatives did not. Alexis himself wasn't born until a decade later, but his parents were psychologically scarred for the rest of their lives, and Tocqueville grew up with perpetual reminders of his family's ordeal.

And so it is no surprise when, in the very first chapter of *Democracy in America*, the author confesses that the "irresistible revolution" sweeping across the West fills his soul with "a kind of religious terror."[30] This was not hyperbole. Tocqueville knew in his gut that democracy can end in tyranny as well as liberty. Its moral consequences aren't inevitably just.

Tocqueville's understanding of human nature reinforced this basic insight. If democratic outcomes aren't reliably just, it's because humans aren't reliably virtuous and discerning. In *Democracy in America*, he observes that men and women invariably harbor a combination of "good instincts" and "wicked inclinations," but our dominant motive is simple self-interest. "Private interest controls most human actions." It's "the interest of the moment" that "rules" us. Self-interest is "the principal if not the sole motive of human action."[31]

Have you heard anything like this before? Tocqueville sounds for all the world like the Framers of the US Constitution, doesn't he? And like the Framers, Tocqueville's view of human nature persuaded him that power is always a threat to liberty and justice. This probably seems obvious under a monarchy or dictatorship, but Tocqueville is warning us that it holds no less true for a democracy.

The mantra of monarchy, that "the king is never wrong," and the dogma of democracy, that "the people are always right," are *both* false. To assert either "is to speak the language of a slave."[32] Human nature is no different in a democracy

---

[29]Tocqueville, *Democracy in America*, 8, 815.

[30]Ibid., 7, 6.

[31]Ibid., 282, 593, 304, 613.

[32]Zunz, *Tocqueville and Beaumont in America*, 307; Tocqueville, *Democracy in America*, 288.

than in any other social state, Tocqueville insists. None of us can be trusted with power as individuals, and our character doesn't improve when we become part of a majority, regardless of what the politicians seeking our votes may tell us.

Tocqueville already held to this view when he arrived in the United States. What surprised him during his stay was the realization that power could be just as concentrated in a democracy as in an absolute monarchy, indeed even more so. "My chief complaint against democratic government as it has been organized in the United States is not that it is weak," he explains, "but rather that its strength is irresistible."[33]

In his native France, monarchists regularly condemned democracy as tantamount to anarchy. They couldn't have been more wrong, Tocqueville maintains. To drive home his point, he repeatedly likens the American majority to a European monarch. The majority's political power is "irresistible." Its "moral ascendancy" is unquestioned.[34] What king on his throne could ask for more?

Tocqueville labels this concentration of power "the omnipotence of the majority." *Omnipotence* is his term for unlimited power. We need to distinguish it from *tyranny*, which is his label for cruel or unjust oppression. So defined, omnipotence isn't intrinsically unjust, but it's always intrinsically dangerous. This may be the single most important point that Tocqueville wants us to hear: in a democratic society, "the *omnipotence* of the majority" can readily become "the *tyranny* of the majority."[35]

The reason is simple. Agreeing with the Framers of the Constitution, Tocqueville believed that we're neither reliably good nor wise. "Only God can be all-powerful without danger," Tocqueville reminds us, "because his wisdom and justice are always equal to his power." In all other instances, unlimited power is "a bad and dangerous thing." It matters little whether it is wielded by a king, a dictator, or a popular majority. In unlimited power "lies the seed of tyranny." Always.[36]

By Tocqueville's reckoning, the majority in Jacksonian America possessed near limitless power in two respects. On the one hand, it possessed "immense *actual* power." Due to its influence at the ballot box, the majority dictated the overall course of public policy and controlled the coercive apparatus of the state.

---

[33]Tocqueville, *Democracy in America*, 290.
[34]Ibid., 284.
[35]Ibid., 283-91.
[36]Ibid., 290.

But it also enjoyed "a power of *opinion* that is almost as great," informally shaping popular values and establishing the boundaries of acceptable belief. As Tocqueville conceives them, "actual power" controls behavior, while "power of opinion" constrains thought. The first operates primarily on the body. The second "goes straight for the soul."[37]

While it's tempting to celebrate the majority's power in Jacksonian America as the hallmark of a robust democracy, Tocqueville would have us shudder instead of cheer. He warns us in no uncertain terms that "the consequences of this state of affairs are dire and spell danger for the future."[38] But what about in the meantime? Did Tocqueville actually find instances of tyranny in Jacksonian America or was his warning purely hypothetical, exaggerated perhaps by memories of the guillotine and the frenzy of revolutionary France?

As always with Tocqueville, the answer is complex. We can hear him apparently assuring us that the Jacksonian majority was omnipotent but *not* tyrannical. Indeed, in the section of volume one headed "Tyranny of the Majority," Tocqueville seems to state this explicitly. "I am not saying that recourse to tyranny is frequent in America today," he clarifies, "only that no guarantee against it can be found."[39]

Wrenched from its context, this quote not only holds out hope for democracy in the long run—something Tocqueville very much wanted to do. It can also be heard as an assertion of American exceptionalism. It seems to imply that the American majority had proved Tocqueville wrong by consistently pursuing justice even while wielding unchecked power. This was decidedly not Tocqueville's goal. When it comes to what it tells us about human nature, *Democracy in America* always warns more than it congratulates.

In context, when Tocqueville observes that "recourse to tyranny" is infrequent in Jacksonian America, what he's actually saying is that the *white* majority rarely exercises its "actual power" to tyrannize over other *whites*. With the exception of a single protracted chapter at the end of volume one, *Democracy in America* is tacitly an analysis of democracy among whites in America. Unfortunately, Tocqueville fails to make this explicit until we've read nearly four hundred pages.

He narrows his focus in this way for two reasons. First, recall Tocqueville's confession that he "did not write a single page without thinking of France." Toward the

---

[37]Ibid., 285 (italics added), 294.
[38]Ibid., 285.
[39]Ibid., 291.

end of volume one, he acknowledges that he has ignored the experience of "Indians and Negroes" in order to concentrate on what was generically "democratic" in the United States as opposed to what was particularly "American." As important as the topic was, it was of "tangential" relevance to his French countrymen.[40]

Second, Tocqueville informs us in a footnote that he doesn't want to compete with the work of his good friend and traveling companion, Gustave de Beaumont. After completing the report on American penitentiaries for the French government, Beaumont had begun work on a book that "seeks primarily to make French readers aware of the situation of Negroes vis-à-vis the white population in the United States." Beaumont's book will be published shortly, Tocqueville explains, and "goes into depth about an issue that my subject allows me only to touch on."[41] *Marie, or Slavery in the United States* would appear the same month as volume one of *Democracy in America*. Unfortunately, Beaumont trapped its penetrating racial analysis inside a mediocre novel, and almost no one remembers it today.

Tocqueville momentarily dropped his reticence at the end of volume one and crafted a lengthy chapter on "the present state and probable future of the three races that inhabit the territory of the United States." Twenty-first-century readers will cringe at some of his language, which reflects the ethnocentrism that most human beings have exhibited for most of human history. Native Americans are self-evidently "savage." Blacks are self-evidently "inferior." "The white man" is "man par excellence" and ranks above the other races "in enlightenment, power, and happiness."[42]

Yet Tocqueville is also unsparing in his indictment of the white majority. In the world's most democratic nation, "oppression has deprived the descendants of Africans of nearly all the privileges of humanity." "Oppression" similarly describes the fate of Native Americans. They are being driven from their ancestral homes, Tocqueville reports, by "the most civilized—and, I would add, the greediest—people on earth."[43]

Simply put, "Indians and Negroes" in the United States "both suffer the effects of tyranny" and both can blame "the same tyrant." In a devastating summation, Tocqueville extrapolates a larger pattern from his observations of the United States: "Might one not say that the European [Tocqueville's synonym

---

[40]Ibid., 365.
[41]Ibid., 392.
[42]Ibid., 365-68.
[43]Ibid., 366, 382.

for "the white man"] is to men of other races what man himself is to animals? He makes them serve his needs, and when he cannot bend them to his will, he destroys them."[44]

No, Alexis de Tocqueville did not conclude that "it was the 'goodness' of America's people that made America work."[45]

In its immediate context, Tocqueville's decision to bracket the experience of Native Americans and African Americans is understandable. It made sense given his French audience, and it honored the complementary work of his friend and colleague. In the long run, however, *we* would hear him more clearly if he hadn't done so. As it stands, his warning about the "tyranny of the majority" has an abstract, bloodless quality to it. It takes on flesh, we feel its weight, when we integrate the experience of more than two million Native Americans and enslaved blacks into his larger analysis.

Tocqueville's discussion of the plight of the Cherokees, for example, constitutes a powerful illustration of the vulnerability of the minority in a society where the majority reigns supreme. In his chapter on Jacksonian America's "three races," Tocqueville leaves no doubt of his opinion that the tribe can be "civilized." He notes their written language, stable form of government, and impressive newspaper (copies of which he took back to France), and he concludes that they have already "demonstrated as much natural genius as the peoples of Europe."[46]

But—and this is an important qualification—"nations, like men, need time to learn, however intelligent and industrious they may be." Although the Cherokees were steadily progressing from "barbarism" to "civilization," they needed more time if they were to match the white majority in "enlightenment, power, and happiness."[47] Until then, they would be vulnerable.

The problem was that the white majority wouldn't afford the Cherokees the time they needed, and the reason for this was obvious, Tocqueville believes: what they really wanted was the Cherokees' land, not their assimilation. However much they might dress it up in the garb of legality, however much they might

---

[44]Ibid., 366.
[45]Eric Metaxas, *If You Can Keep It: The Forgotten Promise of American Liberty* (New York: Viking, 2016), 59.
[46]Tocqueville, *Democracy in America*, 381, 385.
[47]Ibid., 385.

justify it in the language of benevolence, what lay at the bottom of "Indian removal" was a combination of greed and the power to act on it. And as James
Madison had posited a half century earlier, "Wherever there is an interest and
power to do wrong, wrong will generally be done."[48]

Earlier in volume one, Tocqueville had tried to illustrate the danger posed by
an omnipotent majority by inviting readers to imagine an individual who has
been mistreated in some way. "To whom can he turn?" Tocqueville asks. How
can he seek redress except by throwing himself on the mercy of the majority?
This is the case if he seeks justice through the legislature, for it "represents the
majority and obeys it blindly." Ditto if he appeals to the executive, whom the
majority elects as "its passive instrument." The same is even true if he seeks
justice through the courts, since juries consist of members of "the majority invested with the right to pronounce judgment."[49]

The Cherokees' struggle was still ongoing when Tocqueville completed
volume one, but from hindsight we can see that Tocqueville's thought experiment is like a checklist of the tribe's strategy after the passage of the Indian
Removal Act. To whom could they turn, indeed?

The Cherokees had done their best indirectly to put pressure on Congress,
with Elias Boudinot turning out editorials in the *Phoenix* and leaders like John
Ridge speaking in churches and lecture halls across the Northeast. Cherokee
delegations had also directly lobbied lawmakers in Washington, while John Ross
and the Cherokee council had blanketed both Congress and President Jackson
with written memorials and appeals. And of course they had hired one of the
country's foremost attorneys to plead their case before the Supreme Court.

In the end they hadn't succeeded, and what Tocqueville wants us to see is that
this was predictable, maybe even inevitable. With the white majority against
them, there was simply no failproof safeguard against injustice. In effect, the
Cherokees were living out Madison's maxim in *Federalist* no. 51: "If a majority be
united by a common interest, the rights of the minority will be insecure."[50] We
can imagine ways to have protected the Cherokees' rights, but as long as the
majority of the country supported removal, any solutions we might think of
would share one trait in common: they would have thwarted the will of the
majority. By Tocqueville's reasoning, that would make them undemocratic.

---

[48]James Madison to Thomas Jefferson, 17 October 1788, Founders Online, National Archives,
https://founders.archives.gov.
[49]Tocqueville, *Democracy in America*, 290.
[50]James Madison, *Federalist #51*, in Alexander Hamilton, James Madison, and John Jay, *The Federalist*, ed. J. R. Pole (Indianapolis: Hackett, 2005), 282.

For example, we might fantasize for a moment and see Andrew Jackson in our mind's eye, face livid with righteous indignation and fist raised to heaven as he swears "by the Eternal" that he will personally lead an army into Georgia to protect the Cherokee and uphold the Constitution. (This is more or less how he did respond in 1832 when the state of South Carolina threatened to disregard federal tariff laws.) But we need to recognize that, in behaving so heroically in defense of the Cherokees, it's very likely that Jackson would have been contradicting the will of the white majority, not to mention his own desire. It would have been undeniably courageous. The Founding Fathers would have called it virtuous. But we should hesitate to call it "democratic."

Just as the Cherokees' experience vividly illustrates the unlimited "actual power" of the white majority, the racial attitudes that Tocqueville describes at the end of volume one constitute a telling example of the majority's "power of opinion." Except for two extended stays in the nation's capital, Tocqueville and Beaumont spent little time during their American tour in areas where slavery was still legal by the 1830s. They had planned an extended foray into the plantation South, but they had to cancel those plans when the French government abruptly cut their travels short.

But if they had comparatively little opportunity to observe black bondage in the slave states, they had abundant opportunity to observe white racism in the free states. "Racial prejudice seems to me stronger in the states that have abolished slavery than in those where slavery still exists," Tocqueville reports in his conclusion to volume one, "and nowhere is intolerance greater than in states where servitude was unknown."[51]

The result, as Tocqueville describes it, is that a black man in the North is legally free, but by custom "he cannot share the rights, pleasures, labors, or sorrows—not even the tomb—of the person whose equal he has been declared to be." More to the point, any *white* person—not to mention any individual of color—who dared to challenge this racial hierarchy would be met with "a kind of horror" and, quite probably, with physical violence.[52]

Here Tocqueville anticipates much of the argument of Beaumont's *Marie, or Slavery in the United States.* The protagonist in this sentimental novel is a beautiful, chaste young mulatto woman living in Baltimore, Maryland. The great, great granddaughter of an enslaved woman (of 1/32 African descent, in other

---

[51]Tocqueville, *Democracy in America*, 395.
[52]Ibid., 396.

words), Marie easily passes for white, but she lives in constant fear that her secret will be exposed and her life ruined.

When this predictably comes to pass, a sympathetic character rails against public opinion as "the cruelest of tyrants when it persecutes." The narrator echoes this lament, condemning the "prejudice . . . which dominates America, with no voice raised against it." For his part, Tocqueville commends *Marie* to "anyone interested in knowing the tyrannical excesses to which men may gradually be impelled."[53]

These "tyrannical excesses" assaulted the mind as much as the body. A king's power is purely material, Tocqueville observes, but in a democracy the majority's power of opinion is "moral as well as material." It "erects a formidable barrier around thought," discouraging dissenting views on questions about which the majority has made up its mind. The result is devastating to the life of the mind, and Tocqueville pulls no punches in denouncing it: "I know of no country where there is in general less independence of mind and true freedom of discussion than in America."[54]

Tocqueville is not claiming that those who contradicted the majority in Jacksonian America would be violently silenced, although Jacksonian mobs were not infrequent. To use a recent catch phrase, he is describing an oppressive "cancel culture" that rigorously enforces reigning orthodoxies. Tocqueville contends that all but the most courageous individuals will voluntarily police themselves, respecting the lines that the majority forbids them to cross. It will require extraordinary strength of character to "believe what the masses reject and to profess what they condemn."[55]

No one who wanted to be accepted in society, for example, would openly criticize Christianity or Christian morality. No one with ambitions for political office would publicly doubt the innate wisdom and goodness of the people. And no one with hopes for social acceptance, public office, or physical safety would advocate true racial equality. As a fictional Frenchman remarks bitterly in *Marie*, "In America, the black race submits to the sovereignty of hatred and scorn. Everywhere, I found this tyranny of the people's will."[56]

---

[53]Gustave de Beaumont, *Marie, or, Slavery in the United States* (1835; repr., Baltimore: Johns Hopkins University Press, 1999), 77, 71; Tocqueville, *Democracy in America*, 392.

[54]Tocqueville, *Democracy in America*, 293.

[55]Ross Douthat, "Ten Theses About Cancel Culture," *New York Times*, July 14, 2020; Tocqueville, *Democracy in America*, 758.

[56]Beaumont, *Marie*, 77.

Five years later, Alexis de Tocqueville added to his list of democracy's potential dangers. Near the very end of volume two of *Democracy in America*, he warns readers of a different kind of tyranny, if *tyranny* is the right word. He has in mind a softer, subtler oppression than the "tyranny of the majority" he had written about at length in volume one, not an oppression that democratic majorities impose on a vulnerable minority but a loss of liberty that they willingly accept for themselves.

In the end, the wordsmith Tocqueville was unable to craft a precise definition of the danger he alludes to, so he settles for describing it at length. He begins by picturing a typical democratic society in time to come. He sees an "innumerable host" of individuals, "all alike and equal, endlessly hastening after petty and vulgar pleasures with which they fill their souls. Each of them . . . is virtually a stranger to the fate of all the others. For him, his children and personal friends comprise the entire human race." Tocqueville labels this decay of community "individualism," and he believes that it is a predictable if not inevitable feature of democratic society.[57]

This is dreary enough, but Tocqueville's greater concern is how this multitude of lonely strangers might relate to their government. In his mind's eye he imagines standing over them

> an immense tutelary power, which assumes sole responsibility for securing their pleasure and watching over their fate. . . . It works willingly for their happiness but wants to be the sole agent and only arbiter of that happiness. It provides for their security, foresees and takes care of their needs, facilitates their pleasures, manages their most important affairs, directs their industry, regulates their successions, and divides their inheritances.

Its liberty gradually, imperceptibly, inexorably eroding, the nation is in the end reduced to "nothing but a flock of timid and industrious animals, with the government as its shepherd."[58]

Volume two of *Democracy in America* differs so significantly from its predecessor that we might consider it an entirely separate book, as we would surely do if Tocqueville had stuck with his original plan for the book's title. Not long

---

[57]Tocqueville, *Democracy in America*, 818.
[58]Ibid., 818-19.

before it went to press, Tocqueville told the British philosopher John Stuart Mill that his forthcoming work would be titled *The Influence of Equality on Man's Ideas and Sentiments*.[59] He abandoned the title at the last minute—perhaps to capitalize on the popularity of volume one—but it's an accurate description of the volume's actual contents.

As the original title hints, volume two differs from volume one in crucial respects. Thematically, Tocqueville shifts his primary focus from politics to culture. Spatially, he broadens his view to include Europe as well as the United States. Volume one is concretely rooted in Jacksonian America, as Tocqueville extrapolates on what he observed in the United States to form conclusions about democracy more generally. In volume two he theorizes at length about democracy in general and turns frequently to Jacksonian America for examples.

The version of tyranny that Tocqueville describes in volume two is *not* one of those examples. He's predicting, not describing. If he eerily foretells major features of the United States in the 2020s—in particular the feebleness of civil society and the boundless reach of government—he is not describing what he actually observed during the 1830s. In Jacksonian America, individuals were "constantly joining together in groups" to work toward common goals. And while the central government was powerful in matters pertaining to the whole country, it otherwise allowed localities to "manage their own affairs unfettered." Underlying both features was Americans' widespread belief that they should overcome most of "life's woes and impediments" without governmental aid.[60]

We live in a different world, don't we?

Note that the soft tyranny that Tocqueville warns us about is not forcibly imposed on a democratic society by some outside power. In the scenario that he imagines, the people meekly submit to their own servitude, not consciously or all at once but as the result of a series of transactions in which they progressively exchange portions of their liberty for goods that they value more highly.

Remember Tocqueville's declaration that his "one passion" was the "love of liberty and human dignity"? He's insinuating here that few of us share his passion, at least not when it's inconvenient. As in the Old Testament story of Esau, the man favored of God who exchanged his birthright for a bowl of stew when he was hungry, Tocqueville fears that we're inclined to sell our liberty cheaply.[61]

---

[59]Zunz, *Tocqueville and Gustave de Beaumont in America*, 583.
[60]Tocqueville, *Democracy in America*, 595, 215; Tocqueville, *Letters from America*, 109.
[61]Genesis 25:29-34.

I'll reiterate here that, as a Christian, I don't consider liberty our highest goal or greatest good. It's definitely not an *absolute* good, meaning it's not intrinsically wrong to forfeit a part of it in exchange for something else. In truth, we have no choice—unless we're content to live our lives alone in a cave. (Of course, if we could find a cave with Wi-Fi, we might be willing to do that.) Society is inconceivable apart from restraint, and living in society requires that we accept tradeoffs in which we swap a portion of our liberty for other benefits that society affords. Having said that, as a Christian I also view liberty as a blessing never to be taken for granted, and this demands that we think long and hard about the tradeoffs we accept.

Some are more defensible than others. To cite a prime example, a strong case can be made that it is appropriate to limit liberty, at least in the short run, to ward off great danger or potential calamity. During the First and Second World Wars, for instance, Americans accepted conscription, taxation, rationing, wage and price controls, government takeover of key industries, and extensive limitations of First Amendment rights and invasions of privacy as the legitimate price of national survival. More recently, many Americans (though far from all) acquiesced to a host of limitations on their daily routines as necessary to curb the spread of Covid-19.

During the debate over the Constitution, Alexander Hamilton succinctly characterized such transactions as an exchange of liberty for safety. "Safety from external danger is the most powerful director of national conduct," he observed in *Federalist* no. 8. "To be more safe" during times of protracted danger, nations "become willing to run the risk of being less free."[62] A half century later, Tocqueville observed something similar in volume one of *Democracy in America*. When nations are embroiled in major wars, he notes, they ultimately conclude that they must increase the powers of government if they are to survive. When they do so, they intentionally risk despotism because they fear defeat more.

We might disagree on the specifics of the tradeoff, but most of us can imagine a scenario in which we could justify exchanging some portion of our liberty in return for some increase in safety and security. We would surely argue over the details of the exchange, but few of us would *absolutize* liberty. It's the rare bird who would rather die in a terrorist attack than allow the government to scan our luggage at the airport.

---

[62]Alexander Hamilton, *Federalist* #8, 37.

It's not just that we can all imagine a scenario in which it is *reasonable* to exchange a measure of our liberty for something else. We can all imagine a scenario in which it is *right* to do so, in which doing so is essential to the common good, a selfless expression of love of country or love of neighbor. To use the language of the Founding Fathers, we can imagine circumstances in which forfeiting a measure of our liberty is *virtuous*.

But we're not virtuous by nature, and Tocqueville's warning about soft tyranny reminds us of that. Because we're fallen, a powerful majority pursuing its self-interest may oppress the minority. But Tocqueville also wants us to see that, because we're fallen, a powerful majority pursuing its self-interest can also gradually forfeit its own liberty. He envisions a servitude in which "each individual allows himself to be clapped in chains."[63]

Tocqueville predicts that a democratic people will embrace soft tyranny out of a love of comfort, convenience, and immediate gratification. Self-government is difficult. "Nothing is harder than the apprenticeship of liberty." In theory, we desire to remain free, but in practice it is easier to be led, and so we consciously gravitate not toward tyrants but "protectors."[64] The danger is that they can turn out to be one and the same.

The lure of this Faustian exchange is all the more seductive because we are shortsighted as well as self-interested. A people who have never known oppression can become blind to liberty's benefits. Then when challenges come, as they invariably will, the temptation to sell their liberty cheaply will be great, as the short-term advantage of doing so will seem to outweigh the costs. As Tocqueville explains, "Despotism often presents itself as the remedy for all ills suffered in the past. It is the upholder of justice, the champion of the oppressed, and the founder of order. Nations are lulled to sleep by the temporary prosperity to which it gives rise, and when they are awake, they are miserable."[65]

This has been a chapter about Tocqueville's fears. I'd like to close it by sharing a fear of my own, if you'll allow me to speak candidly. I fear that Tocqueville's warnings will fall on deaf ears. I can imagine this happening in three ways: We might simply dismiss Tocqueville entirely. We might listen to him selectively. We might understand him superficially. All three responses would be tragic.

---

[63]Tocqueville, *Democracy in America*, 819.
[64]Ibid., 275, 819.
[65]Ibid., 275.

Tocqueville, for his part, originally doubted that we would listen to him. Realizing that he was often "severely critical" of America, he predicts in volume one that his American readers "will speak out to condemn me."[66] In truth, if we're at all proud of our country, it isn't easy to hear Tocqueville claim that Jacksonian Americans were "the greediest people on earth," that they were given to "tyrannical excesses," that they systematically oppressed one-seventh of the country's population. Who does this arrogant Frenchman think he is?

None of us likes criticism, and our temptation is to respond to it defensively. While that's our natural inclination in the best of times, we live in a cultural moment that magnifies it beyond measure. One of the unintended consequences of the rise of social media is how it's enabled us to withdraw into cocoons of the like-minded. With an abundance of news sources to choose from, we can build custom-tailored "information bubbles" that shield us from alternative perspectives. Barricaded within the echo chambers of our choice, we "experience whatever version of reality we prefer."[67] And because we no longer have to take alternative perspectives seriously, we gradually forget how to respond to criticism constructively. It's an unnatural skill. When we don't practice it, we lose it.

Compounding the problem is our hyperpartisan political climate. "I often say harsh things," Tocqueville conceded to John Stuart Mill in describing *Democracy in America*, "but I say them as a friend."[68] Today's politicians and pundits would sneer and call Tocqueville a liar. By their example, they teach us relentlessly that there is no such thing as a sympathetic critic, a principled political opponent, or a true friend who dares to question our judgment.

We hear instead that those who differ with us politically are extremists or idiots, "socialists" or "racists," "enemies of America" or "traitors" who "hate our country."[69] Listening to them respectfully is a form of moral compromise. Denouncing them unmercifully is an expression of righteous conviction. From

---

[66]Ibid., 480, 297.

[67]Sophia Rosenfeld, *Democracy and Truth: A Short History* (Philadelphia: University of Pennsylvania Press, 2019), 153; Sean Illing, "The Post-Truth Prophets," *Vox*, November 16, 2019, www.vox.com/features/2019/11/11/18273141/postmodernism-donald-trump-lyotard-baudrillard.

[68]Zunz, *Tocqueville and Gustave de Beaumont in America*, 583.

[69]"Amid Multiple Crises, Trump and Biden Supporters See Different Realities and Futures for the Nation," Public Religion Research Institute, October 19, 2020, www.prri.org/research/amid-multiple-crises-trump-and-biden-supporters-see-different-realities-and-futures-for-the-nation; Edward-Isaac Dovere, "Joe Biden Names His Enemies," *The Atlantic*, June 2, 2020, www.theatlantic.com/politics/archive/2020/06/bidens-trump-speech-and-real-enemies-america/612550/; "Trump Attacks Cummings' District," *Chicago Tribune*, July 28, 2019, section 1, 2.

across the years, Tocqueville warns us that such a mindset is disastrous for democracy and fatal to liberty. "Faithful are the wounds of a friend," the book of Proverbs tells us.[70] If you love liberty and human dignity, consider Tocqueville a friend. You don't have to agree with him, but please listen to him.

But I beg you not to listen *selectively*, which is actually a second way to dismiss him. As it turned out, Tocqueville was overly pessimistic about the reception of *Democracy in America*. "I please many people of conflicting opinions," Tocqueville marveled to a close friend shortly after the publication of volume one. This was "not because they understand me," he hastened to explain, "but because they find in my work, by considering it only from a single side, arguments favorable to their passion of the moment."[71]

His contemporaries were good at "cherry-picking," in other words. So are we. It's tempting to treat *Democracy in America* as a handy collection of standalone quotes for every occasion rather than as an extended, integrated argument by a single author. When we give in to that temptation, however, the voice we hear is no longer truly Tocqueville's. It's an echo of our own.

Let me generalize broadly. If we tend toward the liberal end of the political spectrum, we may agree with Tocqueville when he denounces the removal of Native Americans and castigates white racism. But since we're more likely to be enthusiastic about government activism, we may be inclined to pass over Tocqueville's warning about soft tyranny and the dangers of a suffocating paternalism. No sense in complicating his message.

Conversely, if we gravitate toward more conservative political views, we'll likely cheer when Tocqueville condemns creeping governmental power and its capacity to degrade those it protects. At the same time, we may reflexively dismiss his warning about the oppression of marginalized groups as political correctness or "wokeness," and his caution about the tyranny of the majority as so much liberal elitism.

Both responses make Tocqueville into a ventriloquist's puppet who mouths what we want to hear. I'm not arguing that if we accept *anything* Tocqueville says that we have to accept *everything*. Every human argument, no matter how wise, is leavened with a mixture of error. But I am reminding us that Tocqueville viewed democracy as a package deal, and he was convinced that the

---

[70]Proverbs 27:6.
[71]Roger Boesche, ed., *Alexis de Tocqueville: Selected Letters on Politics and Society* (Berkeley: University of California Press, 1985), 99-100.

true friend of democracy must be prepared to combat its dangers as well as bask in its blessings.

But even when we purpose not to dismiss Tocqueville out of hand, or to listen to him selectively, we can still miss the deeper truth embedded in his message: the potential for popular majorities to inflict oppression and injustice—on others or on themselves—will ever remain one of democracy's features. This is democracy's greatest peril, and the more we disregard it, the more perilous it becomes.

We'll miss this deeper truth as long as we hear Tocqueville's message under the influence of *democratic faith*, the dogma that there is nothing wrong with democracy that more democracy won't correct. We'll miss this deeper truth as long as we hear Tocqueville's message as converts to the *democratic gospel*, the welcome news that we are individually good and collectively wise.

Make no mistake: because he rejects the democratic gospel, Tocqueville is resolved to puncture our democratic faith. But he does so in order to replace it with something more modest, more sustainable, and more consistent with human nature. We've heard about Tocqueville's fears. Now let's listen to his hopes.

— 8 —

NURTURING HOPE
FOR DEMOCRACY

By now you may have concluded that Alexis de Tocqueville is not the most encouraging conversation partner. In his defense, Tocqueville told us up front that the rise of democracy filled him with "a kind of religious terror."[1] His fears for the future of democracy are great, and when we listen to him, *really* listen to him, our hearts should pound and our chests grow tight. But don't give up on him. Tocqueville really does have words of hope to share with us.

Be forewarned, however: Tocqueville's words of hope may not be as reassuring as we'd prefer. That's because we've been indoctrinated to abhor complexity. The all-or-nothing rhetoric of our polarized politics won't allow it. We're subjected to a torrent of perpetual hyperbole. Every contest for the presidency becomes an "Armageddon showdown," a "battle for the soul of America," a "Flight 93" emergency in which we must storm the cockpit or die trying. Civilization hangs in the balance. We teeter on the brink between triumph and catastrophe, either gloriously preserving all that we hold most dear or taking the "first step into a thousand years of darkness."[2]

---

[1]Alexis de Tocqueville, *Democracy in America*, ed. Olivier Zunz (New York: Literary Classics of the United States, 2002), 6.

[2]Eric Metaxas, foreword to David Brody and Scott Lamb, *The Faith of Donald J. Trump: A Spiritual Biography* (New York: HarperCollins, 2018), ix; Matthew Choi, "'Democracy Prevailed': Biden Urges Unity as He Condemns Efforts to Overturn Election," Politico, December 14, 2020, www.politico.com/news/2020/12/14/biden-election-coronavirus-attention-445216; Publius Decius Mus [Michael Anton], "The Flight 93 Election," *Claremont Review of Books*, September 5, 2016, http://claremont.org/crb/basicpage/the-flight-93-election; Paul Waldman, "Republicans Accuse Majority of Americans of Hating America," *Washington Post*, January 9, 2020, www.washingtonpost.com/opinions/2020/01/09/republicans-accuse-majority-americans-hating-america/.

The populist strand in our contemporary politics reinforces this do-or-die narrative. The evils that assail us are great. The battle to overcome them will be fierce. But once "the people" recognize our true enemies and mobilize to defeat them, then the clouds will lift and our dreams will become reality. After all, no social ill is truly complicated. All that's required is to "drain the swamp" or "dump Trump" and then apply the fixes that common sense commends. The struggle to vanquish our foes may be ugly and bitter, but once we have conquered them, the solutions to our problems will be simple and easy.[3]

Tocqueville has no patience with such fairy tales. It's not that he doubts that the stakes are high. No one has thought them higher. Democracy can end in "servitude or liberty, enlightenment or barbarism, prosperity or misery."[4] What he wants to purge from our minds (and hearts) is the misguided belief that the dangers that assail us lie wholly outside of us. As long as democracy remains an expression of who we are, the perils that most threaten a democratic society are inseparable from democracy itself. They're features, not bugs, which is why faith in democracy is always misguided.

Yet hope for democracy is possible. As we've learned, Tocqueville's fears concerning democracy were born in inherited memories of the French Revolution. His hopes for democracy first took root during his visit to the United States. In Tocqueville's terminology, the white majority in Jacksonian America was *omnipotent*—its power was nearly unlimited. But it wasn't as *tyrannical* as he would have expected given the absence of reliable barriers against oppression. In this discrepancy lay the seed of hope.

Let's be clear about Tocqueville's discovery before going further. His conclusion was not that oppression was absent in Jacksonian America. As we heard in the last chapter, he leaves no doubt that both "Indians and Negroes" in the 1830s daily "suffer the effects of tyranny." That's upward of two million people, or roughly one-seventh of the population of the United States at the time. It's when Tocqueville narrows his focus to the white population that the grounds for his optimism emerge. Only then can he marvel that there is not a freer people to be found "anywhere in the world."[5]

Admittedly, the white male majority exercised an intellectual tyranny over public opinion, discouraging dissenting views on questions about which the

---

[3]Sophia Rosenfeld, *Democracy and Truth: A Short History* (Philadelphia: University of Pennsylvania Press, 2019), 99, 101.
[4]Tocqueville, *Democracy in America*, 834.
[5]Ibid., 366, 625.

majority had made up its mind (about white supremacy, for example). But Tocqueville saw no evidence of extensive physical intimidation against white men, or assaults on their property, or efforts to impose discriminatory laws designed to benefit a majority of white males at the expense of the remainder. For white men in Jacksonian America, the rise of democracy meant, on the whole, an expansion of liberty. This was hardly inevitable, and Tocqueville was determined to explain it.

From our twenty-first-century vantage point, the fact that Tocqueville's discovery applied only to white Americans may render it meaningless. Why be impressed because a group of whites a couple of centuries ago mostly limited their acts of oppression to people of color? The key for us lies in regaining Tocqueville's perspective; to understand what he argued, we must see as he saw.

To begin with, when Tocqueville contemplated the population of Jacksonian America, he was astounded at its diversity. Reflecting modern terminology, I've been casually referring to "whites" or "white men" as if they were an undifferentiated mass. Tocqueville was dumbfounded by what we so easily miss or forget. The United States that he visited was a country of immigrants.

Confessing to be "dazed" by what he saw, Tocqueville struggled to capture the difference in a letter to a close friend back home. "Imagine a society compounded of all the nations of the world," he related in wonder. "People each having a language, a belief, different opinions: in a word, a society lacking roots, memories, prejudices, habits, common ideas, a national character."[6] Race was only one of innumerable fault lines in such a society.

What is more, Tocqueville knew that, in his far more homogeneous homeland, Frenchmen had turned viciously against Frenchmen in the name of "liberty, equality, and fraternity." Democracy had unleashed its most "savage instincts," even though oppressor and victim were both the "offspring of a single family."[7] Nothing comparable seemed to be occurring in a far more heterogeneous Jacksonian America. Why was this? he wondered.

This brings us to the concrete question about the United States that Tocqueville wrestled with in volume one of *Democracy in America*: Given that self-interest is "the principle motive" of human behavior, and considering that the American majority exercised "irresistible" power, why was tyranny in the United

---

[6]Alexis de Tocqueville, *Letters from America*, ed. Frederick Brown (New Haven, CT: Yale University Press, 2010), 66.
[7]Tocqueville, *Democracy in America*, 8, 366.

States comparatively limited? Or to put the question another way, what had allowed white Americans to remain as free as they were? In listening to Tocqueville's explanation, we'll hear his answer to the question we purposed to ask him in this chapter—namely, "With regard to democracy's impact on liberty and human dignity, what grounds do we have for hope?"

Let's start with one possibility that we might think of that Tocqueville dismisses out of hand. If liberty is comparatively extensive in the United States, he's convinced that it has nothing to do with the quality of the country's current political leaders and political parties.

Tocqueville would be mystified by our habit of pinning our hopes on the victory of a particular candidate or party. He admires the energy of Jacksonian politics, and he finds that one of Jacksonian America's greatest strengths is the broad proportion of its citizens who seek to educate themselves on public issues and play an active role in shaping public policy. Without such grassroots activism, "self-government" is just a figure of speech. But Tocqueville is withering in his criticism of America's parties and politicians.

Some of this was probably instinctive and reflected views that predated his visit. Thomas Jefferson had condemned partisan loyalty as "the last degradation of a free and moral agent," and Tocqueville heartily concurred. "I could not march behind a party standard, no matter which one," he confessed in a letter to an old friend in the midst of his American tour. Parties consisted of mindless true believers and unscrupulous "rogues." As someone with a "mind and some scruples," he wouldn't fit in. Ouch. Tocqueville was more charitable in private. He conceded in his journal that "there are decent people in almost all parties," but he held to his conviction that "there is no party of decency."[8]

Nothing in his tour of the United States altered these views. In his chapter "Parties in the United States," Tocqueville distinguishes between "great" and "minor" parties. Great parties "dedicate themselves more to principles than to consequences." They are loyal to ideas, not to leaders. They have "generous passions" and "genuine convictions." Minor parties, in contrast, "do not feel

---

[8]Richard Hofstadter, *The Idea of a Party System: The Rise of Legitimate Opposition in the United States, 1780–1840* (Berkeley: University of California Press, 1969), 122-23; Tocqueville, *Letters from America*, 216; Olivier Zunz, ed., *Alexis de Tocqueville and Gustave de Beaumont in America: Their Friendship and Their Travels*, trans. Arthur Goldhammer (Charlottesville: University of Virginia Press, 2010), 342.

ennobled and sustained by any great purpose." Self-interest is their North Star, and "their tactics are squalid, as is the goal they set for themselves."[9]

You can decide for yourself whether today's Democratic and Republican parties qualify as "great" or "minor" parties according to these definitions. Tocqueville had no doubt of the answer in the 1830s: "America has had great parties in the past, but today they no longer exist."[10]

Tocqueville was particularly unimpressed by the leaders of these "minor" parties. European advocates of democracy often argued that free elections based on universal suffrage would reliably select worthy individuals for positions of leadership. "For my part," Tocqueville responds, "I must say that what I saw in America gives me no reason to believe that this is the case." In the most democratic nation on earth, talent was common among the people but rare among their leaders. As a general rule, "the most outstanding men are seldom called to public office."[11]

And why not? Part of the explanation lay in the people's capacity to select the best leaders, especially in national elections. It was necessarily limited, Tocqueville believes, not by their intelligence but by the limited time and information available for studying the issues and assessing the candidates. In an era when information was comparatively scarce and expensive, the time and information required to be a truly educated voter in state and national elections was a real barrier. "What a lengthy period of study and variety of ideas are necessary to form an exact idea of the character of a single man!" Tocqueville exclaims. "The greatest geniuses fail at this, yet the multitude is supposed to succeed!"[12]

But more important than the people's *capacity* to elect individuals of merit was their *desire* to do so—or more precisely, their lack of desire to do so. So strong was Americans' passion for equality that they detested all appearances of superiority in others, up to and including those they elected to office. "No form of superiority is so legitimate that the sight of it is not wearisome to their eyes," Tocqueville observes. "They do not fear great talents but have little taste for them."[13]

Echoing Tocqueville's assessment, Gustave de Beaumont has a character in *Marie* explain, "To please the American people one must be simple to the point

---

[9]Tocqueville, *Democracy in America*, 199.
[10]Ibid.
[11]Ibid., 225.
[12]Ibid., 226.
[13]Ibid., 226, 227.

of coarseness."[14] And so John Quincy Adams's education and expertise became liabilities. Henry Clay wore a coat full of holes to appear common. Today he would have worn a ball cap and peppered his public speeches with profanity.

Just as the electorate was rarely drawn to the most worthy, so the most worthy were less and less inclined to public service. In the same way that "the natural instincts of democracy lead the people to banish distinguished men from power, an instinct no less powerful leads distinguished men to shun careers in politics." The reason, according to Tocqueville, is that in a democracy "it is so very difficult to remain entirely true to oneself or to advance without self-abasement."[15] Translation: individuals with integrity don't rise to the top.

Those who *do* rise are like "courtiers," Tocqueville says. That's a calculated slap in the face that we're likely to miss because the term is foreign to us. His French audience would have gotten it immediately. A courtier was an individual who lived at the king's court, dined at the king's table, and flattered the king shamelessly as the price of those privileges.[16]

Jacksonian politicians didn't bow and scrape before an actual king, of course. They knelt at the feet of a democratic monarch: the voters on whose favor they depended. The result, Tocqueville thinks, was both tragic and pathetic. The leaders of the American founding had been "remarkable men," patriots characterized by "virile candor" and "manly independence of thought." A half century later, the political leaders of Jacksonian America were "lackeys" who told their "masters" whatever they wanted to hear. At bottom, they were "sycophants"—a nineteenth-century synonym for "toady" or "lickspittle."[17]

By Tocqueville's reckoning, in other words, the quality of American political leadership was in steep decline by the time of his American tour. In 1787, the Constitutional Convention "included the finest minds and noblest characters the New World had ever seen." Two generations later, American officeholders were "often inept and sometimes contemptible." Even the president of the United States was "a man of violent character and middling ability." For all his popularity, "nothing in his career demonstrates that he possesses the qualities required to govern a free people."[18]

---

[14]Gustave de Beaumont, *Marie, or, Slavery in the United States* (1835; repr., Baltimore: Johns Hopkins University Press, 1999), 100.
[15]Tocqueville, *Democracy in America*, 227.
[16]Ibid., 295-98.
[17]Ibid., 296, 297, 298.
[18]Ibid., 128, 268, 320.

This is one of those spots in *Democracy in America* where the temptation to cherry-pick can be overwhelming. To anyone frustrated with the partisan gridlock in Washington today—if opinion polls are correct, that's most of us—it can be fun to savor the abuse that Tocqueville heaps on politicians. They're sometimes "vile." They often lack "true patriotism." They "debase" themselves by pretending to be guided by principle rather than cowardice and ambition.[19] There's a slew of ready-made internet memes here, juicy quotes to circulate on social media as we look to the next election to "throw the bums out," "clean house," or "drain the swamp."

But let's stop again and be clear about what Tocqueville is saying. He's identifying a troubling trend—"over the past half century the race of American statesmen has singularly shrunk in stature"—but he's not pointing to it as evidence of the deterioration of American democracy. The stature of American statesmen was shrinking *at the same time* that the country was becoming *more* democratic. It gets worse. Tocqueville contends that the stature of American leaders had shrunk *because* the country had grown more democratic: "The steadily increasing effect of the despotism of the majority is, I believe, the chief reason for the small number of remarkable men in American politics."[20]

One of the dominant subtexts of drain-the-swamp crusades is that our leaders in Washington don't sufficiently mirror our values. They're captive to special interests and don't speak for us. And in large measure, that's often true. But Tocqueville's unwelcome message is that our leaders *do* mirror our values in important respects. For example, when we insist on simple answers to complex problems, we reward candidates who make simplistic promises. And so we end up either with officeholders who didn't understand the problem when we elected them—"who knew that health care was so complicated?"—or who were willing to deceive us to gain our votes. Pick your poison.

In the same vein, when we punish candidates who dare to tell us what we *need* to hear, we get officeholders who only tell us what we *want* to hear. Voters who are convinced that they're individually good and collectively wise won't recognize a difference between the two. Tocqueville, who rejects the democratic gospel, knows that the difference can be immense. But he also believes that the individual who dares to challenge the majority—a majority that basks

---

[19]Ibid., 297, 298.
[20]Ibid., 225, 296.

"in perpetual self-adoration"—has "no chance of a political career."[21] In the end, Tocqueville is pointing out that we punish political courage more than we reward it. It may crop up from time to time, but we shouldn't be shocked that it's rare, nor should we be surprised when we find cowardice in its place.

In 1787, James Madison expressed the hope that the proposed US Senate would consist of citizens "whose wisdom may best discern the true interest of their country, and whose patriotism and love of justice will be least likely to sacrifice it to temporary or partial considerations." The problem, Tocqueville believes, is that democratic societies "have little taste" for that type of leader.[22] If tyranny is relatively limited in Jacksonian America, the explanation lies elsewhere.

Tocqueville points instead to three broad factors, or clusters of factors, to account for the impressive extent of liberty in the United States. The least important of the three, though one that still contributed powerfully, is what he variously labels "circumstances," "physical causes," or more fully, "the peculiar, and accidental, situation in which Providence has placed the Americans."[23]

Chief among these is simple geography. One of the reasons that white Americans are so free, Tocqueville reasons, is that government is much smaller in the United States than among European nations, and the main reason it's smaller is geographical. As a Baltimore lawyer explained to Tocqueville, Americans "have no neighbors."[24] Canada and Mexico would have disagreed, of course, but you get his meaning. Neither country posed a threat to American security, and the United States was protected from the leading military powers of the time by a vast ocean. In the early nineteenth century this removed the most compelling rationale for a large government. Because of where God had situated them, Jacksonian Americans required neither a large army nor the high taxes required to sustain one.

A second crucial "circumstance" is the great natural resources that Americans enjoy. In the 1830s, the United States could boast more cultivable land relative to its population than any other nation in the world. All things equal, this made it easier for the average person to prosper, and that in turn made government more

---

[21]Ibid., 295, 293.

[22]James Madison, *Federalist* #10, in Alexander Hamilton, James Madison, and John Jay, *The Federalist*, ed. J. R. Pole (Indianapolis: Hackett, 2005), 52; Tocqueville, *Democracy in America*, 227.

[23]Tocqueville, *Democracy in America*, 319, 352, 353.

[24]Zunz, *Tocqueville and Beaumont in America*, 262.

stable and active government less necessary. (Americans' greater material prosperity meant less social conflict, and less social conflict meant less excuse for government to intrude on the people's liberties to ensure order and foster security.)
In the United States, Tocqueville marvels, "nature herself works for the people."
Or more precisely, "It was God himself who, by giving them a boundless continent, granted them the means to remain equal and free for a long time to come."[25]

Tocqueville argues that the vastness of the United States rewarded character
traits that in Europe would be considered threats to social stability. "In Europe,"
he reminds his countrymen, "we are in the habit of looking upon restlessness of
spirit, immoderate desire for wealth, and extreme love of independence as great
social dangers." Tocqueville found all three traits in abundance in the American
character, but he concluded that, in a sparsely populated continent, they stimulated westward migration rather than undermining the social order. This is just
one other way that Americans are peculiarly blessed, he concludes, for they inhabit a land where their "vices" are actually "useful to society."[26]

More important than "circumstances" is a second cluster of explanatory
factors that Tocqueville groups under the broad heading of laws and institutions.
In this category he includes the structure of the US Constitution, which he lavishly praises for its checks and balances. (The tragedy, in Tocqueville's view, is
that the state constitutions are typically far inferior.)

He similarly affirms the important role accorded the courts as a conservative
check on a radical majority. While juries are merely an expression of popular
sovereignty, lawyers at their best serve as a much needed "counterweight to democracy." Because the US judicial system is based on precedent (unlike that in
France), American attorneys combine "a taste and respect for what is old with a
liking for what is regular and legal." And so, "when the American people allow
themselves to become intoxicated by passion or to be carried away by their own
ideas," the legal profession almost instinctively applies the brakes.[27]

We might pause here for a moment and stress that neither the circumstances
nor the laws that Tocqueville highlights were reflections of Americans' character. Tocqueville alternately describes the circumstances that he underscores
as "accidental" and "providential," the gifts of "nature herself" or "God himself."
Either way, they are "independent of man's will," even though the Americans he

---

[25]Tocqueville, *Democracy in America*, 322.
[26]Ibid., 328.
[27]Ibid., 307, 309.

conversed with often wanted to take credit for them.[28] From a Christian perspective, it makes sense to think of them as instances of unmerited divine favor, reflections of God's grace rather than American goodness.

And as for the laws and institutions that helped to temper the majority, they were the bequest of the Founding generation, not the product of Jacksonian America. The Founding Fathers had been masters of "the art of liberty," statesmen adept at crafting laws and institutions that reflected the will of the majority without being "the slave of its passions." The Jacksonian generation continued to benefit from the Founders' "brilliance," but they had banished such individuals from government and rejected the heart of their worldview.[29] To the degree that laws and institutions were helping to perpetuate liberty, Jacksonian America was reaping where it hadn't sown.

Tocqueville understood that the "circumstances" that helped to perpetuate liberty in America could be fleeting. Hopefully, her laws and institutions would be long-lasting, but alone they were hardly enough. "Would to God I believed more in the omnipotence of institutions!" Tocqueville expostulated to a friend toward the end of his life. "I am quite convinced that political societies are not what their laws make them, but what sentiments, beliefs, ideas, habits of the heart, and the spirit of the men who form them, prepare them in advance to be."[30] This same conviction infuses *Democracy in America*. If liberty is comparatively extensive among white Americans, the most important reason, according to Alexis de Tocqueville, lies in their *mores*.

"The importance of mores . . . is a truth central to all my thinking," Tocqueville informs us in volume one, "and in the end all my ideas come back to it."[31] We need to slow down and wrestle with this third explanatory category, not only because Tocqueville would want us to but also because this is the part of his argument where individuals who listen to him selectively or carelessly are most inclined to go astray.

This is partly a problem of terminology. Who uses the word *mores* anymore? It's a slippery concept at best, and Tocqueville conceives of it so broadly that it can be hard to pin down. He defines the term multiple times in volume one. At

---

[28]Ibid., 319, 320.

[29]James T. Schleifer, *The Chicago Companion to Tocqueville's Democracy in America* (Chicago: University of Chicago Press, 2013), 66; Tocqueville, *Democracy in America*, 291, 296.

[30]Roger Boesche, ed., *Alexis de Tocqueville: Selected Letters on Politics and Society* (Berkeley: University of California Press, 1985), 366.

[31]Tocqueville, *Democracy in America*, 356.

its most sweeping, *mores* refers to "the whole moral and intellectual state of a people." It includes our "notions" and "ideas," our "practical experience, habits, and opinions." It encompasses "the whole range of ideas that shape habits of mind," the "whole range of intellectual and moral dispositions that men bring to the state of society."[32]

To make it more manageable, let's think of the term as denoting the common beliefs and values that shaped the ways that whites in Jacksonian America interacted with each other and with their government. Tocqueville would want to complicate our working definition, I'm sure, but I think he could live with it.

Part of the challenge we'll face in following Tocqueville's argument stems not from the vagueness of the term itself but from the baggage we bring to the conversation—especially our appetite for simple answers and our hope for political ammunition. In contending for the primacy of mores, Tocqueville is insisting that a major reason that liberty was comparatively extensive in Jacksonian America involved the popular beliefs and values of the time. Once we hear that, unfortunately, our minds will start to race, and unless we're careful, we'll stop listening to Tocqueville so that we can start quoting him. Surely, he must be making a case for *our* beliefs. Obviously, he has to be advocating *our* values. The sooner we start tweeting and posting the good news, the better.

Do you remember Tocqueville's wry conclusion after the publication of volume one, that the main reason so many of his readers agreed with him was that they didn't understand him? Let's be sure that we understand him before deciding that he agrees with us. As with every other topic he touched on, Tocqueville's assessment of American mores is complicated, and if we "consider it only from a single side," we may well miss his point.

Because his primary goal is always to understand the "output" of democracy, he is particularly interested in aspects of the American character that were either influenced by equality or shaped the effects of equality. A handful stand out. Two we've already come across. Tocqueville tells us that Americans in the 1830s tend to think very highly of themselves and, in the abstract, to think very highly of human nature. They harbor a deep and abiding "faith in man's good sense and wisdom" and "in the doctrine of human perfectibility." They also exhibit an intense passion for equality itself. They treasure it above all else. They love it "with a love that is eternal."[33]

---

[32]Ibid., 331, 353, 356.
[33]Tocqueville, *Letters from America*, 87; Tocqueville, *Democracy in America*, 60.

Beyond this, Americans as Tocqueville finds them are acquisitive and mate-rialistic, individualistic (up to a point), independent-minded and resistant to authority, rational in their pursuit of self-interest, and religious. Of these habits of heart and mind, Tocqueville reasons that all but the last two are probably detrimental to liberty in the long run. If popular mores undergird liberty in Jacksonian America, then the cornerstones are the majority's rational pursuit of self-interest—what Tocqueville labels "self-interest properly understood"—in tandem with their Christian convictions.[34] The first trained them to believe that their short-term desires could betray their long-term self-interest. The second warned them that what they had the power to do was not always morally proper to do.

What unified these seemingly disparate dispositions is that they both incul-cated what Tocqueville calls "habits of restraint."[35] In essence, both their reli-gious beliefs and their commitment to "self-interest, properly understood" con-ditioned Americans to question the wisdom of their natural impulses. To the degree that they did so, they discouraged a supremely self-confident and all-powerful majority from becoming agents of tyranny.

It's simpler, more flattering, and surely more effective in campaign speeches to remember Tocqueville praising American virtue and goodness as the key to American democracy. "America is great, because Americans show habits of re-straint" hardly carries much punch, and it's a stretch to imagine a sea of sign-waving convention delegates erupting in cheers when they hear it. Yet it's "habits of restraint" that Tocqueville particularly praises. They "singularly favor the tranquility of the American people and the duration of the institutions they have founded."[36]

We've noted already Tocqueville's view that humans are relentlessly self-inter-ested. He arrived in the United States convinced that "personal interest" is "the only fixed point in the human heart." Nothing in his tour caused him to question that. As we've seen, he quickly concluded that Jacksonian Americans were "not a virtuous people." What changed during his visit was his assumption that virtuous self-denial was essential for a free and just society to endure. Put

---

[34]Tocqueville, *Democracy in America*, 611.
[35]Ibid., 337.
[36]Ibid.

differently, one of Tocqueville's key discoveries during his American tour was that self-interested behavior—of a sort—could still serve the common good.[37]

Tocqueville had begun to glimpse this possibility within a month of his arrival, although it would take years to make complete sense of what he was seeing. What could explain the prosperity and harmony of "a society compounded of all the nations of the world," Tocqueville queried a friend in a letter from New York City. "What binds such diverse elements together and makes a nation of it all?" An answer was beginning to form in his mind: "Self-interest. That is the key."[38]

Tocqueville was initially struck by how unabashedly Americans pursued their self-interest. They made no effort to hide it, no effort to excuse or apologize for it. The pursuit of self-interest seemed to function as a "social theory."[39] But over time Tocqueville gradually refined this insight. It wasn't the mere fact that Americans pursued their self-interest that eventually impressed him most. It was *how* they did so.

Although he didn't use their exact terminology, Tocqueville thought about human motivation much as the Framers of the US Constitution a half century earlier. As you'll recall, they also accepted that self-interest is the driving force of human behavior, but they thought more precisely in terms of a "hierarchy of motives."[40] The most common they called *passion*, essentially the reckless or irrational pursuit of self-interest. The next most prevalent was *interest*, by which they meant the prudent, rational pursuit of personal well-being. The least common by far was *virtue*, understood as the rational promotion of the common good above personal advantage.

Like the Framers, Tocqueville recognized the power of the irrational. If reason is too often overwhelmed by "momentary passion," he maintains, it's because humans typically "feel far more than they reason." And yet one of the things that surprised him about Americans was how frequently they overcame passionate impulses to pursue their self-interest in an "enlightened" way. If self-interest reigned in American hearts as elsewhere, and it did, to an impressive degree it was an "enlightened" self-interest.[41]

---

[37]Ibid., 274; Arthur Schlesinger Jr., "Individualism and Apathy in Tocqueville's Democracy," in *Reconsidering Tocqueville's Democracy in America*, ed. Abraham S. Eisenstadt (New Brunswick, NJ: Rutgers University Press, 1991), 96.

[38]Tocqueville, *Letters from America*, 66.

[39]Ibid.

[40]Daniel Walker Howe, "The Political Psychology of *The Federalist*," *William and Mary Quarterly*, 3rd ser., vol. 44 (1987): 491.

[41]Tocqueville, *Democracy in America*, 262, 256.

Tocqueville discovered that Americans frequently lived by the maxim that short-term self-denial leads to long-term gain. They seldom spoke of the beauty of self-sacrifice for the common good, but they lavishly praised the utility of temporary self-denial as the surest way to maximize their long-run wealth and well-being. "Instead of blindly yielding to his first desires," Tocqueville observes, the typical American "has learned the art of combating them and has become accustomed to easily sacrificing the pleasure of the moment to the permanent interests of his entire life."[42] (Credit cards hadn't been invented yet.)

Let's be clear here: as Tocqueville defines it, the pursuit of "self-interest properly understood" is *not* disinterested. The affection at its core isn't love of God, or love of neighbor, or love of country. It's love of self. Individuals guided by "self-interest, properly understood" are displaying an "enlightened love of themselves," Tocqueville tells us. In effect, they were guided by an "enlightened" selfishness. "Self-interest, properly understood" is neither classical virtue nor Christian love.[43]

Yet it mimics their social effects, up to a point. By preaching the usefulness of short-term self-denial, "self-interest, properly understood" promotes the de-velopment of citizens "who are disciplined, temperate, moderate, prudent, and self-controlled."[44] Apart from their personal benefits, these traits are a blessing to the larger society. Most of us would be thankful to see them in our children or our neighbors, our coworkers or our elected officials, maybe even in the president of the United States. And if you're Alexis de Tocqueville, and your parents had barely escaped the wrath of the mob during the French Revolution, they surely must have seemed desirable. By inculcating "habits of restraint," such traits can serve, albeit imperfectly, to mitigate democracy's potential for majoritarian tyranny.

Tocqueville also suggests that "self-interest, properly understood" can coun-teract another of democracy's intrinsic weaknesses—namely, its propensity to promote *individualism*. Did you catch that? Those of us born in the United States have been culturally conditioned to view individualism positively. Just as we exalt the individual as the constituent unit of American society, we as-sociate individualism with admirable character traits such as self-reliance and personal initiative.

---

[42]Ibid., 615.
[43]Ibid., 611-12.
[44]Ibid., 612.

Tocqueville understood individualism differently, in large part because he thought about it comparatively and historically, situating it in the flow of change over time. While aristocracy "linked all citizens together in a long chain from peasant to king," democracy "breaks the chain and severs the links." It places citizens side by side but can leave them "without a common bond to hold them together."[45]

Owing nothing to anyone, expecting nothing from anyone, men and women can gradually withdraw from society into the cocoon of the family. (Tocqueville's "individualism" is not far from what some today call "privatism.") Those who turn inward may not be consciously selfish when they do so, but the long-run consequences of their withdrawal is an erosion of community and the development of a way of life in which "the common good" becomes a meaningless abstraction. As Tocqueville defines it, individualism is not intrinsically selfish, but if left unchecked, it leaves men and women with little else but selfishness to motivate them.[46]

The good news is that Americans in the 1830s largely offset this tendency with a penchant for joining with others to accomplish specific tasks. They do so, Tocqueville is convinced, thanks to the pervasive influence of the doctrine of "self-interest, properly understood." He marvels that Americans are "constantly joining together in groups" to work toward goals they can't accomplish individually, such as the erection of a hospital, the improvement of a school, or the building of a road.[47] When they do, they are promoting the common good, even though their primary motivation may be the expectation of personal benefit.

Having found so little virtue during his tour of the United States, Tocqueville eventually concluded that it would be rare in *any* democratic society. The idealization of virtue is the hallmark of aristocracies, he contends in volume two, not democracies. "Moralists" in the United States had pretty much abandoned "the idea of sacrifice and no longer dared hold it up for the human mind to contemplate."[48] But they were willing to argue that there are times when serving the general welfare and advancing personal interest go hand in hand. This was something. In a society that had given up on virtue, "self-interest, properly understood" could help to ward off some of democracy's intrinsic dangers.

---

[45]Ibid., 586, 590.
[46]Wilfred M. McClay, *The Masterless: Self and Society in Modern America* (Chapel Hill: University of North Carolina Press, 1994), 43.
[47]Tocqueville, *Democracy in America*, 595.
[48]Ibid., 610.

But alone it was not enough. Tocqueville finds another, more reliable source of "habits of restraint" permeating Jacksonian America: religious belief. Religion "must be considered as the first of America's political institutions," Tocqueville announces in volume one, "for even if religion does not give Americans their taste for liberty, it does notably facilitate their use of that liberty."[49]

These are strong words. But you should know in advance that Tocqueville's views on the relationship of Christianity and democracy are characteristically complicated. If you listen carefully, I can pretty much guarantee you'll be offended. For Americans who think religion should be a wholly private affair—don't ask, don't tell; keep the public square relentlessly secular—Tocqueville counters that liberty cannot survive without religious belief. But to Christians eager to see a "moral majority" wield political power, he points to the soul-costs of influence, and he cautions that the Christianity of Jacksonian America was being shaped by the surrounding culture as much as the other way around. The salt was losing its savor.

Even Tocqueville's words of encouragement come with warnings.

Before we listen to him at length, it will help to have four contextual details in mind. First, Tocqueville didn't come to the United States with the intention of systematically studying Americans' religious beliefs and practices, nor did he do so. His correspondence and journals suggest that he attended a few religious services during the course of his visit, but for the most part his observations were drawn from the interviews he conducted.

Second, Tocqueville's focus was always on the external social and political consequences of religious belief. In *Democracy in America* he comments on religious belief in much the way that a political scientist or sociologist might today. He overtly declines to say whether he thinks Americans' religious beliefs are either true or genuine—"for who can read the bottom of men's hearts?"—and he considers the question irrelevant for his purposes.[50]

Third, it's almost impossible to nail down Tocqueville's personal religious convictions. From the hints that he left behind, historians have described him as everything from an "agnostic" to a "believing Catholic" to a "non-practicing

---

[49]Ibid., 338.
[50]Ibid.

Christian," whatever that is.[51] He was raised in a Catholic home and tutored by a Catholic priest as a boy, but by his own account he experienced a crisis of faith in his teens. He appears to have wrestled with doubt for the remainder of his life, although it's hard to tell whether he was a believer plagued with doubt or a doubter who longed to believe.

Tocqueville denied being a Christian at the time of his visit to the United States. That much is sure. "*If ever I become Christian,*" he wrote to his future wife in the midst of his American tour, "I believe that it will be through you." A decade later he was still describing himself as "unbelieving," and when his father died yet another decade later, Tocqueville confessed that it filled him "with the strongest desire to believe. But alas," he lamented, "who is able to do so, if god does not move it?"[52]

None of this adds up to a strong case for remembering Alexis de Tocqueville as an orthodox Christian, although he may well have been "Christ haunted," as the Christian writer Flannery O'Connor once described the American South.[53] What we can say with confidence is that, whatever his innermost beliefs, Tocqueville admired the ethical teachings he associated with Christianity. In a letter to a prominent religious skeptic written a few years afterward, he described the Gospels as "admirable books." Their doctrines are "pure and grand," he maintained. They constitute "the great source of modern morality."[54]

Beyond this, Tocqueville also clung to a view of human nature consistent with traditional Christian teaching. He didn't speak of "the fall," but as we've seen, he believed that self-interest "stands out as the only fixed point in the human heart." He didn't use the language of *imago Dei* and original sin, but he looked on humankind as a composite of "angel" and "beast." And while he longed to see the angel "predominate"—as he put it in a letter to a close friend— he confessed that he was "no more detached from the beast than anyone else."[55] This was a self-awareness that many of the Americans he encountered lacked.

[51]Leo Damrosch, *Tocqueville's Discovery of America* (New York: Farrar, Strauss, and Giroux, 2010), 6; D. H. Leon, "'The Dogma of the Sovereignty of the People': Alexis de Tocqueville's Religion in America," *Journal of Church and State* 14 (1972): 279; Cushing Strout, "Tocqueville and American Religion: Revisiting the Visitor," *Political Theory* 8 (1980): 15.

[52]Tocqueville, *Letters from America*, 38, italics added; Doris S. Goldstein, "The Religious Beliefs of Alexis de Tocqueville," *French Historical Studies* 1 (1960): 383; Arthur Kaledin, *Tocqueville and His America: A Darker Horizon* (New Haven, CT: Yale University Press, 2011), 78.

[53]Flannery O'Connor, "The Grotesque in Southern Fiction," in *Collected Works* (New York: Library Classics of the United States, 1988), 818.

[54]Alexis de Tocqueville, *"The European Revolution" and Correspondence with Gobineau*, ed. and trans. John Lukacs (Gloucester, MA: Peter Smith, 1968), 206, 208.

[55]Tocqueville, *Democracy in America*, 274; Tocqueville, *Correspondence with Gobineau*, 27-28.

Finally, you should know that Tocqueville tends to speak of religion and Christianity interchangeably. In the context of Jacksonian America, this would have been a distinction without a difference. Excepting the country's Native American tribes, followers of non-Christian religious sects were almost unknown. In our far more diverse religious context, however, it's important to acknowledge that Tocqueville is not mounting a concerted argument for the necessity of Christianity specifically.

Although he admired Christian morality greatly, it's Christianity's emphasis on the immortality of the soul that is key to its political benefits, Tocqueville maintains, and at times he seems to endorse any religious system that promotes such belief. "Society has nothing to fear from the other life, and nothing to hope for," he explains, "and what matters most to it is not so much that all citizens profess the true religion as that each citizen profess some religion."[56] In 1831, a lot of Americans were doing that.

"When I arrived in the United States," Tocqueville writes in volume one, it was the country's religious aspect that first captured my attention."[57] No wonder. Tocqueville arrived in the country at the crest of a wave of evangelical revivals that we remember today as "the Second Great Awakening." Although perhaps as few as one-tenth of free adults in the United States were officially church members at the time of the ratification of the Constitution, by the middle of the 1800s the proportion had risen to between a third and two-fifths. Probably two-thirds or more of free Americans were "adherents," meaning they attended church services with some frequency and would have identified themselves as Christians.

Zealous Christ-followers were also the driving force behind any number of collective efforts to reform American society at the time. Eager to usher in the millennium, motivated believers in Jacksonian America were mobilizing to banish alcohol, abolish slavery, and alleviate poverty, among other ills. Their efforts made evangelical Christians easily "the largest, and most formidable, subculture in American society."[58]

---

[56]Tocqueville, *Democracy in America*, 335.
[57]Ibid., 340.
[58]Richard J. Carwardine, *Evangelicals and Politics in Antebellum America* (New Haven, CT: Yale University Press, 1997), 44.

The vitality of Christianity in the United States surprised Tocqueville, but what surprised him even more was how universally Americans viewed this as a boon to liberty. In France, the most forceful champions of democracy took for granted that religious belief was incompatible with political freedom. The Enlightenment philosopher Jean Jacques Rousseau, for example, had insisted that the very concept of a "Christian republic" was inconceivable since "each of the terms excludes the other. Christianity preaches only servitude and dependence," Rousseau insisted, and "its spirit is too favourable to tyranny."[59]

Lending credence to such views was the fact that, for centuries, church and crown had been intimately intertwined in France. This led progressive writers and thinkers to assume that the only way to vanquish one was to eliminate both. Tocqueville always knew that this was a mistake. He came to the United States convinced that some sort of "positive religion" was necessary for human flourishing, and he never doubted that Christianity was the best, if not the only alternative available.[60]

But during his tour of America, Tocqueville also began to see how Christianity's ethical teachings could be especially valuable to a democracy. Everywhere he went in the United States, he heard Americans making precisely the opposite argument to what he had heard in France. His travel notebooks are filled with the same repetitive assertions: "The freer men are, the more necessary religion becomes." "If a people is to be republican, it must be . . . religious." "Religion is our best security for liberty." It is "among the most important reasons why we are able to support republican institutions." Tocqueville summarizes these views in volume one by observing that "Americans so completely confound Christianity with liberty that it is almost impossible to induce them to think of one without the other."[61]

And so, in volume one of *Democracy in America*, Tocqueville offers one of the most eloquent arguments for the importance of religious belief to political liberty ever penned. In the introduction, he notes that in France "friends of liberty attack religion." They would do well to "invoke the aid of religion," he contends, because "without morality freedom cannot reign and without faith

---

[59]Sanford Kessler, "Tocqueville on Civil Religion and Liberal Democracy," *Journal of Politics* 39 (1977): 122-23.

[60]Tocqueville, *Correspondence with Gobineau*, 206.

[61]Zunz, *Tocqueville and Gustave de Beaumont in America*, 220, 234, 246, 286; Tocqueville, *Democracy in America*, 338.

there is no basis for morality." (Os Guinness has christened this "the golden triangle of freedom.")[62]

In the United States, Tocqueville informs his French readers, "liberty looks on religion as its comrade in battle." "The *spirit of religion* and the *spirit of liberty*" are "marvelously combined." America was simultaneously "the freest and most enlightened" of nations and the land where "Christianity maintains more actual power over souls . . . than anywhere else."[63] At the very least, this proved that religion and liberty aren't inevitably at odds.

But Tocqueville goes further. There was a general principle at work: "Despotism can do without faith, but liberty cannot." Democracy *needs* religion to flourish. By "teaching men the immortality of the soul," religion encourages the citizens of democratic societies to delay gratification and practice "habits of restraint."[64] In the process, it reduces the likelihood that the majority will abuse its power and promote injustice.

Furthermore, because Christianity "reigns without impediment, no one in the United States has yet dared to propose the maxim that everything is permitted in the interest of society—a wicked maxim that seems to have been invented in an age of liberty to legitimize all the tyrants of the future." Even though the law was powerless to restrain the majority, "there are some things that religion prevents them from imagining or forbids them to attempt."[65]

To paraphrase Dostoyevsky, when you believe in God, not everything is permitted.

So what, then, does this require of the true friend of liberty in a democratic time and place? Tocqueville is adamant. Such individuals must "apply themselves unstintingly to the task of uplifting souls and keeping them intent on heaven." Remember that Tocqueville isn't saying this because of his own Christian zeal, but because of his self-professed love of liberty and human dignity. And with that passion foremost in his mind, he warns us to beware of any worldview that denies the immortality of the soul. More than that, "You must regard those who profess such theories as natural enemies of the people."[66]

---

[62]Ibid., 13, 12; Os Guinness, *A Free People's Suicide: Sustainable Freedom and the American Future* (Downers Grove, IL: InterVarsity Press, 2012), 100.

[63]Tocqueville, *Democracy in America*, 49, 48, 336.

[64]Ibid., 340, 635.

[65]Ibid., 337-38.

[66]Ibid., 635.

It can be tempting to stop here. Up to this point, Tocqueville's message about the critical necessity of religious belief has been clean, unequivocal, and politically invaluable. All that's left now is to spread the word. *#Democracy-Needs-Religion*. *#Enemies-of-the-People*. Take that, secular humanists! Take that, godless liberals!

But to stop here would be unfair to Alexis de Tocqueville and dangerous to us. It would be unfair to Tocqueville because he isn't through yet, and by interrupting him in the middle of his reflections we'll misrepresent him. It would be dangerous to us because we're likely to hear him as justifying precisely the sort of behavior that he hopes to save us from.

Here's one way to think of it. When it comes to the Frenchman's assessment of American Christianity, we can almost imagine two Tocquevilles. We just finished listening to the first Tocqueville. This one underscores the vital importance of religion to democracy, commends people of faith for their contribution to the American republic, and offers hope for its future. But there's also a second Tocqueville, one who admonishes and warns Christians more than he congratulates them. Until we've heard from this second Tocqueville we'll never understand the first. Until Christians hear Tocqueville's admonitions, in other words, we will misunderstand his encouragement and misplace our hope.

By declaring those who deny the immortality of the soul "enemies of the people," Tocqueville seems to be calling people of faith to a religious war for the future of democracy. In our hyperpartisan environment, for too many of us that can mean only one thing: our enlistment in the service of "God's party" or "God's candidate." That's the last thing he has in mind. The absolutely, positively, very last thing.

If "it was the country's religious aspect that first captured" Tocqueville's attention when he arrived in America, this was in part because French philosophers had been predicting that religious belief would decline as liberty increased. In the United States exactly the opposite was occurring, and Tocqueville was determined to know why. What explained the vitality of religious belief in the world's most democratic country?

Tocqueville posed this question repeatedly to "the faithful of all communions"—clergy and laity both—and repeatedly the same answer came back. "They assigned primary credit for the peaceful ascendancy of religion in their country to *the complete separation of church and state*."[67]

---

[67]Ibid., 341, italics added.

Today, the term "separation of church and state" is politically loaded and historically confusing: politically loaded because of its implications for religious liberty, historically confusing because it has changed in its commonsense meaning over time. Two centuries ago, no one understood it to mean that prayer should be banned from public schools, the Ten Commandments banished from courthouses, or Christmas trees removed from public squares.

By describing what he encountered, Tocqueville provides us with a tolerable understanding of what many Jacksonian Americans did think it meant. In his conversations with clergy, he "found that most of its members seemed to steer clear of power voluntarily." They took "a sort of professional pride in having nothing to do with it." He heard them "blast ambition and bad faith" in both of the major parties, and he learned "that in God's eyes no one is damnable for his political views so long as those views are sincere." Above all, he saw that the clergy "carefully mark their distance from, and avoid contact with, *all* parties."[68]

The irony is that this restraint was one of "the principle causes of religion's power in America." American clergy in the 1830s recognized what so many contemporary Christian leaders have forgotten—namely, that political influence always comes at a cost to the church. When Christians ally themselves with a particular political leader or party, the church "increases its power over some but gives up hope of reigning over all." The reason for this is straightforward: "Religion cannot share the material might of those who govern without incurring some of the hatred they inspire."[69]

It is by keeping all political parties at arms' length, Tocqueville concludes, that America's religious leaders have helped to make religion "the first of America's political institutions." By eschewing power, they have grown in influence. But note that this influence is *indirect*. "Religion in the United States never intervenes directly in government," Tocqueville explains. "One cannot say" that it "influences the laws or the specifics of political opinion." What it does is influence American mores, and it influences mores because "Christianity maintains more actual *power over souls* in America than anywhere else."[70]

In sum, Tocqueville's hopeful message about religious influence in a democracy comes with an enormous qualifier. Religious belief *can* help to sustain liberty in a democratic republic, but it won't do so necessarily. It does so only

---

[68]Ibid., 342, italics added.
[69]Ibid., 340, 343.
[70]Ibid., 338, 336, italics added.

when people of faith—and religious leaders especially—exhibit the "habits of restraint" that their religious convictions are supposed to inculcate. When believers seek to add to their influence through "the artificial might of the law" or the "support of the powers that govern society," they "sacrifice the future for the sake of the present."[71] It's a devil's bargain.

But that's not his only warning. In private, Tocqueville confessed skepticism about the depth and substance of Christian belief in the United States. Seven weeks into his tour, he summarized his initial impressions of American "beliefs" in a lengthy letter to a cousin in France. Upon their arrival, he and Beaumont had quickly sensed that "religious enthusiasm runs high," but now he was starting to "doubt that religious opinions hold as much sway as I originally thought they did."[72]

Americans were strict in observing the Sabbath, and Tocqueville saw numerous other examples of external zeal, but he remained unconvinced of Christianity's grip on their hearts. "Unless I'm sadly mistaken, these external forms conceal a reservoir of doubt and indifference," he conjectured. "Faith is obviously inert," he went on. "Enter any church . . . and you will hear sermons about morals; not one word about dogma—nothing at all likely to fluster one's neighbor or awaken the idea of dissent." By mid-summer, he was musing in his journal that the typical American minister struck him less as "truly the pastor of his flock" than as "an entrepreneur in the religious industry."[73]

Tocqueville was more circumspect about what he shared in public, but he still peppered *Democracy in America* with observations that should give Christian readers pause. For example, even while emphasizing the compatibility between Christianity and political liberty, he implies that Americans had so conflated the two that they tended to support Christianity as an expression of patriotism. "In the United States, religion never ceases to warm itself at patriotism's hearth," he writes. One of the arguments that religious leaders trumpeted on behalf of the gospel, in other words, was that it serves the interest of the nation. "They are forever pointing out how religious beliefs foster liberty and public order."[74]

Note that Tocqueville actually agrees with this argument. By fostering "habits of restraint," religious belief can mitigate tyranny and help to perpetuate the republic. This is one of the most important lessons he wants his *irreligious* French

---

[71]Ibid., 342-43.
[72]Tocqueville, *Letters from America*, 40, 88.
[73]Ibid., 88-89; Zunz, *Tocqueville and Gustave de Beaumont in America*, 317.
[74]Tocqueville, *Democracy in America*, 339, 616.

readers to hear. What disturbs him is how frequently *religious* Americans defended their faith on these same instrumental grounds. In the pages of *Democracy in America*, we encounter a worldview that intertwines democracy and Christianity, the United States and the church, temporal benefits and eternal rewards. Does any of this sound familiar?

Tocqueville relates that he spoke with numerous missionaries to the American West during his journey and found that "eternity is only one of their concerns." They viewed their efforts as a means of spreading American values and protecting America's borders. "If you were to question these missionaries of Christian civilization," he tells us, "you would be quite surprised to hear how frequently they speak of the goods of this world, and you would find politicians where you had thought there were only men of religion."[75]

This emphasis on Christianity's earthly benefits was widespread, Tocqueville reports. "American preachers refer to this world constantly." They "can avert their eyes from it only with the greatest of difficulty . . . and in listening to them it is often difficult to tell whether the chief object of religion is to procure eternal happiness in the other world or well-being in this one." The prosperity gospel is not a recent invention.[76]

What's lurking here is Tocqueville's hint that there was a fair amount of conforming to the world among Jacksonian-era believers. It's no coincidence that Tocqueville uses his observation about the worldly focus of American ministers as a segue into his chapter "On the Taste for Material Well-Being in America." The central theme of this chapter is that "love of well-being has become the national and dominant taste."[77]

This had been his impression since his first arrival in the United States. "Here we are truly in another world," he marveled in a letter to his brother Edouard less than three weeks after going ashore. "Political passions are only superficial. The one passion that runs deep, the only one that stirs the human heart day in and day out, is the acquisition of wealth."[78]

Some of his initial impressions would change by the time he sat down to write *Democracy in America*, but this one only hardened. "The desire to acquire the goods of this world is the dominant passion of Americans." Their yearning for material well-being is insatiable, "an anxious, burning passion that grows even

---

[75]Ibid., 339.
[76]Ibid., 616.
[77]Ibid., 617, 619.
[78]Tocqueville, *Letters from America*, 44.

as it is satisfied." The quintessential American "clings to the goods of this world as though assured of not dying," but then "death comes at last, catching him before he has tired of this futile pursuit of a complete felicity that remains forever out of reach."[79]

But wait a minute. How can we square Tocqueville's observation that Christianity "reigns" in Jacksonian America "by universal consent" with his pronouncement that there is "no other country where the love of money occupies as great a place in the hearts of men"? Tocqueville's answer is that Americans had learned to combine a taste for "material gratifications" with "a kind of religious morality." In the United States, he concludes, "people want to be as well off as possible in this world without renouncing their chances in the next." Jesus taught that "it is easier for a camel to go through the eye of a needle than for a rich man to enter the kingdom of God."[80] Tocqueville thinks Americans were willing to take their chances.

Finally, we must note that neither Americans' religious convictions nor their rational pursuit of self-interest was sufficient to protect the Cherokees or any of the other Native American tribes driven from their homes during the 1830s. Religious beliefs fostered a measure of genuine sympathy for the tribes targeted for removal, but American Christians divided between those who consequently opposed the policy and those who favored it—over the objections of the Native Americans themselves—because they decided it was in the tribes' best interest. Whites' commitment to "self-interest, properly understood" was equally ineffective. The consensus was that Native American removal would serve the material interests of the white majority, and that made enlightened selfishness worse than useless as a deterrent to injustice.

In sum, even when Tocqueville is praising American mores, he would have us see that they *lessened* oppression in Jacksonian America. They didn't *eliminate* it. And the "habits of restraint" that he singles out for praise seem primarily to have influenced how white men treated other white men. By the 1830s, the white majority had arrived at the conclusion that Native Americans "were, and will ever be" inferior, and in such a context, even the Golden Rule loses much of its force. "Do unto others as you would have them do unto you" is an exacting standard, but we understand its demands differently when we see the "others" in question as *wholly* other.

---

[79]Tocqueville, *Democracy in America*, 623, 326, 625, 626.
[80]Ibid., 337, 57, 621; Matthew 19:24.

No, "America is great, because she is good" is not a "brilliant summation" of *Democracy in America*.

Alexis de Tocqueville mocks our storylines of heroes and villains and simple solutions. The "religious terror" that grips him is grounded in his knowledge of the human heart—your heart and mine. The threat to liberty and human dignity that most concerns him isn't somewhere outside of us. It isn't embodied in a rival nation with ambitions for world domination. It isn't lurking in an invisible "Deep State" that conspires against the people or in a homegrown demagogue with dreams of dictatorship. It dwells within each of us. This makes the potential for oppression and injustice inescapable and ever present, and this sobering truth necessarily tempers the encouragement that he can offer us.

And so Tocqueville comes to us with the proverbial good news/bad news message. The bad news, which he refuses to soft-pedal, is that democracy carries an *intrinsic* potential for oppression and injustice. In this sense, it's like every form of government in our fallen world. Plausibly, logically, majority rule can end in tyranny. The good news, the hope that we cling to, is that it doesn't *have* to. "I see great dangers that can be warded off," Tocqueville tells us on the very last page of *Democracy in America*, "and great evils that can be avoided or held in check."[81]

---

[81]Tocqueville, *Democracy in America*, 834.

"Trump Supporters Hold 'Stop the Steal' Rally in DC Amid Ratification of Presidential Election," January 6, 2021. Shortly after this photograph was taken, angry protesters stormed the capitol and clashed violently with police, resulting in five deaths and several hundred arrests.

PART FIVE

REMEMBERING, REMINDING, RESPONDING

Lessons for Today

THIS HAS BEEN THE HARDEST SECTION TO WRITE. I began collecting my thoughts for it just as the first cases of the novel coronavirus appeared in the United States early in 2020. Then on the very day that I had planned to begin writing—during my college's spring break—word arrived that the campus was closing and that in two weeks' time I would be teaching online. As the death toll climbed, and tens of millions of Americans were thrown out of work, and "normal" life came to a halt, I told myself that the pandemic changed everything, that the project I had been working on for years no longer mattered.

It was a temporary delusion, a momentary triumph of emotion over reason that ended as my heart came to accept what my mind already knew: life's most important questions *abide*. They may assume different guises in different contexts, but they are rooted in what T. S. Eliot called "Permanent Things"—the presence of God, the dignity of human beings, the reality of human sin—and as such they are never truly eclipsed by emergencies.[1] If anything, they are magnified.

---

[1] Andrew A. Tadie and Michael H. McDonald, eds., *Permanent Things: Toward the Recovery of a More Human Scale at the End of the Twentieth Century* (Grand Rapids, MI: Eerdmans, 1995).

Certainly the circumstances that initially propelled me to write this book didn't recede as the virus spread. Notwithstanding the chorus of claims that "we're all in this together," we continued to be deeply suspicious of our government and of each other, impatient with constitutional restraints, and susceptible to populist demagoguery.

And in exposing the fragility of our democracy, the pandemic underscored many of the questions at the heart of *We the Fallen People*: Are we by nature unselfish enough to promote the common good when it's costly or even just inconvenient? Are society's most vulnerable protected when the majority has its way? Is power always a threat to liberty, or is that true only when "the other side" wields it? At what price, and under what circumstances, will we exchange liberty for greater security? Such questions are as urgent as ever.

But even as I reassured myself of this truth, I wrestled with a different psychological hurdle, one that had less to do with the immediate global emergency than with years of acculturation to the academy. I've been taught my entire professional life that the kind of concluding remarks I feel compelled to share are precisely the sort that an academic historian should never relate. I've had no training for what follows and few models to imitate.

Academic historians are trained to be "objective." We invariably fall short of that goal, sometimes badly, but we generally maintain that objectivity is our noblest ideal and pursuing it faithfully is our highest responsibility. And I wholeheartedly agree, depending on how we define the term.

If it means anything at all, objectivity surely includes a commitment to be intellectually honest. Historians worthy of respect don't invent evidence to support their conclusions or ignore evidence that contradicts them. They strive to be balanced, thorough, careful, and fair-minded. I aspire to each of these qualities, and I'm convinced that the law of love would require them even if the academy didn't. Up to this point, in other words, I'm all in.

But the academy demands more than this. It insists that objective historians are dispassionate. They keep their personal opinions and moral convictions to themselves. They recognize that their religious beliefs have no place in respectable scholarship, and they view all efforts to glean wisdom from the past as hopelessly naive and old-fashioned. They refuse to discuss the contemporary implications of their research, knowing that only amateurs and cranks find clearcut lessons for today in a complicated and distant past.

In the pages that follow I violate every one of these precepts.

I don't do so lightly, but rather impelled by religious conviction and a deep sense of vocation. As a *Christian* historian, I operate on three basic beliefs. I believe that the past is a sphere of human experience that God sovereignly ordains and superintends. I believe that individuals who lived in the past were like us in that they were made in God's image and marked by the fall, which means that there are truths in their stories that we can relate to and learn from. And from these beliefs it follows—I am absolutely persuaded—that remembering the past rightly is crucial to living in the present faithfully.

As a Christian *historian*, I feel called to help further this goal. To do so, I have come to believe that I must always ask two basic questions: "What can we learn *about* the past?" and "What can we learn *from* the past in order to live more wisely in the present?" The first is safe and unexceptional. The second is risky and invites controversy, but it can also lead to the highest form of knowledge, the kind that not only changes what we know but also how we think and act. It's the second question that we'll turn to now.

A final word before we do so: In the introduction, I noted how pleased I would be for individuals who don't share my faith to pick up this book. If you fall into this category and have stuck it out this far, I'm thankful. Please don't stop. Even as we turn our attention from past to present, from observation to application, I think you'll find questions worth contemplating and recommendations worth considering. There's something here for you.

But I'll be directing much of what follows specifically to Christian readers. As I related in the beginning, I have a deep burden for the American church. I lament her "historylessness." I grieve for her testimony in the public square. Yet I am hopeful that we can learn from our past—I wouldn't be writing otherwise— and I am certain that the past has much to teach us, if God grants us eyes to see and ears to hear.

WE THE *FALLEN* PEOPLE

Renewing Our Thinking

M y premise in *We the Fallen People* has been that, by returning to the days when American democracy was new and strange, we might see our contemporary democracy, and the assumptions we bring to it, with new eyes. Taking inspiration from Abraham Lincoln, in the introduction I suggested that the crisis of democracy that grips our nation calls us to *see* anew, in order to *think* anew, in order that we might *act* anew. Now, having completed our journey, we can use these same categories to clarify what we've learned and what it requires of us. What have we seen? How should it alter our thinking? How might it transform our behavior? We'll take up the first two of these questions in this chapter and save the third for the chapter to follow.

The answer to the first question (What have we seen?) may seem obvious. One insight looms above the rest: what I have labeled "the Great Reversal." Within a half century of the creation of the Constitution, the American people had utterly renounced the view of human nature that informed its every line.

The delegates who gathered in Philadelphia in 1787 knew that officeholders could be corrupted by power. They recognized that their constituents could be misled by ambitious leaders, follow passion rather than reason, and pursue self-interest at the price of justice. The Framers knew that there would be no angels in the government, and no angels in the electorate, and they planned accordingly. They designed a Constitution for *fallen* people. Its genius lay in how it held in tension two seemingly incompatible beliefs: first, that the majority must generally prevail; and second, that the majority is predisposed to seek personal advantage above the common good.

Two generations later, Jacksonian politicians resolved this tension by denying the second premise. They preached a democratic gospel, insisting that we are naturally virtuous. They proclaimed a democratic faith, insisting that our collective will is reliably just. In his farewell address in 1837, Andrew Jackson rejoiced that "the people" are "enlightened" and "patriotic," marked by "good sense and practical judgment," distinguished for "their intelligence," and renowned for "their high tone of moral character." They are "uncorrupted and incorruptible," Jackson concluded, and "the cause of freedom will continue to triumph" as long as they remain "true to themselves."[1]

America is great, because Americans are good.

But the Jacksonian repudiation of the Founding generation isn't, in fact, what we most need to see. What we most need to see is that, in observing Jacksonian America, we've been observing *ourselves*. For all the weighty differences that distinguish the politics of the 1820s and 1830s from our own, when it comes to our understanding of human nature, contemporary American democracy *is* Jacksonian democracy. What Jacksonian politicians preached two centuries ago, modern-day Americans wholeheartedly believe.

Decades ago, the writer Tom Wolfe famously labeled baby boomers the "Me Generation." *Time* magazine later christened their millennial descendants the "Me, Me, Me Generation." Columnist David Brooks recently lumped both into the age of "the Big Me." For years we've heard prophetic voices deprecating Americans' obsession with self-fulfillment and demand for instant gratification, decrying the individualism, relativism, self-satisfaction, and self-absorption of our "therapeutic," "narcissistic," "selfie" nation.[2]

None of these traits makes sense apart from an optimistic view of human nature. Think about it: why emphasize self-fulfillment and self-gratification if the self isn't morally reliable? What makes our narcissism logically consistent is what Brooks labels "the gospel of self-trust," and a slew of opinion polls show just how widely we now accept it.[3]

At the turn of the century, for example, a *New York Times* poll found that 73 percent of Americans believed that humans are born good.[4] A 2014 Lifeway

---

[1]James D. Richardson, comp., *A Compilation of the Messages and Papers of the Presidents* (New York: Bureau of National Literature, 1897), 3:1515, 1517, 1521, 1525, 1513.

[2]Fareed Zakaria, *In Defense of a Liberal Education* (New York: W. W. Norton, 2015), 151; David Brooks, *The Road to Character* (New York: Random House, 2015), 6, 7.

[3]Brooks, *Road to Character*, 7.

[4]Mark Ellingsen, *Blessed Are the Cynical: How Original Sin Can Make America a Better Place* (Grand Rapids, MI: Brazos Press, 2003), 132.

survey found that two-thirds (67 percent) of respondents believe that "most people are by nature good." A YouGov poll from the following year reached a nearly identical conclusion, finding that 68 percent of respondents with an opinion believe that the majority of people around the world are good. These dry statistics underscore what is now a fundamental pillar of the American mindset. In the words of one study, a positive view of human nature "has become the generally accepted presupposition for modern American thinking."[5]

This applies as much to the church as to the larger culture. Polls conducted over the past three decades have consistently found that self-identifying Christians mirror their neighbors in their optimistic assessments. If anything, American Christians can be more likely than non-Christians to believe that men and women are naturally good.

If we go back a generation, a 1991 poll by the Barna Research Group found that 77 percent of self-identifying Christians believed people are basically good. A decade later a poll by the same organization revealed that 74 percent of Christian respondents agreed that "when people are born they are neither good or evil" but "make a choice between the two as they mature." That's not the same as contending that we are naturally good, but it does indicate a wholesale rejection of the traditional Christian doctrine of original sin.

More recently, a 2014 Lifeway poll found that mainline Protestants were more likely than non-Christians to agree that "most people are by nature good" (76 percent to 70 percent), while even a slight majority (51 percent) of American evangelicals hold to this view. Polls by the Ligonier Institute in 2016, 2018, and 2020 arrived at the same conclusion, finding that just over half of self-described evangelicals agree that "most people are good by nature."[6]

These findings dovetail with the research of sociologist Christian Smith of the University of Notre Dame. Beginning in the early 2000s, Smith and his team of researchers undertook a decade-long investigation known as the National Study of Youth and Religion. Starting with a survey of more than three thousand teenagers in 2003, the team reconnected with the same respondents in 2005, 2008, and 2013. The result was a remarkably detailed map of the evolving religious beliefs of American millennials.

Most pertinent to our conversation is how respondents appraised their own moral sensibilities. Although inept at articulating moral principles, they were

---

[5]Ibid., 181.
[6]Ligonier Institute, "The State of Theology," https://thestateoftheology.com.

"confident in their ability to determine right and wrong" on their own. Rare was the respondent who acknowledged that her moral code "comes from outside of herself."[7] The rest took for granted that the heart is a reliable guide to righteous living and that they generally lived up to its standards. Indeed, Smith found that almost none of the professing *Christians* among the respondents showed an inkling that a "holy and almighty God" might call them "to a turning from self." Simply put, theirs "is not a religion of repentance from sin."[8]

In sum, what we most need to see in observing "the Great Reversal"—the insight that truly matters—is not that Jacksonian Americans rejected the Framers' understanding of human nature. It's that *we* have done so, or at least most of us, anyway. The conclusion is undeniable. What we now have to ask is, "So what?" It's a daunting question.

The place to begin is by returning to the metaphor of history as a form of conversation with the dead. In parts one and two of this book, we listened in as the Framers of the Constitution and leading Jacksonian democrats made conflicting arguments about human nature. The former told us that we are "neither wise nor good."[9] The latter reassured us that we are both. Both can't be right.

When we view their disagreement as an obscure debate from a distant past, it remains irrelevant to our lives. We make it alive and powerful and transformative when we enter into the conversation ourselves, and we can do that simply by allowing the dead to ask us two questions: "Which of these views of human nature is *true*, or at least closer to the truth?" and "*Why*, exactly, do you think so?" The first question forces us to join the debate rather than passively observe it. The second requires us to defend our position, pushing us to make our response more thoughtful and coherent than it might otherwise be.

And we need to be pushed. One of the most haunting passages in *Democracy in America* is Alexis de Tocqueville's observation that most of us fall short in our thinking about life's biggest questions. By his reckoning, most of us will either "believe without knowing why, or not know precisely what [we] ought to believe."[10]

---

[7]Melinda Lundquist Denton and Richard Flory, *Back-Pocket God: Religion and Spirituality in the Lives of Emerging Adults* (New York: Oxford University Press, 2020), 49, 50.

[8]Christian Smith with Melinda Lundquist Denton, *Soul Searching: The Religious and Spiritual Lives of American Teenagers* (New York: Oxford University Press, 2005), 154, 163.

[9]John Jay to George Washington, 27 June 1786, Founders Online, National Archives, https://founders.archives.gov.

[10]Alexis de Tocqueville, *Democracy in America*, ed. Olivier Zunz (New York: Literary Classics of the United States, 2004), 213.

But given the centrality of our thoughts about human nature to how we see the world, how can we possibly settle for either state? This goes double for Christians called to bring "every thought into captivity to the obedience of Christ."[11]

Here is a sobering truth: the chances are good that our views on the matter will come less from sustained reflection than from a kind of osmosis in which we unconsciously absorb the values of our culture. This is what prompted the British writer Samuel Taylor Coleridge—a contemporary of Tocqueville's—to lament that most of us go through life "like bats, but in twilight." Unless we actively combat it, Coleridge is warning us, we'll stumble blindly through life, guided by values that we feel more than see.[12] The more this describes us, the greater the probability we'll disagree with the Framers about human nature, although it won't be because we've thought through their position systematically and found it wanting. It will be because we were born into a world that long ago stopped listening to them.

All this is to say that there is undoubtedly a personal benefit to what I'm recommending. Seriously wrestling with these questions—approaching them as if your life depended on it, which in a sense it does—is the kind of "inner work" that can challenge and change us.[13] At the same time, recognize that doing so is also the essential first step in answering the "So what?" question about the Great Reversal. If the Framers were wrong about human nature, then our rejection of their view is cause for celebration. We can rest assured knowing that, by conforming to the culture, we're reinforcing the truth rather than undermining it. (There's a comforting thought.) But if the Framers were on to something, and we've based our approach to democracy on false assumptions about who we are, then we've got some serious rethinking to do.

I hope you'll take to heart the exhortation to join the conversation, clarifying your view and thinking long and hard about why you hold it. In the meantime, though, I'm going to tell you what I believe. This won't settle the debate, but I hope it will stimulate your thinking, even where we disagree, perhaps *especially* where we disagree. Ideally, the remainder of this book will "become a place where my best thoughts and yours will meet, sometimes clash, and in the process

---

[11]2 Corinthians 10:5.

[12]Samuel Taylor Coleridge, *Essays on His Own Times, Forming a Second Series of the Friend* (London: William Pickering, 1850), 708-9.

[13]E. F. Schumacher, quoted in Parker Palmer, *To Know as We Are Known: Education as a Spiritual Journey* (New York: HarperSanFrancisco, 1983), 36.

sharpen each."[14] It may not be pleasant—sparks fly when "iron sharpens iron"—but the Scripture tells us to look for blessing when that happens.[15]

And it's with the Scripture that I feel compelled to begin. I don't believe that the Bible speaks *directly* to every political question that we face, but I accept that where it speaks directly it also speaks finally and authoritatively. In part one I argued that, whatever their private religious convictions, the Framers' understanding of human nature corresponds closely to what the Bible unequivocally teaches. The Scripture does not describe us as basically good beings who occasionally "let ourselves down" by making "poor choices." It teaches instead that we come into the world bearing not only the image of God but also the imprint of the fall, propelled through life by the determination to govern ourselves and please ourselves. Although they didn't use the language of *imago Dei* or original sin, the Framers' sense of who we are sounds a lot like the Bible's description of fallen humanity.

Now let me go further: it's possible to acknowledge the similarity between the teaching of Scripture and the views of the Framers while dismissing both as false. I am convinced, however, that what the Bible teaches about human nature is *true*, and this leads me inexorably to the conclusion that the Framers were far closer to the truth than the Jacksonian democrats who trumpeted the essential goodness of the people. More to the point, they were far closer to the truth than the majority of Americans today. The Great Reversal is a tragedy, not primarily because we have turned our backs on the Founding Fathers—that's not intrinsically wrong—but because we have exchanged the truth about ourselves for a lie.

In saying this, I am acutely aware that, if the survey data are accurate, there will be large numbers of professing Christians who disagree with me. I take no pleasure in contradicting them, but the gospel is not a personal philosophy that we shape to our individual taste. Scripture describes it as "the faith which was once for all delivered to the saints," and inseparable from its good news is the very bad news that we're rebels against the King of the universe. Apart from God's mercy and grace, we're all in a boatload of trouble.[16]

Remember George Whitefield's blunt assessment? "If you have never felt the weight of original sin," the evangelist thundered, "do not call yourselves Christians." Or Reverend John Witherspoon's caution about the centrality of the fall

---

[14]Maryanne Wolf, *Reader, Come Home: The Reading Brain in a Digital World* (New York: Harper, 2018), 14.

[15]Proverbs 27:17.

[16]Jude 3.

to the gospel? Take away the "clear and full conviction of the sinfulness of our nature and state," this signer of the Declaration of Independence insisted, and "all that is said in scripture of the wisdom and mercy of God in providing a Saviour is without force and without meaning."[17] The fall is a load-bearing beam; remove it, and the gospel edifice collapses.

This is what the eminent theologian H. Richard Niebuhr famously concluded almost a century ago. Religious liberals' discovery that we are naturally "benevolent" and "altruistic" had been a crucial step in their dismantling of historic Christian orthodoxy. When they were finished, all that remained was a pseudo-gospel in which "a God without wrath brought men without sin into a kingdom without judgment through the ministrations of a Christ without a cross."[18] And this is why, after discovering that neither Christian millennials nor their parents gave much thought to repentance from sin, the National Study of Youth and Religion concluded that "a significant part of Christianity in the United States is actually only tenuously Christian in any sense that is seriously connected to the actual historical Christian tradition."[19]

The conclusion of Christian Smith and his team is almost certainly correct. What it means for the vitality of American Christianity is a question that goes far beyond the scope of our conversation here, but we at least can ponder the implications for American democracy. With that end in mind, it makes sense to conduct a hypothetical thought experiment. *If* the Framers' understanding of us as naturally selfish is correct, *if* orthodox Christianity's belief about the effects of the fall are true, how might that logically direct our own political attitudes and behavior?

Three caveats before we go on. First, what follows is hardly a systematic theology of politics. My goal is to get us thinking and to jump-start a conversation. Second, as will become evident, my primary concern is not with our awareness of sins but of original sin, not with our ability to combat specific sins plaguing our culture but with our willingness to acknowledge the sin nature that dwells within each of us. Finally, I am directing the remarks that follow to *all* who

---

[17] Alan Jacobs, *Original Sin: A Cultural History* (New York: HarperCollins, 2008), 133; Carl J. Richard, *The Founders and the Bible* (Lanham, MD: Rowman & Littlefield, 2016), 264-65.

[18] H. Richard Niebuhr, *The Kingdom of God in America* (New York: Harper & Row, 1939), 191, 193.

[19] Smith and Denton, *Soul Searching*, 171. See also Ed Stetzer, who concludes from different US survey data that "the majority of people who claim to be Christian do not have a Christian worldview." *Christians in the Age of Outrage: How to Bring Our Best When the World Is at Its Worst* (Carol Stream, IL: Tyndale Momentum, 2018), 64.

profess Christian faith. Although, historically, the repudiation of original sin has been a hallmark of theological liberalism and most notable in mainline Protestantism, when it comes to our political involvement, I see little evidence that American evangelicals take the doctrine any more seriously, with consequences just as tragic.

So how would we think differently about democracy, how would we act differently within our democracy, if we were to take original sin seriously? What would change if we conceived of ourselves as "We the *Fallen* People"?

Let's begin with our thinking. I have several suggestions.

To begin with, if we took original sin seriously, we would be more alert to the false assumptions about human nature, implicit and explicit, that are intertwined with democracy as we practice and experience it. To say that the Framers were much closer to biblical truth than the majority of Americans today is another way of saying that American democracy preaches a false gospel. James Madison was right. We're not angels, and we should be offended by those who seek our votes while implying that we are. In the *Federalist*, Alexander Hamilton wrote that it was a mark of "good sense" when citizens "despise the adulator" who tells them that their judgment is invariably right.[20] It is also a mark of biblical wisdom.

Let me be clear about what I am *not* saying. I am not arguing that democracy is intrinsically un-Christian or that it inevitably proclaims what Scripture denies. Never forget C. S. Lewis's observation that confidence in human goodness isn't the only possible foundation for democracy. As Lewis observed, we could just as plausibly advocate universal enfranchisement and majority rule on the grounds that, precisely because we are not good, it isn't safe to entrust power solely to individuals or minority factions. In this light, it would make sense instead to distribute power as broadly as possible, even though the majority itself, like each of us individually, is hardly infallible. This line of reasoning would be logically consistent, but it isn't very flattering, and Americans have preferred a different justification.

But this is precisely the line of reasoning we must cultivate. In *Common Sense*, Thomas Paine told American patriots that the state of nature was democratic and suggested that humans fell *from* democracy as kings and strongmen robbed them of their natural rights. We would be closer to the mark to think of

---

[20]Alexander Hamilton, *Federalist* #71, in Alexander Hamilton, James Madison, and John Jay, *The Federalist*, ed. J. R. Pole (Indianapolis: Hackett, 2005), 383.

democracy as something that we fall *to*. Writing during the Second World War, theologian Reinhold Niebuhr (Richard's brother) drove home this point, rebuking as "foolish" those who defended democracy while dismissing original sin. If our "capacity for justice makes democracy possible," Niebuhr observed, it's our "inclination to injustice" that "makes democracy necessary."[21]

This side of eternity, we'll need to remind ourselves of this truth perpetually. If democracy doesn't *necessarily* proclaim a false gospel, until humans become angels it will *typically* do so. We naturally "suppress the truth," as the apostle Paul explains, including the truth about ourselves, and we're happy for our elected officials to help us. Let me correct that: we *demand* that they do so. As Paul warned Timothy, we're drawn to voices that tickle our "itching ears"—that tell us what we want to believe—and if this is true in our religious lives, it's most assuredly true in our politics.[22]

As long as the majority rewards them, in other words, there will be more than enough office seekers willing to tell us how good and wise we are. As long as we cheer them, there will be more than enough politicians and pundits eager to portray the other side as the sole repository of evil. The democratic gospel isn't going away anytime soon, but if we aspire to think Christianly, we must resist being shaped by it or contributing to it.

If we took original sin seriously, we would reject democratic faith as well as the democratic gospel. The core assumption of democratic faith, you'll recall, is the conviction that "genuine" democracy is intrinsically just and good. Democratic faith imagines a state of society in which the people not only rule but in which they rule righteously, reliably promoting the common good and securing "liberty and justice for all." To use the language of our Founding Fathers, democratic faith assumes that we are naturally *virtuous*. But remember that neither the Framers nor Tocqueville believed that, and neither should anyone who believes what the Bible teaches about the human heart.

We must nurture instead a democratic philosophy, conceiving of democracy simply as a process of self-government that is inevitably imperfect, like all human institutions, and learning to measure its strengths and weaknesses against our more fundamental commitments and convictions. As we try to do so, it will help if we drop all efforts to define "true" democracy by the outcomes it produces.

---

[21]Jared Hickman, "The Theology of Democracy," *New England Quarterly* 81 (2008): 177-217; Reinhold Niebuhr, *The Children of Light and the Children of Darkness: A Vindication of Democracy and a Critique of Its Traditional Defense* (Chicago: University of Chicago Press, 1944), 10, xxxii.

[22]Romans 1:18; 2 Timothy 4:3.

When we define democracy by its output, the concept soon becomes useless. We expand it to include "all kinds of things we like," until we end up with "a pile of everybody's pet concerns."[23] When Donald Trump and Nancy Pelosi can both champion "democracy," we can be pretty sure they're not thinking of the same thing.

We'd be better off to follow Tocqueville's example and define democracy in terms of input. Although you can make a case for a more complicated definition than Tocqueville's, I think there's much to be said for his simple definition of democracy as the process by which the will of the majority becomes public policy. "The very essence of democratic government," Tocqueville tells us, is that "the majority has absolute sway."[24] Not much ambiguity there.

Even more important than its precision is how Tocqueville's conception of democracy helps us in thinking about the human heart and the human condition. When we define democracy as a set of desirable outcomes, we're making a statement about who "We the People" *aspire* to be. That's never a bad thing. But if we take original sin seriously, we should be at least as concerned about who "We the *Fallen* People" *are inclined* to be. Tocqueville's approach is superior for that purpose. It teaches us more truthfully about our hearts.

The key is Tocqueville's insight that democracy is morally indeterminate instead of intrinsically just. If democracy is the implementation of the will of the majority, then whatever the majority wills is "democratic." But because the majority consists of individuals who are simultaneously children of the living God and rebels against him, the range of democratic outcomes can vary from the morally upright to the morally indefensible.

Accustomed as we are to thinking about democracy through the lens of democratic faith, we can recoil against a definition of democracy that allows it to result in egregious injustice. What if the majority supports the removal of Native Americans, or slavery, or racial segregation, or an unprovoked war, or the internment of American citizens without trial? (All of which it has done before.) Is that "democracy"? Can such acts be "democratic"? Such a definition can seem worse than useless, for it leaves no reliable boundary between democracy and tyranny.

From across the centuries, we can hear Tocqueville reply, "That's precisely my point."

---

[23]Yascha Mounk, *The People vs. Democracy: Why Our Freedom Is in Danger & How to Save It* (Cambridge, MA: Harvard University Press, 2018), 26; Robert Wiebe, *Self-Rule: A Cultural History of American Democracy* (Chicago: University of Chicago Press, 1995), 2.

[24]Richardson, *Messages and Papers of the Presidents*, 3:1011; Tocqueville, *Democracy in America*, 283.

It was partly to drive home this truth that we revisited the removal of the Cherokee Nation. A decided majority of white Americans supported the policy championed by "the People's President," while the vast majority affirmed the racist assumptions marshaled to justify it. By Tocqueville's reckoning, this made Native American removal as it unfolded in the 1830s a democratic policy. What is indisputable is that it was popular, and that should be sobering. When we take original sin seriously, we will understand, with Tocqueville, that the majority is ever capable of great injustice.

But although we will be grieved by such episodes, we will not be shocked. "A small knowledge of history depresses one with the sense of the everlasting weight of human iniquity," J. R. R. Tolkien once remarked.[25] When we take original sin seriously, we know that the depravity that distressed Tolkien has never been confined to specific moments or particular lands. It stretches across the entirety of the past into our present; it extends across all national boundaries, including our own. This doesn't mean that all cultures are somehow morally equivalent—not remotely!—but it does mean that no age is "golden," and no nation is righteous. The lingering effects of the fall mark every era, and every land, and every era in every land.

If we take original sin seriously, we'll not purge its effects from our national story nor condemn those who refuse to do so. There's nothing unpatriotic about acknowledging moral failures in our country's past. G. K. Chesterton emphasized this truth over a century ago in his classic work *Orthodoxy*. In its essence, patriotism is less an expression of pride than a commitment to love a particular human community, and authentic love "is not blind," Chesterton observed. "That is the last thing that it is. Love is bound; and the more it is bound, the less it is blind."[26] Never for a minute accept the false dichotomy that pits patriotism against an honest acknowledgment of America's failures and flaws. Because love binds rather than blinds, we are free to criticize our country without somehow betraying it.

I'll go further. I think that Christians *must* do so. Because we are created in the image of God *and* disfigured by moral corruption—because we simultaneously reflect both *imago Dei* and original sin—all human communities exhibit

[25]Humphrey Carpenter, ed., *The Letters of J. R. R. Tolkien* (New York: Houghton Mifflin Harcourt, 1981), 80.

[26]G. K. Chesterton, *Orthodoxy* (1908; repr., New York: Image Books, 2001), 70.

these twin realities in varying proportions. We're right to celebrate what is honorable in our past, but we err when that's all we acknowledge. A sanitized national history purged of moral failures isn't just inaccurate. It teaches "bad religion," contradicting what orthodox Christianity has always taught about human nature and the human condition.[27]

If we take original sin seriously, it will not only inform how we remember our past; it will also transform the significance that we attach to it. As I write this, I'm mindful of Jesus' parable about two men who went into the temple to pray. The first, a Pharisee, proudly thanked God for his own righteousness. The second, a despised tax collector, grieved over his sin and pleaded with God for mercy. It was the latter, Jesus explained, who "went down to his house justified."[28]

These are our only choices when we observe injustices in our history. Jesus' command in the Sermon on the Mount, "judge not, that you be not judged," doesn't prohibit us from measuring the actions of others against the yardstick of Scripture.[29] In fact, we're required to exercise such discernment. But Jesus clearly taught that we jeopardize our hearts when we go beyond the appraisal of behavior to the assessment of souls, when we conclude that we're more righteous than others and less in need of God's grace.

Consider the removal of Native Americans. The historical record testifies that much about it was immoral. But in condemning the actions of our forebears, we must beware against assuring ourselves that we would have behaved differently. What is that but the Pharisee's prayer, "God, I thank You that I am not like other men"?

The late Robert Remini, arguably the premier historian of Jacksonian democracy, concluded that removal was "harsh, arrogant, racist—and inevitable." There was simply "no way the American people would continue to allow the presence of the tribes in the fertile hills and valleys that they coveted." And as for the denigration of Native Americans so frequently used to justify the policy? It "crossed party lines, crossed sectional lines, and crossed social and economic lines," Remini observed. "It was a near-universal attitude that most Americans accepted as commonplace."[30]

Why would we expect to respond differently if we had been born at the same time, shaped by the same culture, and constrained by the same circumstances?

---

[27]Ross Douthat, *Bad Religion: How We Became a Nation of Heretics* (New York: Free Press, 2012).
[28]See Luke 18:9-14.
[29]Matthew 7:1.
[30]Robert V. Remini, *Andrew Jackson and His Indian Wars* (New York: Penguin, 2001), 237, 223.

Don't misunderstand my point. To concede that we probably would have supported the removal of Native Americans had we been alive two centuries ago doesn't exonerate those who did so at the time. *It implicates us.* When we wrestle with this rightly, when we not only concede but *confess* this reality, our prayer shifts to that of the tax collector, "God, be merciful to me a sinner!" And when this becomes our heart's cry, Native American removal becomes more than just a regrettable episode in the distant past. It becomes an urgent warning—to *us, today.* Although the circumstances would surely be different, we are just as capable of condoning injustice and rationalizing it as righteous, of depriving others of their liberty and calling ourselves good. In a democracy, the minority is never truly safe from the majority.

But we are also just as capable of forfeiting our own liberty, which is why, in a democracy, the majority is never truly safe from itself. "I have no confidence in the spirit of liberty that seems to animate my contemporaries," Alexis de Tocqueville confessed in *Democracy in America*.[31] Should we have such confidence in *our own* contemporaries? More to the point, should we have that confidence in *ourselves*?

Not if we take original sin seriously. If we think otherwise, it's probably because we confuse liberty with license. Augustine tells us that the two telltale signs of our fallen nature are our desires to please ourselves and to rule ourselves, to pursue "happiness," as we define it, without interference or accountability. That's the very definition of license, and in our fallenness, we delight in it. (We delight in it for ourselves, that is. We're less enamored of it for others.) But liberty is not the freedom to do what we *want*. It's the freedom to do what we *ought*.

Secular political philosophy has often distinguished liberty from license by defining liberty as the freedom to enjoy our rights *while respecting the rights of others*, but from a Christian perspective, that's still an impoverished understanding. When the apostles defied the order of the Jewish Sanhedrin to stop teaching in the name of Jesus, their justification was simply, "We ought to obey God rather than men."[32] Christian liberty is less about self-assertion than obedience, less the freedom to exercise rights than to honor obligations. The Puritan minister John Robinson put it well in a letter to the Pilgrims of Plymouth

---

[31]Tocqueville, *Democracy in America*, 815.
[32]Acts 5:29.

Colony: a Christian's liberty is to "to serve God in faith, and his brethren in love."[33] When we have complete freedom to love God and love our neighbors, we are enjoying liberty to the full.

But such liberty is as fragile as it is precious, and if it is to survive we must be faithful and vigilant stewards. We must exercise our liberty responsibly, not allowing it to degenerate into license. We must treasure it dearly, refusing to sell it cheaply for short-term advantage. We must never risk it unnecessarily, tolerating (or applauding!) the concentration of power when we believe that will further our interests.

The problem is that our love of self makes all of this difficult, which is why Tocqueville could speak of "the burden of liberty."[34] Because we are naturally selfish, we are also naturally short-sighted (preferring immediate gratification to self-denial), and that makes us susceptible to foolish bargains. When we expect to benefit in the short run—by a temporary increase in order or security or prosperity or comfort—we can be persuaded to jeopardize our liberty in the long run.

This surely is one of the primary lessons of the Bank War. While it has become customary in recent years to condemn Andrew Jackson for his enthusiastic support of Native American removal and southern slavery, we are more likely to give the general a pass for his assault on the Constitution's checks and balances during his campaign against "the Monster." The "People's President" wasn't consciously trying to create an "executive despotism," but his authoritarian instincts and boundless self-righteousness led him inexorably in that direction.[35]

Today's "imperial presidency" is "an office with no fixed limits," as a constitutional scholar puts it, with powers so far beyond what the Framers envisioned that "we've witnessed something of a creeping constitutional coup."[36] It was Jackson who set that gradual, relentless process in motion. Whatever his intentions, the general expanded the power of the presidency at the expense of Congress and the courts.

If the Framers were right about human nature, this undermining of the Constitution's checks and balances was a threat to liberty and should have been

---

[33]*Governor William Bradford's Letter Book* (Bedford, MA: Applewood Books, 2001), 23.

[34]Tocqueville, *Democracy in America*, 108.

[35]Sean Wilentz, *The Rise of American Democracy: Jefferson to Lincoln* (New York: W. W. Norton, 2005), 399.

[36]Saikrishna Bangalore Prakash, *The Living Presidency: An Originalist Argument Against Its Ever-Expanding Powers* (Cambridge, MA: Belknap Press, 2020), 3.

controversial, and it was, but not in a way that would reassure us. With limited exceptions, it was controversial *along partisan lines*, with Whigs denouncing a tyrant and Democrats praising a hero. This would set the mold for a pattern that continues to this day. While the Framers concluded that power is a threat to liberty regardless of who wields it, we have tended to be suspicious of power primarily when it's controlled by the other side.

Arguably more important than Jackson's actions in expanding executive power was his justification for doing so. He was the first president to anoint himself the only "direct representative of the American people."[37] He was the first president to proclaim that the people are innately virtuous and that their preferences (as *he* defined them) are intrinsically good. He was the first to claim a popular mandate and equate it with moral authority.

What was novel precedent two centuries ago is hoary tradition today. In democracy as Americans have known it ever since, politicians routinely pay tribute to the wisdom of the people. They regularly impute moral authority to the decision of the majority. They universally present themselves as the best representative of the people, and they predictably claim that the majority, if well informed, will be on their side.

Jackson's populist rhetoric went beyond this, however. What populism adds to the mix, above all, is fear—fear that the people are being attacked, that they are being threatened by an enemy, that defeat at the polls will mean the downfall of the republic or the "end of the country as we know it."[38] The people are still virtuous, but there is a palpable evil that threatens them and that justifies extraordinary measures to avoid calamity.

In his populist justification for the bank veto, Jackson didn't simply offer a description of the conflict that was wildly inaccurate. More seriously, he was teaching his followers to see themselves and their world in a way that is incompatible with an open, pluralistic society. I noted earlier that populists are "dichotomizers" who routinely divide society into two groups. This isn't what makes them unique. The heart of their message is that *only one of these two groups is legitimate.* One of them consists of "the people" and is righteous. The other consists of the people's enemies—of "the Monster," however defined, and its malevolent allies and unwitting accomplices.

---

[37]Richardson, *Messages and Papers of the Presidents*, 3:1309.

[38]Glenn Beck, quoted in Jeremy W. Peters, "The 'Never Trump" Coalition That Decided Eh, Never Mind, He's Fine," *New York Times*, October 5, 2019, www.nytimes.com/2019/10/05/us/politics/never-trumper-republicans.html.

A democratic mindset doesn't have to become populist, but when our commitment to democracy is founded on a positive view of human nature that externalizes all evil, the boundary between them can be tissue thin. Even when our public life seems tranquil, populism is always just one national crisis and charismatic leader away. This should concern us all, regardless of our religious beliefs, regardless of whether we feel called to think Christianly in the public square.

To the degree that we believe what populists tell us, Americans will have less patience with complicated solutions, less motivation for constructive engagement with other perspectives, less openness to compromise across the aisle, less space for genuine pluralism, and less willingness to submit peacefully to electoral defeat. In the process, we will find ourselves more prone to intolerance, more accepting of concentrated power, and more susceptible to authoritarianism. Many of us would find that tragic, I have no doubt. Alexis de Tocqueville certainly would, but he wouldn't see it necessarily as a contradiction of democracy. He'd warn us that it is always a possible trajectory of democracy.

To sum up, democracy isn't *intrinsically* intolerant and authoritarian, but it *can* be. The question for us is, *Will* it be?

I noted in the introduction G. K. Chesterton's warning that "nothing so much threatens the safety of democracy as assuming that democracy is safe."[39] If there was a silver lining in the cascading crises that assailed us in 2020, it may be that they made us more acutely aware of how fragile liberal democracy can be, even in the United States. As I write this, I'm skeptical that democracy per se is in imminent danger in this country—we're not on the verge of a military coup— but whether in the future American democracy will provide a "domain of liberty" for the preservation of human dignity is an open question.[40]

As it must always be. This is one of the truths that Tocqueville most wants us to hear. It is the truth that filled his heart with "a kind of religious terror." Because the human heart harbors both "angel" and "beast," because "only God can be all-powerful without danger," the possibility that democracy will devolve into tyranny is ever present. It's a threat that we must never ignore, a danger that

---

[39]Kent R. Hill, "Chesterton, Democracy, and the Permanent Things," in *Permanent Things: Toward the Recovery of a More Human Scale at the End of the Twentieth Century*, ed. Andrew A. Tadie and Michael H. McDonald (Grand Rapids, MI: Eerdmans, 1995), 94.

[40]Tocqueville, *Democracy in America*, 834, italics added; Hugh Heclo, *Christianity and American Democracy* (Cambridge, MA: Harvard University Press, 2007), 8.

never goes away.[41] This is not a flaw that can be eliminated by "more democracy." The work of sustaining liberty is hard, and it never ends, not only because we live in a fallen world but because each of us is fallen as well.

As a Christian, I say "amen" to Tocqueville's insight that democracy in and of itself cannot be our salvation. It's not an antidote to human iniquity or somehow immune to it. It just reflects who we are. If the lingering effects of the fall touch every era and every land, they also mar every system of government, democracy included. For the Christian, to think otherwise is not just misguided. It's a form of idolatry.

I'm also thankful for the hope that Tocqueville offers us, because I think that it's entirely reconcilable with Christian truth. For two thousand years, traditional Christian doctrine has given believers *hope for* humanity while warning against *faith in* humanity.[42] In a similar way, Tocqueville rejects *faith in* democracy while inviting us to embrace *hope for* democracy. And what is that modest, humble hope? That despite our fallen nature, democracy can significantly, if imperfectly, promote both liberty and human dignity. That's huge. But whether it succeeds in doing so won't depend on some moral trait intrinsic to democracy. Humanly speaking, it will depend mostly on what we believe and how we behave. That should scare us, because we're not as good as we think.

---

[41]Tocqueville, *Democracy in America*, 6, 290; Alexis de Tocqueville, *"The European Revolution" and Correspondence with Gobineau*, ed. and trans. John Lukacs (Gloucester, MA: Peter Smith, 1968), 27-28.

[42]Heclo, *Christianity and American Democracy*, 57.

— 10 —

WE THE *FALLEN* PEOPLE

Transforming Our Behavior

*I*t's supremely ironic that we ever imagined Alexis de Tocqueville attributing the success of American democracy to Americans' goodness. Given his actual conclusion that "Americans are not a virtuous people," our claim that he concluded that "America is great, because she is good" is not just a little bit off. It's one of those cruel tricks that Voltaire said the living sometimes play on the dead.[1]

As we have seen, Tocqueville attributed the harmony and prosperity of Jacksonian America not to the prevalence of virtue but to the primacy of a particular kind of selfishness. To the degree that Americans avoided tyranny and promoted liberty, Tocqueville credited their success to "habits of restraint" shaped by "self-interest properly understood." For all their nationalist hubris, for all their theoretical claims about human perfectibility, a critical mass of Americans had learned in their day-to-day behavior to doubt the first impulses of their hearts. To the degree that democracy "worked" in Jacksonian America, it was less because Americans were naturally good than because enough of them knew that they weren't. What would that mindset look like today?

I confessed in the introduction that I have no comprehensive solution to offer for the political polarization, governmental gridlock, and popular frustration that plague our country. The problems we face are manifold and complex. Crafting a comprehensive solution, if it exists, is beyond me. Yet I have no doubt that we would benefit by adjusting our thinking to take original sin seriously.

---

[1]Alexis de Tocqueville, *Letters from America*, ed. Frederick Brown (New Haven, CT: Yale University Press, 2010), 70.

However ironic it may sound, having less faith in ourselves—reconceiving ourselves as "We the *Fallen* People"—would constitute a sizable step toward a healthier democracy. If nothing else, taking our fallenness seriously would immunize us from the self-satisfaction and complacency that G. K. Chesterton warned against, the mindset that endangers democracy by assuming that democracy is not in danger.

But thinking should also lead to action, and it makes sense to explore briefly how our political *behavior* might change if we took original sin to heart. So here are a few suggestions of what it might look like for Christians to bring this truth with them into the public square. You should know that I've intentionally kept them broad, I've intentionally saved them to the end, and I've intentionally made them brief because of the single most striking thing that I've noticed about the Bible's teaching on politics: there isn't much of it.

As Jonathan Leeman observes in his wonderful book *How the Nations Rage*, "most of the political questions citizens face today are biblically unscripted."[2] Scripture tells us much about the heart of God—the Lord loves justice and mercy, grace and truth—but it doesn't spell out how to infuse those values into public policy in a twenty-first-century democracy. In a similar way, the Bible tells us much about the human heart—it testifies to human fallenness, most notably—but it doesn't specify how to make allowances for our sinful nature in order to craft an effective constitution or promote a flourishing democracy.

Questions such as these can't be answered unequivocally by biblical precepts. They require the application of biblically informed wisdom, and that means we're inevitably going to disagree about them. But we can disagree without being divided, without effectively excommunicating brothers and sisters in the faith who don't arrive at our conclusions. And so, while I'm going to make the strongest argument that I can for the recommendations that follow, I'm not going to imply that if you disagree with me you're apostate, heretical, or in the grips of demonic possession. I hope you'll return the favor.

One caveat before we proceed: what follows is not a road map for Christian political success. I'm not remotely interested in trying to craft such a strategy. No offense, but our recent efforts to wield political influence have done less to Christianize politics than to politicize Christianity, and I want no part of that.

---

[2]Jonathan Leeman, *How the Nations Rage: Rethinking Faith and Politics in a Divided Age* (Nashville: Nelson Books, 2018), 85.

I love my country, and I fear for the future of American democracy, but my greatest concern is for the church and for her witness. And so I want us to consider together what it might look like for Christians who take original sin seriously to live out that truth politically. I believe that living out that truth would honor God and bless our neighbors, and I also happen to believe that, in the mercy of God, it would benefit American democracy. But if my suggestions seem politically naive, I can live with that. If you doubt that they would enhance our leverage with party politicians, I can live with that too. I'm not sure when Christian political success becomes an indicator of Christian faithfulness, at any rate. And it's faithfulness that God calls us to, not results.[3]

So here goes: to live out a heartfelt conviction of original sin, we must run from every effort to meld Christianity with a particular political party, movement, or leader. The reason for this is twofold: For one, we'll recognize the folly of placing unlimited confidence in any earthly deliverer. If the effects of the fall touch every era in every land, they also mark every political institution we revere, every political party we champion, every incumbent we cheer, every candidate we vote for. But because we know that the effects of the fall also linger in *us*, we'll know that we can be lured into political idolatry all the same, and we'll be on guard against that perpetual danger.

As late as the 1970s, white Christian voters split fairly evenly between the two major parties, and if anything, they tilted slightly Democratic. Over the past half century, however, white evangelicals have shifted dramatically toward the Republican Party, and today we are so "locked into our political identity" that seemingly nothing can shake our allegiance, not even the GOP's nomination for president in 2016 of a serial adulterer and casino owner with no experience in government and no apparent qualifications for the office beyond impersonating a successful businessman on TV.[4] For a vast swath of white American evangelicals, a key component of our identity as Christ followers is that we vote for the Republican Party, come hell or high water.[5]

---

[3]Ibid., 173.

[4]Steven Levitsky and Daniel Ziblatt, *How Democracies Die* (New York: Crown Publishing, 2018), 171; Ezra Klein, *Why We're Polarized* (New York: Avid Reader Press, 2020), xiv.

[5]A national survey conducted the month before the 2020 election found that 46 percent of white evangelical Protestants claimed that there was "almost nothing" Donald Trump could do to lose their support. See Public Religion Research Institute, "Amid Multiple Crises, Trump and Biden Supporters See Different Realities and Futures for the Nation," October 19, 2020, www.prri.org/

Not that we always admit that so baldly. Part of the mark of the fall in our lives is a talent for self-justification, and so we look for creative ways to rationalize our reflexive allegiance as principled and discerning. In the case of Donald Trump, one path was to insist against all evidence that he, too, was a Christ follower, albeit one who had learned to hide it well. When Trump admitted at a Christian political conference that he had never asked God for forgiveness, this contingent marveled at his honesty and integrity for saying so. When he revealed his unbounded ignorance of Scripture—"the Bible means a lot to me, but I don't want to get into specifics"—they assured themselves of his "God consciousness."[6]

Another common tack was to focus on policy as paramount. By this line of thinking, the right candidate is simply the candidate whose platform most closely aligns with our priorities. Outcomes mean everything. This is a conception of politics as transaction, a mutually beneficial exchange in which citizens swap their votes for specific governmental actions. In both 2016 and 2020, for example, countless evangelicals justified ignoring Donald Trump's numerous, well-documented moral lapses on the grounds that he would oppose abortion, defend religious liberty, and fast-track conservative judicial nominees. The unofficial slogan of this group came from Jerry Falwell Jr.: "We're not electing a pastor, we're electing a president."[7]

If only it were that simple. The reality is that every *transaction* comes embedded with *testimony*, a host of messages about ourselves and about our God. Rather than focusing on political outcomes, we should be asking ourselves constantly, "What is the vote I am casting (or the opinion I am registering, or the post I am liking, or the tweet I am sharing) proclaiming about what it means to follow Jesus, about the nature of the gospel, about the heart of God?

We reveal much about ourselves in our political transactions, for implicit in each is a declaration about what we desire and how much we are willing to pay for it. In recent years, I fear that what many Christians revealed was an overriding pragmatism. In return for the right promises, we were willing to give overwhelming

---

research/amid-multiple-crises-trump-and-biden-supporters-see-different-realities-and-futures-for-the-nation/.

[6]David Brody and Scott Lamb, *The Faith of Donald J. Trump: A Spiritual Biography* (New York: HarperCollins, 2018), 150-51, 158, 209.

[7]Ben Howe, *The Immoral Majority: Why Evangelicals Chose Political Power over Christian Values* (New York: Broadside Books, 2019), 56.

support to a candidate who, in terms of his character, was "the very personification" of the values that evangelicals have historically condemned.[8]

We sanctified this alliance of convenience by insisting that it was the price of combating abortion. That argument fails on two counts. In the realm of moral reasoning, it flirts with the assertion that the ends justify the means, a moral fallacy that is always and everywhere the tool of tyrants and the enemy of the weak and vulnerable. But it fails also to describe political reality. When the Billy Graham Center of Wheaton College conducted a nationwide survey of evangelicals after the 2016 election, only 5 *percent* of respondents identified the candidates' position on abortion as the most important factor in determining how they voted. Respondents were more likely to list as most important the candidates' positions on the economy, health care, immigration, and national security, among other issues.[9] Far from a determination to defend the helpless, it seems that many of us sold our souls for more self-interested reasons.

Which wouldn't surprise us, if we believed in original sin.

Intertwined with this pervasive pragmatism, I'm afraid, was a substantial measure of something that looks a lot like hypocrisy. In 1998, when evidence surfaced that Democratic president Bill Clinton had had sex with a White House intern, evangelical leaders lectured the country on the importance of strong moral character in the nation's highest office. "Character matters," the Christian Coalition's Ralph Reed intoned, "and we will not rest until we have leaders of good moral character." James Dobson reminded the followers of Focus on the Family that "character DOES matter. You can't run a family, let alone a country, without it." Franklin Graham, son of the twentieth century's foremost evangelist, posed a rhetorical question in the *Wall Street Journal*: If the president "will lie to or mislead his wife . . . what will prevent him from doing the same to the American public?" Jerry Falwell Sr., founder of the Moral Majority, concluded that Clinton was "no longer worthy to fulfill his office."[10] Character mattered—then.

Two decades later it had become less important. When it was revealed that the Republican presidential nominee had paid porn star Stormy Daniels $130,000 to hush up an alleged affair, Franklin Graham argued that "this thing with Stormy

---

[8]R. Albert Mohler Jr., "Donald Trump Has Created an Excruciating Moment for Evangelicals," *Washington Post*, October 9, 2016, www.washingtonpost.com/news/acts-of-faith/wp/2016/10/09/donald-trump-has-created-an-excruciating-moment-for-evangelicals/.

[9]Ed Stetzer, *Christians in the Age of Outrage: How to Bring Our Best When the World Is at Its Worst* (Carol Stream, IL: Tyndale Momentum, 2018), 71-72.

[10]Howe, *Immoral Majority*, 75, 76; Franklin Graham, "Clinton's Sins Aren't Private," *Wall Street Journal*, August 27, 1998.

Daniels and so forth is nobody's business." When a video surfaced showing Trump bragging about grabbing women "by the pussy," Reed found the comment "disappointing" but stressed that evangelicals would base their vote on other issues. Dobson labeled it "deplorable" but reaffirmed his endorsement of the Republican nominee. And Jerry Falwell Jr.—who would later be forced by scandal to resign as president of the nation's largest evangelical university— simply dismissed the importance of character outright. After all, we weren't "electing a pastor." Or as Falwell would tweet later, "Christians need to stop electing 'nice guys.'"[11]

It's not a flattering self-portrait, is it? The most charitable thing that can be said of us is that we have foolishly sought "to usher in a kingdom not of this world by using tools that are of this world." The consequences have been both lamentable and predictable. In the words of Christian political theorist Glenn Tinder, the result has been "less a sacralization of society than a degradation of the sacred."[12]

Think about it: what have we proclaimed about the body of Christ? Aren't we telling the world that evangelical Christians are simply another interest group playing politics, pragmatically delivering our votes to any candidate who will make the right promises, and expediently preaching the importance of character only when it helps us and hurts the other side?

More tragic still is what we have proclaimed to the world about God. Make no mistake: when prominent evangelical leaders described Donald Trump as "God's man to lead our great nation," or christened him their "dream president," or praised him as "a knight in shining armor . . . for the evangelical community," they were teaching an unbelieving world about the God we claim to worship.[13] And what were they teaching them? That the man after God's own heart is a textbook narcissist who praises his own "stable genius," calls Mexicans "rapists," deplores immigrants from "shithole countries," mocks Gold Star families, spews misogynistic slurs, detests "losers," demeans the vulnerable, praises dictators and strongmen, and reminisces fondly about the "good old days" when police could crack heads with impunity.

---

[11]David French, "Franklin Graham and the High Cost of the Lost Evangelical Witness," *National Review*, April 25, 2019, www.nationalreview.com/2019/04/franklin-graham-and-the-high-cost-of-the-lost-evangelical-witness/; Howe, *Immoral Majority*, 84; John Fea, *Believe Me: The Evangelical Road to Donald Trump* (Grand Rapids, MI: Eerdmans, 2018), 67-68; Klein, *Why We're Polarized*, 246.

[12]Cal Thomas and Ed Dobson, *Blinded by Might: Can the Religious Right Save America?* (Grand Rapids, MI: Zondervan, 1999), 60; Fea, *Believe Me*, 163.

[13]Brody and Lamb, *Faith of Donald J. Trump*, 210, 300, 311.

What is left of our witness? What is left of our moral authority?

The long-term effects of evangelicals' unshakable alliance with the Republican Party may not be clear for decades, but unless God is merciful they will be tragic. Two centuries ago, Alexis de Tocqueville observed that when religion allies itself with a political power, "it embraces the bitter passions of this world." It "may be forced to defend allies acquired *through interest rather than love*."[14] I call that prophetic.

Tocqueville further warned that such an alliance had devastated the churches of Europe. There, "Christianity allowed itself to become the close ally of temporal powers." Then when those powers began to collapse, Christianity found itself "buried, as it were, beneath their debris." Although still "a living thing," the church was "lashed to cadavers."[15] May God spare us from such a fate.

Next, living out a conviction of original sin will require that we confess the allure of power, acknowledge the danger of power, and work proactively to mitigate the abuse of power. If we accept the reality of original sin, we'll know that the seductiveness of power is fueled by our self-interested nature. In our fallenness, what we want above all is to rule ourselves and please ourselves, and power promises to facilitate what our hearts desire most. The Founding Fathers felt this keenly, which is why their writings reverberate with warnings about "the love of power," the "thirst for power," the "natural lust for power so inherent in man."[16]

Heeding their warning is complicated by two obstacles. First, in our heart of hearts we doubt that it really applies to *us*. Too much power may be dangerous in the hands of Nazis or Democrats or our teenage children, but we're confident that *we* can be trusted. Second, we are blinded by our preoccupation with the present, unaware of how much the fall has left us short-sighted as well as selfish. In his introduction to *Democracy in America*, Alexis de Tocqueville observed that the political parties of his day thought about "tomorrow only," which led them into tragic miscalculations. For his part, Tocqueville "aimed to think about the future." We must follow his example and "try to see further."[17]

---

[14]Alexis de Tocqueville, *Democracy in America*, ed. Olivier Zunz (New York: Literary Classics of the United States, 2004), 343, italics added.

[15]Ibid., 347.

[16]Alexander Hamilton, *Federalist #15*, in Alexander Hamilton, James Madison, and John Jay, *The Federalist*, ed. J. R. Pole (Indianapolis: Hackett, 2005), 79; Bernard Bailyn, ed., *The Debate on the Constitution: Federalist and Antifederalist Speeches, Articles, and Letters During the Struggle over Ratification* (New York: Literary Classics of the United States, 1993), part 2, 514; Carl J. Richard, *The Founders and the Bible* (Lanham, MD: Rowman & Littlefield, 2016), 271.

[17]Tocqueville, *Democracy in America*, 17.

For the Christian, power is never more dangerous, more corrupting in its influence, more beguiling in its appeal than when it is offered directly to the church. This was the misguided alliance of Christendom that Tocqueville lamented, the wedding of the church with the coercive power of the state that characterized much of Europe for a millennium. Americans rejected an established church more than two centuries ago, but politicians continue to offer power to Christians in exchange for their votes, and Christian voters continue to signal their openness to such a deal.

For decades now, Bible-believing Christians in the United States have sensed (correctly) that the country has been drifting away from historic Christian orthodoxy. Some have responded with humility and repentance and godly sorrow, but many have reacted with anger and fear and resentment and demands to have "their country back." And when candidates for office pledge to help them "take back America," they are quite simply offering to deliver cultural power in exchange for political support. It's not that subtle.[18]

President Trump, not surprisingly, was more blunt than most. Early in the 2016 campaign, he introduced his strategy for winning over "the evangelicals": tap into our sense of fear and victimization, pour gasoline onto our smoldering resentment, and promise to help us regain the power, influence, and respect that is rightfully ours. Speaking to an evangelical rally during the run-up to the Iowa caucuses, Trump declared that "Christians in our country are not treated properly." But there was hope. "I want to give power back to the church because the church has to have more power," he told the audience. And if he should be elected, "Christianity *will* have power. . . . If I'm there, you're going to have plenty of power," Trump reiterated. "You don't need anybody else."[19]

Was there no one in the audience who recalled Christ's haunting question, "What will it profit a man if he gains the whole world, and loses his own soul?"[20] Was there no one who remembered that an offer of earthly power was one of the main ways that Satan tempted Jesus in the wilderness?[21] Was there no one brave enough to rise to his feet and say, "Mr. Trump, you know nothing about the kingdom of God"?

I'm going to give you power. You don't need anybody else. To say these words and believe them is the height of hubris. To hear these words and believe them is the

---

[18]Fea, *Believe Me*, chapter 1; Stetzer, *Christians in the Age of Outrage*, 10.
[19]Howe, *Immoral Majority*, 26; Brody and Lamb, *Faith of Donald J. Trump*, 188.
[20]Mark 8:36.
[21]Matthew 4:8-10.

epitome of idolatry. They should evoke horror—not applause—and they would if we took original sin seriously.

Living out the conviction of original sin means more than shunning political power for the church. Out of love for our neighbors, out of love for our country, we must heed the Founders' warnings about power more generally. Among other things, this means that we should jealously protect what remains of the constitutional structure that the Framers designed for a fallen people. We would remind ourselves that the Constitution's federal structure and its separation of powers and checks and balances were intended for our protection. They grew out of an understanding that, human nature being what it is, power is always a threat to liberty, regardless of who wields it, regardless of how we justify it, regardless of who stands to benefit in the short run.

But let's be clear about what this requires. We readily object to the concentration of power when we are in the minority and governmental power is in the hands of our political opponents. We're all zealous constitutionalists in those circumstances, but who wouldn't be? Self-interest and principle speak with one voice.

The true litmus test of our constitutional scruples—and more important, of our belief in human sinfulness—comes when the party we support is in the majority and we can expect immediate benefits from the further concentration of power. At those moments our talent for rationalization kicks in and we can become the world's most calculating pragmatists. If we take original sin seriously, we'll recognize the need for those "habits of restraint" Alexis de Tocqueville wrote about—both to protect the minority in the present and to protect everyone, including ourselves, in the future.

The key to the latter, Tocqueville would tell us, lies in remembering our tendency to "sacrifice the future for the sake of the present." Part of the problem is that we can't foresee the long-term consequences of our actions, but part of the problem is that we don't care. (Tocqueville called this our "contemptible love of present pleasures.")[22] If we take original sin seriously, however, we know that delayed gratification never comes naturally, and given the right combination of fear and resentment, complacency and apathy, we're more than capable of swapping our birthrights of liberty for a bowl of stew. We're hungry *now*.

If we take original sin seriously, then, we will do all that we can to rejuvenate the near-moribund legislative branch of our federal government, even if that

---

[22]Tocqueville, *Democracy in America*, 343, 759.

requires—horror of horrors—that we support congressional candidates willing to cooperate with the other party rather than promising to bludgeon it. But if we take original sin seriously, we will know that this is as it should be, because we will recognize with the Russian dissident Aleksandr Solzhenitsyn that "the line separating good and evil" doesn't separate political parties. It passes "right through every human heart."[23] We might even take to praying for the other party, believing that everyone benefits when both parties in our two-party system are healthy and flourishing. No one-party state has ever truly been free.

Conversely, living out a belief in original sin will require us to push back against the inexorable expansion of the imperial presidency, even when—*especially* when—the current resident of the White House is one of *us*. Regardless of our views on immigration, for example, we will recognize that it is a dangerous precedent when the president can unilaterally redirect congressionally appropriated funds to pay for a border wall that Congress had refused to approve. Regardless of our views on international trade, we will know that something is wrong when the president can bypass the commerce clause and single-handedly instigate a trade war between the world's two largest economies.

When the president of the United States can wield such power without impediment, it is utterly immaterial which political party benefits in the short run or what happens to the stock market, the crime rate, the unemployment rate, or your 401(k). The individual who has paid attention to the Framers, much more so the individual who believes in original sin, will conclude that such power is antithetical to liberty and a threat, in the long run, to everyone. Agreeing with the Framers, echoing Alexis de Tocqueville, we would declare that here "lies the seed of tyranny."[24]

Finally, living out the truth of original sin means insisting that rhetoric matters. Few of us believe that. To the degree that we think about rhetoric at all, we tend to focus on a short list of no-noes. We'd surely object to a politician using the f-word. Some Christians were offended by President Trump's reference to "shithole countries," and a handful of evangelicals publicly scolded him for taking the Lord's name in vain when he joked about "goddamn windmills."[25]

---

[23]Quoted in Alan Jacobs, *Original Sin: A Cultural History* (New York: HarperCollins, 2008), 224.
[24]Tocqueville, *Democracy in America*, 290.
[25]Josh Dawsey, "Trump Derides Protections for Immigrants from 'Shithole' Countries," *Washington Post*, January 12, 2018, www.washingtonpost.com/politics/trump-attacks-protections-for-immi-

But apart from instances of obscenity or profanity, we simply don't think rhetoric is important. We reassure ourselves that it's the policy position that counts, that as long as public figures agree with us on a particular question, how they frame the issue is irrelevant (as long as it's not boring). Megachurch pastor Robert Jeffress expresses this view bluntly: as long as a candidate promotes a pro-Christian agenda, he explains, "I don't care about that candidate's tone or vocabulary." And if we're still uncomfortable with a politician's language, we can always just hit the mute button, as a popular columnist (and former presidential speechwriter!) advised on the eve of the 2020 election. Actions matter. Words don't. Just evaluate the candidates "with the sound off."[26]

This is a tragic misunderstanding of the power of speech. Our words reveal who we are, Jesus proclaimed in the Sermon on the Mount, for they flow "out of the abundance of the heart." But our words also *teach* by example, and in 2016 and 2020 the vast majority of evangelical voters supported a candidate who claimed to follow Christ but whose language consistently modeled contempt for others. The book of James perfectly captures this shameful contradiction, lamenting that with the tongue "we praise our Lord and Father, and with it we curse human beings, who have been made in God's likeness." Rather than excusing or ignoring Donald Trump's contemptuous language (and possibly our own?), we would do better to echo James's conclusion: "My brothers and sisters, this should not be."[27]

But there's more that we must see. The typical political *argument*—the justification for a particular policy or program—is a rhetorical Trojan horse crammed with worldview assumptions. It comes with explicit or implicit assertions about human nature, the structure of society, and the proper role of government, among other things. I'm not talking here about recitations of facts and

---

grants-from-shithole-countries-in-oval-office-meeting/2018/01/11/bfc0725c-f711-11e7-91af-31ac729add94_story.html; Julie Zauzmer, "Trump Uttered What Many Supporters Consider Blasphemy," *Washington Post*, September 14, 2019, www.washingtonpost.com/politics/trump-uttered-what-many-supporters-consider-blasphemy-heres-why-most-will-probably-forgive-him/2019/09/13/685c0bce-d64f-11e9-9343-40db57cf6abd_story.html.

[26]Fea, *Believe Me*, 125; Marc Thiessen, "Trump Is One of the Best Conservative Presidents in Modern History—If You Turn the Sound Off," *Washington Post*, October 29, 2020, www.washingtonpost.com/opinions/2020/10/29/trump-is-one-best-conservative-presidents-modern-history-if-you-turn-sound-off/.

[27]Luke 6:45; James 3:9-10 (NIV). See also Mark Galli, "Why 'Mere' Words Matter: The President's Words—and Our Words About the President," in Ronald J. Sider, ed., *The Spiritual Danger of Donald Trump: Thirty Evangelical Christians on Justice, Truth, and Moral Integrity* (Eugene, OR: Cascade Books, 2020), 3-9.

figures, buttressed by graphs and pie charts. Psychological research suggests that "fact-based arguments don't persuade people very well at all."[28] The most powerful political arguments come packaged as *stories*, narratives that help us to situate our lives, explaining who we are, what we should fear, where our hope lies.

We are bombarded with such stories daily. They are predominantly Us vs. Them stories, churned out ceaselessly by an "outrage-industrial complex" that manipulates our emotions and profits from our anxieties. The details may vary, but the plot line is simple and repetitive: our lives would be better off if not for Them. These scripted melodramas are calculated to generate resentment and disgust, as when a prominent cable news commentator warns that "the worst people in our society have taken control" of America, and "now, they are tearing it down." Americans are "afraid" and "filled with rage," he laments, all the while doing his utmost to stoke fear and rage. The Bible warns us that "the wrath of man does not produce the righteousness of God." That's true, but it can do wonders for ratings.[29]

It doesn't have to be this way, even in the often seamy world of politics. A century and a half ago, as fear and rage propelled a different voting bloc to actions it would later regret, president-elect Abraham Lincoln told Southern secessionists that "we mean to recognize, and bear in mind always, that you have as good hearts in your bosoms as other people, or as we claim to have."[30] Compare that with former president Trump, who often compared himself to our sixteenth president. Trump gushed that Americans on the whole are "good and virtuous people," but his political opponents were "bad people" who "hate our country"—"cowards," "traitors," and "human scum," "unpatriotic," "deranged," "crazy," "wacko," and "crooked as hell."[31]

---

[28]Arthur C. Brooks, *Love Your Enemies: How Decent People Can Save America from the Culture of Contempt* (New York: Broadside Books, 2019), 130.

[29]Ibid., 29; Tucker Carlson, "Our Leaders Have Dithered and Lied About the Riots as the Nation Goes Up in Flames," Fox News, June 2, 2020, www.foxnews.com/opinion/tucker-carlson-nation-flames-leaders-dithered; James 1:20. On "Them," see Ben Sasse, *Them: Why We Hate Each Other—and How to Heal* (New York: St. Martin's Press, 2018).

[30]Abraham Lincoln, *The Collected Works of Abraham Lincoln*, ed. Roy P. Basler, 8 vols. (New Brunswick, NJ: Rutgers University Press, 1953–1955), 4:199.

[31]Ashley Parker, "Trump Pushes Fights over Racist Legacy While Much of America Moves in a Different Direction," *Washington Post*, June 11, 2020, www.washingtonpost.com/politics/trump-pushes-fights-over-racist-legacy-while-much-of-america-moves-in-a-different-direction/2020/06/11/8d4398a4-abf5-11ea-9063-e69bd6520940_story.html; Wagner, "Trump Lashes Out Again"; Miller, "Trump Attacks Cummings' District"; Ted Widmer, "President Lincoln vs. President Trump," *Washington Post*, June 28, 2019, www.washingtonpost.com/news/posteverything/wp/2019/06/28/feature/o-captains-my-captains/.

It was easy to become too focused on Trump's verbal abuse, disturbing as it was, and miss the underlying message of his rhetoric. Like a host of godless ideologies and "isms," it taught that the source of evil in the world lies entirely outside of us, that our most pressing problems can be solved while leaving our hearts unchanged. Strip away the personal attacks, and the sanitized version of his message was still deeply flawed. A staunch defender of the president summarizes his 2016 campaign message this way: "An *innately great people* had let the wrong politicians drive their country into a quagmire. But it still could be led out of the morass to reclaim rapidly its former greatness by simply swapping leaders and agendas."[32]

This gentler, nicer version of "Make America Great Again" has been a mainstay in our politics for two centuries, yet it, too, wholly externalizes evil. It's essentially a modern-day form of Manichaeism, the ancient pagan religion that posited two deities—one evil and one good—and divided the universe between the forces of darkness and the forces of light. At the risk of stating the obvious, this is a profoundly un-Christian conception, yet it infuses a rhetorical strategy that all too many contemporary American Christians find compelling. If we took original sin seriously, we would find it offensive. I'm pretty sure that our Lord does.

We would rise up in righteous anger to condemn a politician who made sure to insist in every speech that "God is dead," or "Christianity is a myth," or "religious faith is a crutch for the weak and feeble-minded." Why then, would we cheer when a public figure proclaims that *we* are good, *they* are evil, and our only hope is in *him*? Aren't such claims just as offensive to the "faith which was once for all delivered to the saints"?[33] Aren't they teaching something just as antithetical to the gospel?

So what will it mean to live out politically a deep conviction of original sin? It won't mean working harder to increase Christian influence in politics. It won't involve bringing "power to the people." It will have nothing to do with efforts to "make America great again" by "draining the swamp" in Washington, nor with campaigns to "make America good again" by placing the other party in power.[34]

---

[32]Victor Davis Hanson, *The Case for Trump* (New York: Basic Books, 2019), 7, italics added.
[33]Jude 3.
[34]"Biden, Harris Have Chance to Make America Good Again," *Rocky Mountain Telegraph*, August 8, 2020.

Each of these responses in some sense *externalizes* evil by placing the fundamental source of our troubles entirely outside of ourselves.

Conversely, it will require agreeing with the Framers that power is dangerous *whoever* wields it, not just when it is controlled by our political rivals. We will know that *we* can be agents of oppression, just as we can be the authors of our own subjugation. As a result, we will be fearful of any leader unwilling to question his own virtue and wisdom, appalled by any politician who dares to proclaim "I alone can fix it," and skeptical of any figure eager to portray political opponents as "enemies."[35]

At bottom, living out politically a conviction of original sin means internalizing Solzhenitsyn's insight about "the line separating good and evil" passing within our hearts. It will daily demand that we make the apostle Paul's declaration our own: "Christ Jesus came into the world to save sinners, *of whom I am chief*."[36]

After years of studying early US history, the best example that I've encountered of this mindset comes from a figure that almost no one has heard of and about whom I know little. In 1788, Samuel Thompson was a fifty-something-year-old delegate to the Massachusetts convention charged with deciding whether that state would ratify the recently proposed Constitution. He hailed from Topsham, Maine (Maine was a part of Massachusetts at that time), had served extensively in the state legislature, and for much of his life earned his living as a tavern keeper.

Thompson was also an anti-federalist, meaning that he opposed ratification. The records of the Massachusetts convention reveal that he was troubled that the Constitution would allow slavery indefinitely. He disliked that it empowered the government to raise a standing army in peacetime. He was alarmed that it would not require annual elections to the House of Representatives, and he objected to the absence of a bill of rights.

These reservations notwithstanding, Thompson generally shared the Framers' skeptical view of human nature. If anything, he thought they were too optimistic. When defenders of the Constitution ridiculed him for conjuring imaginary dangers, he reiterated the principle that undergirded them: "I extremely doubt the infallibility of human nature." And the basis for his doubt? "Sir, I suspect my own heart," Thompson confessed, "and I shall suspect our rulers."[37]

---

[35]"Full text: Donald Trump 2016 RNC Draft Speech Transcript," Politico, July 21, 2016, www.politico.com/story/2016/07/full-transcript-donald-trump-nomination-acceptance-speech-at-rnc-225974.

[36]1 Timothy 1:15, italics added.

[37]Bailyn, *Debate on the Constitution*, part 2, 899-900.

I suspect my own heart. I don't know enough to be certain that this Maine tavern keeper believed literally in original sin, but it sure sounds as if he did. Samuel Thompson's perspective is sorely lacking today, but it doesn't have to be nonexistent. We can model it, by the grace of God, before a watching world.

EPILOGUE

"If America Is Good . . ."

America is great because she is good, and if America ever
ceases to be good, she will cease to be great.

<small>ANONYMOUS</small>

We'll probably never know the exact genealogy of the inspiring testimonial that Dwight Eisenhower shared with the nation on the eve of his election in 1952. Evidence suggests that it evolved gradually and more or less innocently over a period of years, even decades, and when that happens you can end up with something that's not only spurious but also impossible to track down.[1] I do have a theory, though. It's based on a clue buried seven hundred pages into the writings of a foreign dignitary who visited the United States in the 1830s then returned home to write a two-volume account of his travels.

His name was not Alexis de Tocqueville, but rather Andrew Reed, and if you've never heard of him you're not alone. Reed was a liberal Congregational minister and social reformer from London who, along with his colleague James

---

[1] The earliest version of the testimonial I've been able to find dates to 1886 and is contained in a collection of homilies by Philadelphia minister Madison C. Peters. See *Empty Pews & Selections from Other Sermons on Timely Topics* (Philadelphia: A. T. Zeising and Co., 1886), 35. Peters's variant has the French statesman "De Tochneville" searching high and low for the source of American success before finding it in the country's churches, but the wording differs in several instances. The exact paragraph-long anecdote that Dwight Eisenhower shared in 1952 apparently first appeared in print in a 1922 essay by the secretary of the Home Mission Board of the Presbyterian Church, USA. See Reverend John McDowell, "Labor Day Message," *Herald and Presbyter* 93, no. 36 (1922): 8. McDowell explicitly attributed the testimonial to Alexis de Tocqueville. Why Dwight Eisenhower credited a "wise philosopher" can only be guessed.

Matheson, toured the United States in 1834 as a representative of Britain's Congregational and Presbyterian churches. Like Tocqueville, Reed then penned a lengthy set of reflections, both volumes of which came out the very same year as volume one of *Democracy in America*, although with a considerably more unwieldy title: *A Narrative of the Visit to the American Churches by the Deputation from the Congregational Union of England and Wales.*

The first major stop on Reed's American itinerary was Washington, DC. His object in coming to the United States was primarily religious: to visit, observe, and encourage the country's churches. He was important enough, however, to score an invitation to dinner at the White House, and interested enough in politics to spend three days in the galleries of the House and Senate.

The first of these experiences was generally positive. Reed praised President Jackson's informal hospitality, although he noted that the general repeatedly steered the conversation to the "delicate subject" of the Bank of the United States. Reed passed over the particulars of Jackson's political opinions, but in a classically British understatement, he acknowledged that the president "held them with a strong conviction that they were right."[2]

At the other end of Pennsylvania Avenue, Reed was disappointed by "the Congress of this great empire." The congressmen and senators preened and postured and played to the galleries, but they said little of importance and accomplished even less. Echoing Tocqueville, Reed concluded that those who thrived in private life were rarely tempted to forsake their farms and businesses for public service, leaving the seats in the "American Parliament" to "less worthy" persons. Unless the trend were reversed, he warned, the day would come when Americans would awake to find their country "in the hands of a few ambitious and ill-principled demagogues."[3]

Away from the capital, though, Reed found much to admire in the American character. Americans were an energetic, optimistic, adaptable, driven, "can-do" people who turned obstacles into opportunities. Given the great natural resources at their disposal, their potential knew no bounds. But again like Tocqueville, Reed recognized that none of these character traits was intrinsically virtuous. None guaranteed that the majority would preserve liberty or promote the common good.

---

[2] Andrew Reed, *A Narrative of the Visit to the American Churches by the Deputation from the Congregational Union of England and Wales* (New York: Harper, 1835), 1:34.
[3] Ibid., 1:31.

And so this Christian minister finished his report by emphasizing the critical necessity of Christian morality. Maintaining that "religion is requisite to the welfare of any people," Reed predicted that the future of the United States was bright, but only if Americans promoted "universal education" and "universal piety." "AMERICA WILL BE GREAT IF AMERICA IS GOOD," Reed predicts in capital letters in the book's conclusion. "If not, her greatness will vanish away like a morning cloud."[4] Sound familiar?

Here, I suspect, is the long-lost germ of the observation that we've attributed to Alexis de Tocqueville all these years. Yes, there had to be a lot of embellishment over time—with someone picturing Tocqueville searching here, there, and everywhere for the secret of American "greatness and genius"—but it would hardly be the last time that a story has grown in the retelling.

And yes, somewhere along the line, someone had to confuse the identity of the author, but that's not hard to imagine either, given that Reed was scarcely better known in the nineteenth century than he is today. If an educated person heard a quote attributed to a foreign visitor to the United States during the 1830s, it would be reasonable to assume that the writer was Tocqueville, especially if you had never read *Democracy in America*.

This leaves just a little more tweaking to get us from Andrew Reed's assessment to the "words to live by" that Dwight Eisenhower shared with the nation more than a century later. Note that Reed offered a tentative prediction about our potential as a nation: "America *will be* great *if* America is good." At some point we substituted a more self-congratulatory version: "America *is* great because she *is* good." It makes sense. One of the consequences of the fall is that we resist acknowledging the consequences of the fall. It was a telling modification, well suited for a fallen people who prefer to think otherwise.

---

[4]Ibid., 2:197. My thanks to Lynn Betts for first alerting me to this passage.

ACKNOWLEDGMENTS

Research and writing, for me at least, is always a solitary activity but never a solitary undertaking, and it is a privilege to thank the family and friends, colleagues and students who have helped bring this book to completion. At home, my now very grown children—Callie (and Jonathan), Margaret, and Robert—have loved and listened and cared. At work, my colleagues and students at Wheaton College have daily challenged and inspired me. I'm grateful for the research assistance of Jared Marchant, and for the tireless and invaluable encouragement of Miles Veth, who has contributed to this work more than he realizes. The Arthur F. Holmes Chair of Faith and Learning, which I am honored to hold, provided funds to subsidize my research as well as to pay for the permission to use several of the illustrations in this book. At InterVarsity Press, I was blessed to work with two wonderful editors—academic editorial director Jon Boyd, who believed in this project from its inception, and assistant project editor Rebecca Carhart, whose attention to detail and commitment to excellence helped to bring it home.

As I wrestled to put my thoughts on paper, I benefited from the suggestions of James Felak, Timothy Larsen, Bryan McGraw, Mark Noll, Jack Scott, and Tom Wilson, as well as from the feedback of three anonymous reviewers for IVP Academic. Beyond them, two individuals read every word of every chapter as the manuscript unfolded. One is my former graduate student and now longtime friend, Adam Andrews. Adam is a wonderful educator with a passion for the life of the mind, a heart for the church, and a gift for encouragement which he has lavished on me. The other is my wife, Robyn. She, more than anyone else, encouraged me to write this book. Although ill during much of the time that I worked on it, Robyn read multiple drafts, scoured the internet for illustrations, and attacked with relish the mind-numbing work of compiling the index. Above all, for thirty-five years she has known my flaws and believed in me still, and that is surely one of the most precious gifts one human being can give to another.

FIGURE CREDITS

Figure Part 1.1. Junius Brutus Stearns, *Washington as Statesman at the Constitutional Convention*, 1856 / © The Granger Collection Ltd d/b/a GRANGER Historical Picture Archive

Figure Part 1.2. Charles Willson Peale, *Portrait of James Madison*, 1783 / © The Granger Collection Ltd d/b/a GRANGER Historical Picture Archive

Figure 1.1. Joseph Siffred Duplessis, *Benjamin Franklin*, 1785 / National Portrait Gallery, Smithsonian Institution. Gift of the Morris and Gwendolyn Cafritz Foundation

Figure 1.2. John Trumbull, *Alexander Hamilton*, 1806 / National Portrait Gallery, Smithsonian Institution. Gift of Henry Cabot Lodge

Figure 2.1. Title page of the first volume of *The Federalist*, 1788 / © The Granger Collection Ltd d/b/a GRANGER Historical Picture Archive

Figure 2.2. John Trumbull, *John Adams*, 1793 / National Portrait Gallery, Smithsonian Institution

Figure Part 2.1. John Sartain after George Caleb Bingham, *The County Election*, 1854 / National Gallery of Art. Gift of Gaillard F. Ravenel and Frances P. Smythe-Ravenel

Figure 3.1. Francis Kearney, after Charles Bird King, *John Quincy Adams*, 1825 / National Portrait Gallery, Smithsonian Institution

Figure 3.2. James Barton Longacre, *Andrew Jackson*, 1829 / National Portrait Gallery, Smithsonian Institution

Figure 3.3. Artist unknown, *The Hermitage*, lithograph published by Endicott & Co., New York, 1856 / Library of Congress Prints and Photographs Division

Figure 3.4. Charles King, painter, and Peter Maverick, engraver, *Henry Clay*, 1822 / Library of Congress Prints and Photographs Division

Figure 4.1. John Binns, "Some Account of Some of the Bloody Deeds of General Jackson," 1828 / Library of Congress Rare Book and Special Collections Division

Figure 4.2. Risso & Browne Lithography Company, *Andrew Jackson*, equestrian print, 1833 / National Portrait Gallery, Smithsonian Institution

Figure Part 3.1. Robert Lindneux, *The Trail of Tears, 1838*, 1942 / © The Granger Collection Ltd d/b/a GRANGER Historical Picture Archive

Figure 5.1. Front page of the first edition of the *Cherokee Phoenix*, 1828 / © The Granger Collection Ltd d/b/a GRANGER Historical Picture Archive

Figure 5.2. Alfred M. Hoffy, *John Ross—A Cherokee Chief*, 1843 / National Portrait Gallery, Smithsonian Institution. Gift of Betty A. and Lloyd G. Schermer

Figure 6.1. Colored engraving, after William Henry Bartlett, *Second Bank of the United States*, Philadelphia, Pennsylvania, 1839 / Sarin Images, © The Granger Collection Ltd d/b/a GRANGER Historical Picture Archive

Figure 6.2. Henry Dawe, *Nicholas Biddle*, 1837 / National Portrait Gallery, Smithsonian Institution

Figure 6.3. Artist unknown, *King Andrew the First*, 1833 / Library of Congress Prints and Photographs Division

Figure 6.4. Printed and published by H. R. Robinson, *The Downfall of Mother Bank*, 1833 / Library of Congress Prints and Photographs Division

Figure Part 4.1. Theodore Chasseriau, *Alexis de Tocqueville*, 1850 / A Picture Library, © The Granger Collection Ltd d/b/a GRANGER Historical Picture Archive

Figure Part 5.1. "Trump Supporters Hold 'Stop the Steal' Rally in DC Amid Ratification Of Presidential Election," January 6, 2021, photo by Jon Cherry / Getty Images

INDEX